NoSQL For Dummies®

FOR
DUMMIES®
A Wiley Brand

by Adam Fowler

FOR
DUMMIES®
A Wiley Brand

NoSQL For Dummies®

Published by: **John Wiley & Sons, Inc.,** 111 River Street, Hoboken, NJ 07030-5774, www.wiley.com

Copyright © 2015 by John Wiley & Sons, Inc., Hoboken, New Jersey

Media and software compilation copyright © 2015 by John Wiley & Sons, Inc. All rights reserved.

Published simultaneously in Canada

For general information on our other products and services, please contact our Customer Care Department within the U.S. at 877-762-2974, outside the U.S. at 317-572-3993, or fax 317-572-4002. For technical support, please visit www.wiley.com/techsupport.

Wiley publishes in a variety of print and electronic formats and by print-on-demand. Some material included with standard print versions of this book may not be included in e-books or in print-on-demand. If this book refers to media such as a CD or DVD that is not included in the version you purchased, you may download this material at http://booksupport.wiley.com. For more information about Wiley products, visit www.wiley.com.

Library of Congress Control Number: 2014954658

ISBN 978-1-118-90574-6 (pbk); ISBN 978-1-118-90562-3 (epub); ISBN 978-1-118-90578-4 (epdf)

Manufactured in the United States of America

10 9 8 7 6 5 4 3 2 1

Contents at a Glance

Table of Contents

Introduction

I love NoSQL both as a movement and as a technology. It's a fast-paced, constantly changing area. Barely a week goes by without a new NoSQL database being created to handle a specific real-life problem.

As a movement, NoSQL is interesting in that it started wholly independently of any commercial organization. In fact, it was the brainchild of interested individuals who grouped together and shared ideas. Some core ideas certainly came from large commercial organizations, including the Bigtable paper from Google and the key-value store paper from Amazon, but NoSQL was popularized as open source.

The normal process in software development is that several commercial companies form and compete with one another and gradually the field narrows. Then, once the remaining companies prove their worth, they're gobbled up by big boys like Oracle, IBM, and Microsoft. Open-source alternatives appear only during the later phases of this cycle.

That's not the case with NoSQL. Sure, there were a few early commercial players (very early in MarkLogic's case — way back in 2001). However, the majority of publicly available NoSQL products were created in the open before companies incorporated them into their commercial products.

This book encourages a practical approach to evaluating NoSQL as a set of technologies and products. The book tells you how to determine which ones might meet your needs and how select the most appropriate ones. This information enables you to spot business and technical problems that NoSQL databases can solve.

After reading this book, not only will you be able to identify which type of NoSQL database to use, but perhaps more importantly, you'll know the questions to ask vendors about their software and services prior to purchasing one.

This book discusses NoSQL in terms of real-life, complex mission-critical applications. Understanding complex enterprise applications allows you to see the flaws and benefits of each NoSQL database, and within contexts similar to the ones you see in your workplace.

This book guides you through this exciting area of technology and highlights how you and your organization can achieve similar benefits to those described. I hope you enjoy the journey!

Foolish Assumptions

My main aim for the book is to expose many NoSQL databases and point out their common features and specific use cases.

My other aim is to point out that NoSQL databases are ready for the big time! I have gone to pains to point out where things can be configured to support this, or where gaps still exist in offerings.

I hope that large enterprises that have not yet widely adopted NoSQL will be reassured by this book. I also hope that it will act as a call to action to NoSQL database vendors in hardening their offerings to support the key needs of each business sector and use cases in such systems.

As this book is considering enterprise classes of problems, I have to be aware of things like long-term development plans, resilient systems, support, and availability of services.

I've chosen to cover the following NoSQL databases (plus one search engine):

- ✔ Riak: A key-value store
- ✔ MongoDB: An aggregate (document) database that primarily stores JSON
- ✔ Apache Cassandra: A column store (Bigtable clone)
- ✔ Neo4j: A triple and graph store
- ✔ MarkLogic Server: Primarily stores XML documents, also JSON, binary, text. Also provides in memory column indexes, a triple store and a search engine
- ✔ Redis: An in-memory only key-value store
- ✔ Elasticsearch: An Open Source search engine used with many NoSQL databases

I was keen to give a background to a breadth of databases in this book. I also needed to make sure I wasn't covering the same subject multiple times. I decided to cover one database that primarily manages each data type (document, keys/values, column/tables, triple/graph).

I'm keen to ensure that I don't give you the impression that each database in each data type area is created equal. Although I concentrate on just one database of each type, I also mention areas where other similar databases are stronger or weaker where appropriate.

I threw in a couple of wildcards. I want to cover Redis as an in memory database. Although in-memory databases have been around for years, Redis provides a NoSQL version of this which is applicable to a different set of problems.

I also cover a commercial NoSQL solution: MarkLogic Server. I include this database for two reasons. Firstly, and most importantly, MarkLogic Server can handle multiple data types whereas the others in my list only concentrate on one particular domain.

Secondly, I love MarkLogic Server – so much so, I joined MarkLogic as a Senior Sales Engineer. MarkLogic Server is also the market leader by software sales in NoSQL databases. (Most companies behind Open Source NoSQL databases only sell extensions to open source software and services, so this is perhaps to be expected!)

Although not strictly a database, Elasticsearch does use NoSQL approaches to its search engine design. NoSQL databases are often used to store semi-structured and unstructured data. This means search engines are an appropriate area to cover. Indeed, Elasticsearch (and Solr/Lucene) are commonly integrated with Open Source NoSQL databases to provide more advanced information retrieval and indexing services.

Icons Used in This Book

Throughout the book, you'll see these little graphic icons to identify useful paragraphs.

The Tip icon marks tips and shortcuts that you can take to make a specific task easier.

The Remember icon marks the information that's especially important to know.

The Technical Stuff icon marks information of a highly technical nature that you can safely skip over with impunity.

The Warning icon tells you to watch out! It marks important information that may save you headaches. *Warning:* Don't skip over these icons!

Beyond the Book

NoSQL For Dummies includes the following goodies online for easy download:

- **Cheat Sheet:** You can find the Cheat Sheet for this book here:

  www.dummies.com/cheatsheet/nosql
- **Extras:** I provide a few extra articles here:

  www.dummies.com/extras/nosql

Where to Go from Here

With this book, you have all the information you need to get started on your journey. You can start with Chapter 1, or you can take a look at the table of contents and start with a topic that most interests you.

Part I
Getting Started with NoSQL

In this part . . .

- ✔ Discover exactly what NoSQL is.
- ✔ Identifying terminology.
- ✔ Categorizing technology.
- ✔ Visit www.dummies.com for great Dummies content online.

Chapter 1

Introducing NoSQL: The Big Picture

In This Chapter

▶ Examining the past

▶ Recognizing changes

▶ Applying capabilities

The data landscape has changed. During the past 15 years, the explosion of the World Wide Web, social media, web forms you have to fill in, and greater connectivity to the Internet means that more than ever before a vast array of data is in use.

New and often crucial information is generated hourly, from simple tweets about what people have for dinner to critical medical notes by healthcare providers. As a result, systems designers no longer have the luxury of closeting themselves in a room for a couple of years designing systems to handle new data. Instead, they must quickly create systems that store data and make information readily available for search, consolidation, and analysis. All of this means that a particular kind of systems technology is needed.

The good news is that a huge array of these kinds of systems already exists in the form of NoSQL databases. The not-so-good news is that many people don't understand what NoSQL databases do or why and how to use them. Not to worry, though. That's why I wrote this book. In this chapter, I introduce you to NoSQL and help you understand why you need to consider this technology further now.

A Brief History of NoSQL

The perception of the term NoSQL has evolved since it was launched in 1998. So, in this section, I want to explain how NoSQL is currently defined, and then propose a more appropriate definition for it. I even cover NoSQL history background in the side bars.

Amazon and Google papers

NoSQL isn't a single technology invented by a couple of guys in a garage or a mathematician theorizing about data structures. The concepts behind NoSQL developed slowly over several years. Independent groups then took those ideas and applied them to their own data problems, thereby creating the various NoSQL databases that exist today.

Google Bigtable paper

In 2006, Google released a paper that described its Bigtable distributed structured database. Google described Bigtable as follows: "Bigtable is a distributed storage system for managing structured data that is designed to scale to a very large size: petabytes of data across thousands of commodity servers."

Similar to an RDBMS model at first sight, Bigtable stores rows with a single key and stores data in the rows within related column families. Therefore, accessing all related data is as easy as retrieving a record by using an ID rather than a complex join, as in relational database SQL.

This model also means that distributing data is more straightforward than with relational databases. By using simple keys, related data — such as all pages on the same website (given as an example in Google's paper) — can be grouped together, which increases the speed of analysis. You can think of Bigtable as an alternative to many tables with relationships. That is, with Bigtable, column families allow related data to be stored in a single record.

Bigtable is designed to be distributed on commodity servers, a common theme for all NoSQL databases created after the information explosion caused by the adoption of the World Wide Web. A *commodity server* is one without complex bells and whistles — for example, Dell or HP servers with perhaps 2 CPUs, 8 to 16 cores, and 32 to 96GB of RAM. Nothing fancy, lots of them, and cheaper than buying one big server (which is like putting all your eggs in one expensive basket).

The first NoSQL "meetup"

The first documented use of the term NoSQL was by Carlo Strozzi in 1998. He was visiting San Francisco and wanted to get some people together to talk about his lightweight, relational database.

Relational database management systems (RDBMS) are the dominant database today. If you ask computer scientists who have graduated within the past 20 years what a database is, odds are they will describe a relational database.

Carlo used the term NoSQL because his database was accessed via shell scripts, rather than through use of the standard Structured Query Language (SQL). The original meaning was "No SQL." That is, instead of using SQL, it used a query mechanism closer to the developer's source environment — in Carlo's case, the UNIX scripting world.

The use of this term shows a frustration amongst the developer community with using SQL. Although an open standard with massive common support in the prevalent Relational Databases of the time, the term NoSQL shows a desire to find a better way. Or at least, a way better for the poor old developer reading through complex and long SQL queries.

Carlo's meeting in San Francisco came and went. Developers continued to experiment with alternate query mechanisms. Technology appeared to abstract complex queries away from the developer. A prime example is the Hibernate library in Java, which is driven by configuration and enables the automatic generation of value objects that map directly onto database tables, which means developers don't have to worry so much about how the underlying database is structured — developers just call functions on objects.

There's a cost to using SQL. Complex queries are hard to debug, and it's even harder to make them perform well, which increases the cost of development, administration, and testing. Finding an alternative mechanism, or a library to hide the complexities at least, looked like a good way to reduce costs and make it easier to adopt best practices.

Abstraction gets you only so far, though. Eventually, data problems will emerge that require a completely different way of thinking. Existing relational technology didn't work well with such problems, and the explosion of the growth of the Internet and World Wide Web would give rise to these issues.

Moreover, other key things were happening. In 1991, the first public web page was created, just seven years before the NoSQL "meetup." Yahoo and Amazon were founded in 1994. In comparison, Google, which we tend to think has always existed, wasn't founded until 1998. Yes, there was a web before Google — and before Google, remember AltaVista (which was eventually purchased and shut down by Yahoo!) and Ask Jeeves (now known as Ask.com)?

The specification for the language used for system-to-system communication — XML — was released as a recommendation in 1997. The XSLT specification — used to transform XML between formats — came in 1999. The web was young, wild, and people were still just trying to figure out how to make money with it. It had not yet changed the world.

Amazon Dynamo paper

Amazon released a paper of its own in 2007 describing its Dynamo data storage application. In Amazon's words: "Dynamo is used to manage the state of services that have very high reliability requirements and need tight control over the tradeoffs between availability, consistency, cost-effectiveness and performance."

The paper goes on the describe how a lot of Amazon data is stored by use of a primary key, how consistent hashing is used to partition and distribute data, and how object versioning is used to maintain consistency across data centers.

The Dynamo paper basically describes the first globally distributed key-value store used at Amazon. Here the keys are logical IDs, and the values can be any binary value of interest to the developer. A very simple model, indeed.

The second NoSQL "meetup"

Many open-source NoSQL databases had emerged by 2009. Riak, MongoDB, HBase, Accumulo, Hypertable, Redis, Cassandra, and Neo4j were all created between 2007 and 2009. These are just a few NoSQL databases created during this time, so as you can see, a lot of systems were produced in a short period of time. However, even now, innovation moves at a breakneck speed.

This rapidly changing environment led Eric Evans from Rackspace and Johan Oskarsson from Last.fm to organize the first modern NoSQL meetup. Needing a title for the meeting that could be distributed easily on social media, they chose the #NoSQL tag.

The #NoSQL hashtag is the first modern use of what we today all regard as the term NoSQL. The description from the meeting is well worth reading in full — as the sentiment remains accurate today.

"This meetup is about 'open source, distributed, non relational databases'.

Have you run into limitations with traditional relational databases? Don't mind trading a query language for scalability? Or perhaps you just like shiny new things to try out? Either way this meetup is for you.

Join us in figuring out why these newfangled Dynamo clones and BigTables have become so popular lately. We have gathered presenters from the most interesting projects around to give us all an introduction to the field.

This meetup included speakers from LinkedIn, Facebook, Powerset, Stumbleupon, ZVents, and couch.io who discussed Voldemort, Cassandra, Dynamite, HBase, Hypertable, and CouchDB, respectively.

This meeting represented the first time that people came together to discuss these different approaches to nonrelational databases and to brand them as *NoSQL*.

These two papers inspired many different organizations to create their NoSQL databases. There were so many variations that some people thought it necessary to meet and discuss the various approaches being taken (see "The second NoSQL 'meetup'" sidebar).

What NoSQL means today

Today the NoSQL movement includes hundreds of NoSQL database products, which has led to a variety of definitions for the term — some with very common tenets, and others not so common. I cover these tenets in detail in Chapter 2.

This explosion of databases happened because nonrelational approaches have been applied to a wide range of problems where an RDBMS has traditionally been weak (as this book covers in detail). NoSQL databases were also created for data structures and models that in an RDBMS required considerable management or shredding and the reconstitution of data in complex plumbing code.

Each problem resulted in its own solution — and its own NoSQL database, which is why so many new databases emerged. Similarly, existing products providing NoSQL features discovered and adopted the NoSQL label, which makes the jobs of architects, CIOs, and IT purchasers difficult because it's unlikely that one NoSQL database can solve all the issues in a particular business area.

So, how can you know whether NoSQL will help you, or which NoSQL database to choose? The answer to these questions consume the remainder of Part I of this book by discussing the variety of NoSQL databases and the business problems they can solve, beginning with the following section that covers NoSQL features.

Features of NoSQL

NoSQL books and blogs offer different opinions on what a NoSQL database is. This section highlights the common opinions, misconceptions, and hype and fringe opinions.

Common features

Four core features of NoSQL, shown in the following list, apply to most NoSQL databases. The list compares NoSQL to traditional relational DBMS:

- **Schema agnostic:** A database schema is the description of all possible data and data structures in a relational database. With a NoSQL database, a schema isn't required, giving you the freedom to store information without doing up-front schema design.

- **Nonrelational:** Relations in a database establish connections between tables of data. For example, a list of transaction details can be connected to a separate list of delivery details. With a NoSQL database, this information is stored as an aggregate — a single record with everything about the transaction, including the delivery address.

- **Commodity hardware:** Some databases are designed to operate best (or only) with specialized storage and processing hardware. With a NoSQL database, cheap off-the-shelf servers can be used. Adding more of these cheap servers allows NoSQL databases to scale to handle more data.

- **Highly distributable:** Distributed databases can store and process a set of information on more than one device. With a NoSQL database, a cluster of servers can be used to hold a single large database.

Next, I take you through the preceding terms and describe why NoSQL databases have each one and when it's helpful and when it's not.

Schema agnostic

NoSQL databases are schema agnostic. You aren't required to do a lot of up-front design work before you can store data in NoSQL databases. You can start coding and store and retrieve data without knowing how the database stores and works internally. (If and when you need advanced functionality, then you can manually add further indexes or tweak data storage structures.) Schema agnosticism may be the most significant difference between NoSQL and relational databases.

An alternative interpretation of schema agnostic is *schema on read.* You need to know how the data is stored only when constructing a *query* (a coded question that retrieves information from the database), so for practical purposes, this feature is exactly what it says: You need to know the schema on read.

The great benefit to a schema agnostic database is that development time is shortened. This benefit increases as you go through multiple development releases and need to alter the internal data structures in the database.

For example, in a traditional RDBMS, you go through a process of schema redesign. The schema instructs the database on what data to expect. Change the data stored, or structures, and you must reinstruct the database using a modified schema. If you were to make a change, you'd have to spend a lot of time deciding how to re-architect the existing data. In NoSQL databases, you simply store a different data structure. There's no need to tell the database beforehand.

You may have to modify your queries accordingly, maybe add the occasional specific *index* (such as an integer range index to allow less than and greater than data-type specific queries), but the whole process is much less painful than it is with an RDBMS.

Developers allowed to do whatever they want with a database! This sends shivers down the spines of CIOs and DBAs. Lack of control is perceived as inherent risk. But it's a lack of control only if you let developers change production systems without first going through a process of development, functional testing, and user-acceptance testing. I'm not aware that this process is ever bypassed, so just consider this as a theoretical risk.

RDBMS took off because of its flexibility and because, by using SQL, it sped up changing a query. NoSQL databases provide this flexibility for changing both the schema and the query, which is one of the key reasons that they will be increasingly adopted over time.

Even on query, you may not need to worry too much about knowing the schema changes — consider an index over a field account number, where *account number* can be located anywhere in a document that is stored in a NoSQL database. You can change the structure and relocate where *account number* is stored, and if the element has the same name elsewhere in the document, it's still available for query without changes to your query mechanism.

Sometimes, you'll also find the term *schema-less* mentioned, which is a stretch, because there aren't many occasions when you can do a general query without knowing that particular fields are present — for example, a query that is purely full-text search doesn't restrict itself to a particular field.

Note that not all NoSQL databases are fully schema agnostic. Some, such as HBase, require you to stop the database to alter column definitions. They're still considered NoSQL databases because not all defined fields (columns in this case) are required to be known in advance for each record — just the column families.

RDBMS allows individual fields in records to be identified as *null* values (no defined value). The problem with an RDBMS is that stored data size and performance are negatively affected when storage is reserved for null values just in case the record may at some future time have a value in that column. In Cassandra, you simply don't provide that column's data, which solves the problem.

Nonrelational

Relational database management systems have been the dominant way to store application data for more than 20 years. A great deal of mathematical work was done to prove the theory that underpins them.

This underpinning describes how tables relate to each other. A single Order row may relate to many Delivery Address rows, but each Delivery Address row also relates to multiple Order rows. This is a *many-to-many relationship*.

NoSQL databases don't have this concept of relationships between their records. They instead denormalize data. This means that in a NoSQL database would have an Order structure with the Delivery Address embedded. This means the delivery address is duplicated in every Order row that uses it. This approach has the advantage of not requiring complex query time joins across multiple data structures (tables) though.

NoSQL databases don't store information about how individual records relate to other records in the database, which may sound like a limitation. However, NoSQL databases are more flexible in terms of the data structures you can store.

Consider an order from an online retailer. The order could include product codes, quantities, item prices, and item descriptions, as well as information about the person ordering, such as delivery address and payment information.

Relational database basics

Relational databases are designed on the understanding that a row in one table can be related to one or more rows in another table. It's possible, therefore, to build up complex interrelated structures.

Queries, on the other hand, are returned as a single set of rows. This means that a query must use a mechanism to join tables together as required at runtime in order to fit them into a single result structure.

This joining mechanism is well understood and generally predictable from a performance point of view.

Rather than insert ten rows in a variety of tables in a relational database, you can instead store a single structure for all of this order information — say, as a JSON or XML document.

This brings up the question, "Do you really need relationships if all your data is stored in a single record?" For a lot of applications, especially ones that need to store exact state for a point in time, such as financial transactions, the answer is often "No." However, if you're experienced with relational databases, you may have stored the same information more than once, so there's an obvious drawback to storing information in this way.

In relational database theory, the goal is to *normalize* your data (that is, to organize the fields and tables to remove duplicate data). In NoSQL databases — especially Document or Aggregate databases — you often deliberately denormalize data, storing some data multiple times.

You can store, for example, "Customer Delivery Address" multiple times across many orders a customer makes over time, rather than store it once and refer to it in multiple orders. Doing so requires extra storage space, and a little forethought in managing in your application. So why do it?

There are two advantages to storing data multiple times:

- ✔ **Easy storage and retrieval:** Just save and get a single record.
- ✔ **Query speed:** In relational databases, you join information and add constraints across tables at query time. This may require the database engine to evaluate many tables. The more query constraints you have across different tables, the more you reduce your query speed. (This is why an RDBMS has precomputed views.) In a NoSQL database, all the information you need to evaluate your query is in a single document. Therefore, you can quickly determine the list of matching documents.

Relational views and NoSQL denormalizations are different approaches to the problem of data spread across records. In NoSQL, you may have to maintain multiple denormalizations representing different views of the same data. This approach increases the cost of storage but gives you much better query time.

Given the ever-reducing cost of storage and the increased speed of development and querying, denormalized data (aka *materialized views*) isn't a killer reason to discount NoSQL solutions. It's just a different way to approach the same problem, with its own advantages and disadvantages.

Again, there is an exception to this rule! Triple stores and graph databases have the basic concept of relationships. The difference is that every single record (a triple consisting of three things — subject, predicate, and object — such as "Adam likes Cheese") contains a relationship.

NoSQL is a fundamentally different approach to related data, very much different from an RDBMS. Hence, the term *nonrelational* is shorthand for *Non-Relational Mathematics Theory*.

Highly distributable and uses commodity hardware

In many NoSQL databases, a key design decision is to use multiple computers to store data for a single database, rather than have the whole database on a single server.

Storing data across multiple machines and allowing it to be queried is difficult. You must send the query to all the servers and wait for a reply. Hopefully, you set up the machines so that they're fast enough to talk to each other to handle distributed queries!

The main advantage of this approach is in the case of very large datasets, because for some storage requirements, even the largest available single server couldn't store or process all the data you need. Consider all the messages on Twitter and Facebook. You need a distributed mechanism to effectively manage all that data, even if it's mostly about what people had for breakfast and cute cat videos.

An advantage of distributing your database is that you can use cheaper servers, called *commodity servers*, which are cheaper than single very powerful servers. (However, a decent one will still cost you $10,000!) Even for smaller datasets, it may be cheaper to buy three commodity servers instead of a single, higher-powered server.

Another key advantage is that adding high availability is easier; you're already halfway there by distributing your data. If you replicate your data once or twice across other servers in the cluster, your data will still be accessible, even if one of the servers crashes, burns, and dies.

Not all open-source databases support high availability unless you buy the supported, paid-for version of the database from the company that develops it.

An exception to the highly distributable rule is that of graph databases. In order to effectively answer certain graph queries in a timely fashion, data needs to be stored on a single server. No one has solved this particular issue yet.

Carefully consider whether you need a triple store or a graph store. Triple stores are generally distributable, whereas graph stores aren't. Which one you need depends on the queries you must support. You find more on Triple and Graph Stores in Chapter 2.

Not-so-common features

Although some features are fairly common to NoSQL databases (for example, schema agnosticism and non-relational structure), it's not uncommon for a database to lack one or more of the following features and still qualify as a modern NoSQL database.

Open-source

NoSQL software is unique because the open-source movement has driven development rather than follow a set of commercial companies. You therefore can find a host of open-source NoSQL products to suit every need. When developers couldn't find a NoSQL database for their needs, they created one, and published it initially as open-source.

I didn't include this in the earlier "Common features" section because the majority of popular NoSQL solutions are driven by commercial companies, with the open source variant lacking the key features required for mission critical use in large enterprises.

The difference between open-source NoSQL vendors and these wholly commercial companies is that open-source vendors have a business model similar to the Red Hat model. Basically, they release an open-source product and also sell enterprise add-on features, support, and implementation services.

This isn't a bad thing! It's worth noting, though, that people at NoSQL aren't driven purely, or even mainly, by open-source developers working in their spare time — instead, they work for the commercial companies behind the products.

 Buyer beware! When it comes to selecting a NoSQL database, remember "total cost of ownership." Many organizations acquired open-source products only to find that they need a high-priced subscription in order to get the features they want.

BASE versus ACID

Prior to 2014, the majority of NoSQL definitions didn't include ACID transaction support as a defining feature of NoSQL databases. This is no longer true.

ACID-compliant transaction means the database is designed so it absolutely will not lose data:

- ✔ Each operation moves the database from one valid state to another (*A*tomic).

- ✔ Everyone has the same view of the data at any point in time (*C*onsistent).

- ✔ Operations on the database don't interfere with each other (*I*solation).

- ✔ When a database says it has saved data, you know the data is safe (*D*urable).

Not many NoSQL databases have ACID transactions. Exceptions to that norm are FoundationDB, Neo4j, and MarkLogic Server, which do provide fully serializable ACID transactions.

So why do I include ACID compliance as a not-so-common feature? When the Oracle RDBMS was released, it didn't provide ACID compliance either. It took seven versions before ACID compliance was supported across multiple database updates and tables.

Similarly, if you look at the roadmaps of all the NoSQL databases, you'll see that all of them refer to work on transactional consistency. MongoDB, for example, raised $150 million in the fall of 2013 specifically to address this and other enterprise issues. MongoDB has announced a new ACID compliant storage engine. The ACID versus BASE debate is an interesting one, and I cover it in detail in Chapter 3.

Enterprise NoSQL

Let me say up front that I've sold enterprise software for nine years and have implemented it even longer, so as you might guess, I'm passionate on the subject. Over time, I've witnessed its strong focus on development and support, both of which are reassuring to major companies looking to make huge investments in mission-critical software.

How to tell enterprise grade software from popular software — that's the hard bit! It's like those TV shows where they take an old car or motorbike and refit it completely for its owners. Maybe install a plasma TV, some lightning decals down the side, and a bopping stereo system. The result looks awesome, and the smiling owners jump in ready to drive away. The problem is that the shiny exterior may be masking some real internal engine problems.

This book's definition of NoSQL

I apply the highly scientific *duck test* to my definition of NoSQL: *If it looks like a duck, quacks like a duck, ... then it's probably a duck!* This approach will likely be very familiar to duck-type language developers, but my apologies to strictly scientific-minded types.

A piece of software is a NoSQL database if it adheres to the following:

✔ Doesn't require a stringent schema for every record created.

✔ Is distributable on commodity hardware.

✔ Doesn't use relational database mathematical theory.

I can just see a few jaws dropping because of this wide-ranging definition! However, many different approaches to database design and theory are prevalent in today's NoSQL ecosystem, and as author of this book, I feel duty-bound to cover them.

This book introduces you to both the mainstream and the edge cases so that you understand the boundaries of NoSQL use cases. Consequently, I cover many databases, some of which you may decide to use and others you may decide simply aren't for you. In my humble opinion, that's what makes this book stand out from others (no names and titles, of course, or their lawyers might chew me up — and none of us deserves the indigestion that might cause).

The same is true of software. Some software is easy to start using, but will be unreliable in large-scale installations. This is just one example of something to look out for that I include in this book.

The following list identifies the requisite features that large enterprises look for (or should look for) when investing in software products that run the core of their system.

✔ **High availability:** Fault tolerance when a single server goes down

✔ **Disaster recovery:** For when a datacenter goes down, or more likely someone digs up a network cable just outside the datacenter

✔ **Support:** Someone to stand behind a product when it goes wrong (or it's used incorrectly!)

✔ **Services:** Product experts who can advise on best practices and help determine how to use a product to address new or unusual business needs

✔ **Ecosystem:** Availability of partners, experienced developers, and product information — to avoid being locked into a single vendor's expensive support and services contract

Many NoSQL databases are used by enterprises. Just visit the website of any of the NoSQL companies, and you'll see a list of them. But there is a difference between being used by an enterprise, and being a piece of mission-critical *enterprise software*.

NoSQL databases are often used as high-speed caches for web-accessible data on mission-critical systems. If one of these NoSQL systems goes down, though, you lose only a copy of the data — the mission-critical store is often an RDBMS! Seriously question enterprise case studies and references to be sure the features mentioned in the preceding list of enterprise features exist in a particular NoSQL product.

NoSQL databases have come of age and are being used in major systems by some of the largest companies. As always, though, the bar needs to be constantly raised. This book is for the many people who are looking for a new way to deliver mission-critical systems, such as CIOs, software developers, and software purchasers in large enterprises.

In this book, you find the downsides of particular NoSQL approaches and databases that aren't developed sufficiently to produce products of truly enterprise grade. The information in this book helps to separate propaganda from fact, which will enable you to make key architecture decisions about information technology.

Beginning with the following section (and, in fact, in the rest of this book), I talk about NoSQL in terms of the problems related to mission-critical enterprise systems and the solutions to those problems.

Why You Should Care about NoSQL

If you're wondering whether NoSQL is just a niche solution or an increasingly mainstream one, the answer lies in the following discussion. So, it's time to talk about recent trends and how you can use NoSQL databases over and above the traditional RDBMS approach.

Recent trends in IT

Since the advent of the World Wide Web and the explosion of Internet-connected devices, information sharing has dramatically increased. Details of our everyday lives are shared with friends and family, whether they're close or continents away. Much of this data is unstructured text; moreover the structures of data are constantly evolving, making it hard to quantify.

There are simply no end of things to keep track of (for example, you can't predict when a website or newsfeed will be updated, or in what format).

It's true that search engines help you find potentially useful information; however, search engines are limited because they can't distinguish the nuances of how you search or what you're aiming for.

Furthermore, simply storing, managing, and making use of this information is a massive task. What's needed is a set of database solutions that can handle current and emerging data problems, which leads us back to NoSQL, the problems, and the possibilities.

Although there's been an outpouring of enthusiasm by the development community about NoSQL databases, not many killer applications have been created and put on the market. These applications will take time to emerge — right now, NoSQL databases are being used to solve problems that emerge in conventional approaches.

Problems with conventional approaches

During the initial phases of a new project, people often think, "I need to store data, and I have an Enterprise License Agreement for an RDBMS, so I'll just use it." True, relational DBMS have provided great value over the past 25 years and will continue to do so. Relational databases are great for things that fit easily into rows and columns. I like to call this kind of data *Excel data*, and anything that you can put in a Microsoft Excel spreadsheet, you easily store in an RDBMS.

However, some problems require a different approach. Not everything fits well into rows and columns — for example, a book with a tree structure of cover, parts, chapters, main headings, and subheadings. Likewise, what if a particular record has a field that could contain two or more values? Breaking this out into another sheet or table is a bit of overkill, and makes it harder to work with the data as a single unit.

There are also scenarios in which the relationships themselves can hold their own metadata. An RDBMS doesn't handle those situations at all; an RDBMS just relates records in tables using structures about the relationships known at design time.

Each of the preceding scenarios has a type of NoSQL database that overcomes the limitations of an RDBMS for those data types: key-value, columnar, and triple stores, respectively. Turn to Chapter 2 for more on those types of NoSQL database.

Many of the problems are because the main type of data being managed today — unstructured data — is fundamentally different from data in traditional applications, as you'll see in the following sections.

Schema redesign overhead

Consider a retail website. The original design has a single order with a single set of delivery information. What if the retailer now needs to package the products into potentially multiple deliveries?

With a relational system, you now have to spend a lot of time deciding how best to handle this redesign. Do you create an Order Group concept, with each group related to a different delivery schedule? Do you instead create a Delivery Schedule containing delivery information and relate that to Order Items?

You also have to decide what to do with historical structures. Do you keep them as they are, perhaps adding a flag for "Order Structure version number" so that you can decide how to process them?

Developers also must restructure every single one of their queries. Database administrators have to rework all the views. In short, it's a massive and costly undertaking.

If you use a document NoSQL database instead, you can start storing your new structure immediately. Queries on indexes still work because the same data is stored in a single document, just elsewhere within it. You have two sets of display logic for viewing historical orders, but plugging a new view into an application is a lot easier than redesigning the entire application stack's data model. (A stack consists of a database, business application tier, and user interface.)

Managing feeds of external datasets you cannot control is a similar issue. Consider the many and varied ways Twitter applications create tweets. Believe it or not, a simple tweet involves a lot of data, some of it application-specific and some of it general across all tweets.

Or perhaps you must store and manage XML documents across different versions of the same XML schema. It's still a variety problem. You may have to support both structures at the same time. This is a common situation in financial services, insurance and public sectors (including federal government metadata catalogues for libraries), and information-sharing repositories.

In financial services, FpML is an XML document format used extensively for managing trades. Some trades, especially in the derivatives market, last weeks or months and involve many institutions. Each bank uses its own particular version of FpML with its own custom tags.

The same is true for retail insurance. Each insurance company has its own fields and terms, or subset thereof, even if it obeys the same standard, such as those from the ACORD insurance standards organization.

This is where the schema agnostic, or schema on read, feature of NoSQL databases really pays for itself — being able to handle any form of data. If the preceding sentences sound familiar, I highly recommend that you evaluate a NoSQL solution to manage your data.

Unstructured data explosion

I started working in sales engineering for FileNet, an enterprise content management company that's now part of IBM. I was struck at the time by a survey concluding that 80 percent of organizations' data was unstructured in nature, and that this percentage was increasing. That statistic is still used today, nine years later, though the proportion is bound to be more now. Many organizations I've encountered since then still aren't arranging their data holistically in a coherent way in order to answer complex questions that span an entire organization.

Increasingly the focus of organizations has been to use publicly available data alongside their own to gain greater business insight — for example, using government-published open data to discover patterns of disease, research disease outbreak, or to mine Twitter to find how well a particular product is received.

Whatever the motivation, there is a need to bring together a variety of data, much of which is unstructured, and use it to answer business questions. A lot of this data is stored in plain text fields. From tweets to medical notes, having a computer evaluate what is important within text is really, really hard.

For storing this data and discovering relevant information presents issues, too. Databases evaluate queries over indexes. Search engines do the same thing. In NoSQL, there is an ever-increasingly blurred line between where the database ends and the search engine begins. This enables unstructured information to be managed in the same way as more regular (albeit rapidly changing) information. It's even possible to build in stored searches that are used to trigger entity extraction and entity enrichment activities in unstructured data.

Consider a person tweeting about a product. You may have a list of products, list of medical issues, and list of positive and negative phrases. Being able to write "If a new tweet arrives that mentions Ibuprofen, flag it as a medication" enables you to see how frequently particular medications are used or to specify that you only want to see records mentioning the medication Ibuprofen. This process is called *entity extraction*.

Similarly, if the opinion "really cool" is mentioned, you flag it as an opinion with a property of positive or negative attached. Flagging data and then adding extra information is called *entity enrichment*.

Entity enrichment is a common pattern used when a NoSQL database and search-alerting techniques are combined (turn to Chapters 3 and 16 for more on this topic).

The sparse data problem

As I've mentioned, relational databases can suffer from a sparse data problem — this is where it's possible for columns to have particular values, but often the columns are blank.

Consider a contact management system, which may have a field for home phone, cell phone, twitter ID, email, and other contact fields. If your phone is anything like mine, usually you have only one or two of these fields present.

Using an RDBMS requires a null value be placed into unused columns. Potentially, there could be 200 different fields, 99 percent with blank null values.

An RDBMS will still allocate disk space for these columns, though, because they potentially could have a value after future edits of the contact data. This is a great waste of resources. It's also inefficient to retrieve 198 null values over SQL in a result set.

NoSQL databases are designed to bypass this problem. They store and index only what is provided by the client application. No nulls stored, and no storage space previously allocated, but unused. You just store what you need to use.

Dynamically changing relationships

You may discover facts and relationships over time. Consider LinkedIn where someone may be a second-level connection (a friend of a friend). You realize you know the person, so you add her as a first level relationship by inserting a single fact or relationship in the application.

You could go one step further and define subclasses of these relationships, such as worked with, friends with, or married to. You may even add metadata to these relationships, such as a "known since" date.

Relational databases aren't great at managing these things dynamically. Sure you could model the above relationships, but what if you discover or infer a new class of relationship between entities or subjects that wasn't considered during the original system design?

Using an RDBMS for this would require an ever-increasing storm of many-to-many relationships and linking tables, one table schema for each relationship class. This approach would be hard to keep up with and maintain.

Another aspect of complex relationships is on the query side. What if you want to know all people within three degrees of separation of a person? This is a common statistic on LinkedIn.

Just writing the SQL gives you a headache. "Return all people who are related to Person1, or have a relationship with Person2 who is related to Person1, or is related to Person3, who is related to Person4, who is related to Person1. Oh, and make sure there are no duplicates, would you please?" Ouch!

These self-referencing queries where the same table references itself are very difficult to construct a query for in an RDBMS, and typically run poorly.

Triple and graph store NoSQL databases are designed with dynamically changing relationships in mind. They specifically use a simpler data model but at terrific scale to ensure these questions can be answered quickly.

Global distribution and access

We live in an interconnected world, but these interconnects don't have infinite bandwidth or even guaranteed connectivity. To provide a globally high-performance service across continents requires a certain amount of replication of data. For example, a tweet from someone in Wisconsin may result in a cached copy being written in Ireland or New Zealand. This is to make read performance better globally.

Many NoSQL databases provide the capability to replicate information to distributed servers intelligently so as to provide this service. This is generally built in at the database level and includes management settings and APIs to tweak for your particular needs. A lot of the time, though, this replication requires that global copies may have a slightly outdated view of the overall data. This approach is called an *eventual consistency* model, which means you can't guarantee that a person in Singapore sees all of a person's tweets if that person just tweeted in Wisconsin.

For tweets, this lag time is fine. For billion dollar financial transactions, not so much. Care is needed to manage this (turn to Chapter 3, for more on mission-critical issues).

NoSQL benefits and precautions

There's more to NoSQL than simply being the gleam in the eye of agile web developers. Real business value can be realized by using a NoSQL database solution.

NoSQL vendors have focused strongly on ease of development. A technology can be adopted rapidly only if the development team views it as a lower-cost alternative. This perspective results in streamlined development processes or quicker ways to beat traditionally knotty problems, like those in traditional approaches mentioned in this chapter.

Lower total cost of ownership (TCO) is always a favorite with chief information officers. Being able to use commodity hardware and rapidly churn out new services and features are core features of a NoSQL implementation. More so with NoSQL than relational DBMS, iterative improvements can be made quickly and easily, thanks to schema agnosticism.

It's not all about lower cost or making developers' lives easier though. A whole new set of data types and information management problems can be solved by applying NoSQL approaches.

Hopefully, this chapter has whetted your appetite to find out not just what NoSQL is good for, but also how these features are provided in different NoSQL databases.

Chapter 2

NoSQL Database Design and Terminology

In This Chapter

▶ Identifying and handling different types of data

▶ Describing NoSQL and its terminology

▶ Encompassing the range of consistency options available

▶ Integrating related technologies

*N*ew data management challenges have triggered a new database technology — NoSQL. NoSQL thinking and technology mark a shift away from traditional data management technologies. With all the new terms and techniques and the wide variety of options, it's not easy to come up with a succinct description of NoSQL.

NoSQL databases aren't a mere layer on top of existing technologies used to address a slightly different use case. They're different beasts entirely. Each type of NoSQL database is designed to manage different types of data. Understanding the data you want to manage will help you apply the right NoSQL solution.

The popularity of NoSQL databases lies largely in the speed they provide for developers. NoSQL solutions are quicker to build, update, and deploy than their relational forerunners. Their design is tuned to ensure fast response times to particular queries and how data is added to them.

This speed comes with tradeoffs in other areas, including ensuring data consistency — that is, data that has just been added or updated may not be immediately available for all users. Understanding where consistency should and shouldn't be applied is important when deciding to deploy a NoSQL solution.

Modern computer systems don't exist in a vacuum; they're always communicating with someone or something. NoSQL databases are commonly paired with particular complementary computer software, from search engines to semantic web technologies and Hadoop. Leveraging these technologies can make deployment of NoSQL more productive and useful.

Managing Different Data Types

I like to think in lists. When describing something, I list its properties and the values for those properties. When describing a set of objects, I use a table with a row for each object and a column for each property. You probably do something similar, for example, when you use Microsoft Excel or a similar program to store important information about a set of objects.

Sometimes some of these properties relate objects to other objects. Perhaps you have a set of drop-down lists, such as Expense Type, on your personal finance sheet. This Expense Type drop-down list is defined in another sheet called Reference. This linking, therefore, represents a relationship between two sheets, or tables.

The relational database management system (RDBMS) was introduced in the 1970s to handle this exact type of data. Today, the RDBMS underpins most organizations' applications. Examples of such systems include customer relationship management (CRM) systems that hold details on prospects, customers, products, and sales; and banking systems that include a list of transactions on your bank accounts.

NoSQL databases aren't restricted to a rows-and-columns approach. They are designed to handle a great variety of data, including data whose structure changes over time and whose interrelationships aren't yet known.

NoSQL databases come in four core types — one for each type of data the database is expected to manage:

- **Columnar:** Extension to traditional table structures. Supports variable sets of columns (column families) and is optimized for column-wide operations (such as count, sum, and mean average).

- **Key-value:** A very simple structure. Sets of named keys and their value(s), typically an uninterpreted chunk of data. Sometimes that simple value may in fact be a JSON or binary document.

- **Triple:** A single fact represented by three elements:

  - The subject you're describing

- The name of its property or relationship to another subject

- The value — either an intrinsic value (such as an integer) or the unique ID of another subject (if it's a relationship)

For example, Adam likes Cheese. Adam is the subject, likes is the predicate, and Cheese is the object.

✔ **Document:** XML, JSON, text, or binary blob. Any treelike structure can be represented as an XML or JSON document, including things such as an order that includes a delivery address, billing details, and a list of products and quantities.

Some document NoSQL databases support storing a separate list (or document) of properties about the document, too.

Most data problems can be described in terms of the preceding data structures. Indeed, nearly all computer programs ever written fall into these categories. It is therefore important to understand how you can best store, retrieve and query that data.

The good news is that there's now a set of databases to properly manage each different type of data, so you don't have to shred data into a fixed relational schema (by shred, I mean convert complex data structures to simple excel like table structures with relationships, which has always seemed like the wrong thing to do). I don't like writing plumbing code just to store and retrieve data — and that's despite my father being a plumber!

In addition to the preceding NoSQL data types, here are two other developments worth mentioning:

✔ **Search engines:** If you're storing information that has a variable structure or copious text, you need a common way across structures to find relevant information, which search engines provide.

✔ **Hybrid NoSQL databases:** These databases provide a mix of the core features of multiple NoSQL database types — such as key-value, document, and triple stores — all in the same product.

Several search engines and hybrid databases apply general themes present in NoSQL products — namely, allowing variable data types and being horizontally scalable on commodity hardware. As the internal designs of search engines and hybrid NoSQL databases are similar and complementary, I'm including them in this book. (For information on what I'm not covering, see the upcoming sidebar named, you guessed it, "What I'm not covering.")

What I'm not covering

Because the NoSQL world is awash with a range of products, I had to carefully select which products to include and which to exclude. Conversely, I wanted to provide more content than you might find in other NoSQL books.

I mention several products in each type of NoSQL database and complementary technologies. I had to draw the line somewhere, though, so here's what I'm not covering, and why:

- **In-memory and flash databases:** Some great advances have been made in real-time online transaction processing (OLTP) and analytics using in-memory databases. In-memory databases are very specialized and are targeted to particular problem domains. I have, though, mentioned NoSQL databases that take advantage of flash or memory caching to aid real-time analytics.

- **Complex proprietary stacks:** Large multinational vendors may be inclined to think they have a solution that fits in this book. Typically, this solution involves integrating multiple products. I want to cover NoSQL databases that provide a platform, not technical jigsaw pieces that you have to cobble together to provide

similar functionality, which is why these guys aren't included. I do mention single-product commercial NoSQL software such as Oracle NoSQL, MarkLogic, Microsoft's Document DB, and IBM Cloudant, though.

- **NewSQL:** This is a new database access paradigm. It applies the software design lessons of NoSQL to RDBMS, creating a new breed of products, which is a great idea, but fundamentally these products still use traditional relational math and structures, which is why they aren't included. Hopefully, someone will write a *For Dummies* book about these new databases!

- **Every possible NoSQL database out there:** Finally, there are just too many. I picked the ones you're most likely to come across or that I believe provide the most promise for solving mission-critical enterprise problems. I do mention the key differences among many products in each NoSQL category, but I concentrate on one or two real-world examples for each to show their business value.

Columnar

Column stores are similar at first appearance to traditional relational DBMS. The concepts of rows and columns are still there. You also define column families before loading data into the database, meaning that the structure of data must be known in advance.

However, column stores organize data differently than relational databases do. Instead of storing data in a row for fast access, data is organized for fast column operations. This column-centric view makes column stores ideal for running aggregate functions or for looking up records that match multiple columns.

Aggregate functions are data combinations or analysis functions. They can be as simple as counting the number of results, summing them, or calculating their mean average. They could be more complex, though — for example, returning a complex value describing an overarching range of time.

Column stores are also sometimes referred to as Big Tables or Big Table clones, reflecting their common ancestor, Google's Bigtable.

Perhaps the key difference between column stores and a traditional RDBMS is that, in a column store, each record (think *row* in an RDBMS) doesn't require a single value per column. Instead, it's possible to model column families. A single record may consist of an ID field, a column family for "customer" information, and another column family for "order item" information.

Each one of these column families consists of several fields. One of these column families may have multiple "rows" in its own right. Order item information, for example, has multiple rows — one for each line item. These rows will contain data such as item ID, quantity, and unit price.

A key benefit of a column store over an RDBMS is that column stores don't require fields to always be present and don't require a blank padding null value like an RDBMS does. This feature prevents the sparse data problem I mentioned in Chapter 1, preserving disk space. An example of a variable and sparse data set is shown in Figure 2-1.

Order Table

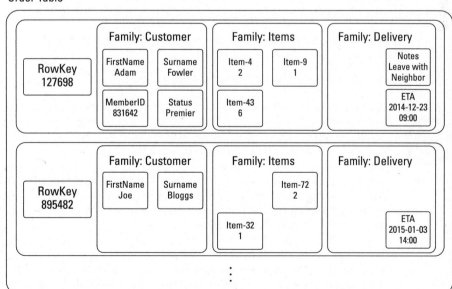

Figure 2-1: Column families at work.

The great thing about column stores is that you can retrieve all related information using a single record ID, rather than using the complex Structured Query Language (SQL) join as in an RDBMS. Doing so does require a little upfront modeling and data analysis, though.

In the example in Figure 2-1, I can retrieve all order information by selecting a single column store row, which means the developer doesn't need to be aware of the exact complex join syntax of a query in a column store, unlike they would have to be using complex SQL joins in an RDBMS.

So, for complex and variable relational data structures, a column store may be more efficient in storage and less error prone in development than its RDBMS ancestors.

Note that, in my *item* column family, each item's ID is represented within the key, and the value is the quantity ordered. This setup allows for fast lookup of all orders containing this item ID. You can find more on structuring your data for fast lookup in Chapters 9 and 10.

If you know the data fields involved up front and need to quickly retrieve related data together as a single record, then consider a column store.

Key-value stores

Key-value stores also have a record with an ID field — the key in key-value stores — and a set of data. This data can be one of the following:

✔ An arbitrary piece of data that the application developer interprets (as opposed to the database)

✔ Any set of name-value pairs (called *bins*)

Think of it as a shared mailbox in an apartment building. All you see from the outside is a set of numbered holes. Using a key, you access whatever is in the mailbox. After looking at the mail, you decide what to do with it (probably just throw it away, if it's junk like most of my mail).

In this way, key-value stores are similar to column stores in that it's possible to store varying data structures in the same logical record set. Key-value stores are the simplest type of storage in the NoSQL world — you're just storing keys for the data you provide.

Some key-value stores support typing (such as integers, strings, and Booleans) and more complex structures for values (such as maps and lists). This setup aids developers because they don't have to hand-code or decode string data held in a key-value store.

In computer science, a "list" is zero or more data values. These values may or may not be stored in a sorted representation that allows for fast match processing.

Maps are a simple type of key-value storage. A unique key in a map has a single arbitrary value associated with it. The value could be a list of another map. So, it's possible to store tree structures within key-value stores, if you're willing to do the data processing yourself.

If you have numerous maps in your key-value store, consider a document store instead, which will likely minimize the amount of code required to operate on your data and make search and retrieval easier.

Key-value stores are optimized for speed of ingestion and retrieval. If you need very high ingest speed on a limited numbers of nodes and can afford to sacrifice complex ad hoc query support, then a key-value store may be for you.

Triple and graph stores

Although it's just now becoming prominent, the concept of triples has been around since 1998, thanks to the World Wide Web Consortium (W3C) and Sir Tim Berners-Lee (one of my British heroes).

Before reading this book you may not have heard of triple (or graph) stores, but if you're experienced with LinkedIn or Facebook, you're probably familiar with the term *social graph*.

Under the hood of these approaches is a simple concept: every *fact* (or more correctly, *assertion*) is described as a triple of subject, predicate, and object:

✔ A *subject* is the thing you're describing. It has a unique ID called an IRI. It may also have a type, which could be a physical object (like a person) or a concept (like a meeting).

✔ A *predicate* is the property or relationship belonging to the subject. This again is a unique IRI that is used for all subjects with this property.

✔ An *object* is the intrinsic value of a property (such as integer or Boolean, text) or another subject IRI for the target of a relationship.

Figure 2-2 illustrates a single subject, predicate, object triple.

Therefore, Adam likes Cheese is a triple. You can model this data more descriptively, as shown here:

Figure 2-2:
A simple
semantic
assertion.

Adam Fowler: Person — likes → Cheese: Foodstuff

```
AdamFowler is_a Person
AdamFowler likes Cheese
Cheese is_a Foodstuff
```

More accurately, though, such triple information is conveyed with full IRI information in a format such as Turtle, like this:

```
<http://www.mydomain.org/people#AdamFowler> a <http://www.mydomain.
        org/rdftypes#Person> .
<http://www.mydomain.org/people#AdamFowler> <http://www.mydomain.
        org/predicates#likes> <http://www.mydomain.org/
        foodstuffs#Cheese> .
<http://www.mydomain.org/foodstuffs#Cheese> a <http://www.mydomain.
        org/rdftypes#Foodstuff> .
```

The full Turtle example shows a set of patterns in a single information domain for the URIs of RDF types, *people, relationships,* and *foodstuffs.* A single information domain is referred to as an *ontology.* Multiple ontologies can coexist in the same triple store.

It's even possible for the same subject to have multiple IRIs, with a *sameAs* triple asserting that both subjects are equivalent.

You can quickly build this simple data structure into a web of facts, which is called a *directed graph* in computer science. I could be a *friend_of* Jon Williams or *married_to* Wendy Fowler. Wendy Fowler may or may not have a *knows* relationship with Jon Williams.

These directed graphs can contain complex and changing webs of relationships, or triples. Being able to store and query them efficiently, either on their own or as part of a larger multi-data structure application, is very useful for solving particular data storage and analytics problems.

Figure 2-3 shows an example of a complex web of interrelated facts.

I focus on triple stores in this book rather than graph stores. I think of graph stores as a subset of triple stores that are optimized for queries of relationships, rather than just the individual assertions, or facts, themselves.

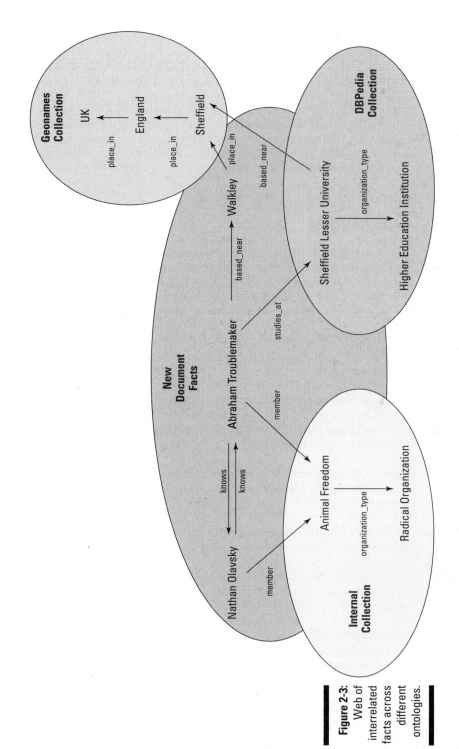

Figure 2-3:
Web of interrelated facts across different ontologies.

Graph math is complex and specialized and may not be required in all situations where storing triples are required. Throughout this book, I point out where the difference matters. The query types supported also affect the design of a graph store, which I talk about in Chapter 19.

If you need to store facts, dynamically changing relationships, or provenance information, then consider a triple store. If you need to know statistics about the graph (such as how many degrees of separation are between two subjects or how many third level social connections a person has), then you should consider a graph store.

Document

Document databases are sometimes called aggregate databases because they tend to hold documents that combine information in a single logical unit — an *aggregate*. You might have a document that includes a TV episode, series, channel, brand, and scheduling and availability information, which is the total set of result data you expect to see when you search an online TV catch-up service.

Retrieving all information from a single document is easier with a database (no complex joins as in an RDBMS) and is more logical for applications (less complex code).

The world is awash with documents. Documents are important as they are generally created for a high-value purpose. Unfortunately many of them are tax documents and bills, but that's totally out of my control. I just help organizations manage the things!

Loosely, a document is any unstructured or tree-structured piece of information. It could be a recipe (for cheesecake, obviously), financial services trade, PowerPoint file, PDF, plain text, or JSON or XML document.

Although an online store's orders and the related delivery and payment addresses and order items can be thought of as a tree structure, you may instead want to use a column store for these. This is because the data structures are known up front, and it's likely they won't vary and that you'll want to do column operations over them. Most of the time, a column store is a better fit for this data.

Some NoSQL databases provide the best of both worlds — poly-structured document storage and fast field (column) operations (see the "Hybrid NoSQL databases" section in this chapter, for details on heterogeneous data management).

This makes a document database a bit of a catchall. Interestingly, because of its treelike nature, an effective document store is also capable of storing simpler data structures.

A table, for example, can be modeled as a very flat XML document — that is, one with only a single set of elements, and no sub-element hierarchies. A set of triples (aka *subgraph*) can be stored within a single document, or across documents, too. The utility of doing so depends, of course, on the indexing and query mechanisms supported. There's no point storing triples in documents if you can't query them.

Search engines

It may seem strange to include search engines in this chapter, but many of today's search engines use an architecture very similar to NoSQL databases. Their indexes and query processing are highly distributed. Many search engines are even capable of acting as a key-value or document store in their own right.

NoSQL databases are often used to store unstructured data, documents, or data that may be stored in a variety of structures, such as social media posts or web pages. The structures of this indexed data vary greatly.

Also, document databases are appropriate in cases where system administrators or developers frequently don't have control of the structures. This situation is common in publishing, where one storefront receives feeds of new books and their metadata from many publishers.

Although publishers use similar standards such as PDF and ePub for documents and ONIX XML files for metadata, they all produce documents in slightly different ways. As a result, consistent handling of data is difficult, and publishing is a great use case for a Document database.

Similar problems occur in the defense and intelligence realms. An agency may receive data from an ally or a terrorist's hard disk in a variety of formats. Waiting six months to develop a revised relational database schema to handle a new type of target is not viable! This is where *document NoSQL databases* can be used.

Storing many structures in a single database necessitates a way to provide a standard query mechanism over all content. Search engines are great for that purpose. Consider search as a key requirement to unstructured data management with NoSQL Document databases.

Search technology is different from traditional query database interface technology. SQL is not a search technology; it's a query language. Search deals with imperfect matches and relevancy scoring, whereas query deals with Boolean exact matching logic (that is, all results of a query are equally relevant).

Hybrid NoSQL databases

Given the range of data types being managed by NoSQL databases, you're forgiven if you think you need three different databases to manage all your data. However, although each NoSQL database has its core audience, several can be used to manage two or more of the previously mentioned data structures. Some even provide search on top of this core all-data platform.

A recent claim in relational circles is that NoSQL databases cannot manage a range of NoSQL data types. Throughout this book, I explain the core capabilities of each type of NoSQL database. Use this information to separate vendor claims from facts.

Hybrid databases can easily handle document and key-value storage needs, while also allowing fast aggregate operations similar to how column stores work. Typically, this goal is achieved by using search engine term indexes, rather than tabular field indexes within a table column in the database schema design itself.

The functionality provided, though, is often the same as in column stores. So, these products have three or four of the preceding types covered: key-value, document, and column stores, as well as search engines.

Many databases are moving in this direction. In Part 7, I highlight the databases that are leading the way.

Available NoSQL products

At my last count, there were more than 250 databases described by analysts in the NoSQL field. With so many (and because of this book's page count, plus the risk of repetitive strain injury), I had to select only a few of them. Here is a condensed list of the leaders in providing NoSQL databases:

- **Columnar:** DataStax, Apache Cassandra, HBase, Apache Accumulo, Hypertable
- **Key-value:** Basho Riak, Redis, Voldemort, Aerospike, Oracle NoSQL
- **Triple/graph:** Neo4j, Ontotext's GraphDB (formerly OWLIM), MarkLogic, OrientDB, AllegroGraph, YarcData
- **Document:** MongoDB, MarkLogic, CouchDB, FoundationDB, IBM Cloudant, Couchbase

- **Search engine:** Apache Solr, Elasticsearch, MarkLogic
- **Hybrid:** OrientDB, MarkLogic, ArangoDB

In Parts II through VII, I deal with each type of NoSQL database in turn, describing the key unique features of each option and reviewing one product of each type in detail.

Describing NoSQL

If you studied databases in school, you may have been indoctrinated in a relational way of thinking. Say *database* to most people, and they think *relational database management system.* This is natural because during the past 30 years, the RDBMS has been so dominant.

Getting your head around NoSQL can be a bit hard, but this book was created to make it as easy as possible.

To aid you on this journey, I want to introduce some key terms that are prevalent in the following chapters, as well as what they mean when applied to NoSQL databases.

- **Database construction**
    - *Database:* A single logical unit, potential spread over multiple machines, into which data can be added and that can be queried for data it contains.

        The relational term *tablespace* could also be applied to a NoSQL database or collection.

    - *Data farm:* A term from RDBMS referring to a set of read-only replica sets stored across a managed cluster of machines.

        In an RDBMS, these typically can't have machines added without down time. In NoSQL clusters, it's desirable to quickly scale out.

    - *Partition:* A set of data to be stored together on a single node for processing efficiency, or to be replicated.

        Could also be used for querying. In this case, it can be thought of as a *collection.*

- **Database structure**
    - *Collection:* A set of records, typically documents, that are grouped together. This is based not on a property within the record set, but within its metadata. Assigning a record to a collection is usually done at creation or update time.

- *Schema:* In RDBMS and to a certain extent column stores. The structure of the data must be configured in the database before any data is loaded.

  In document databases, although any structure can be stored, it is sometimes better to limit the structures by enforcing schema, such as in an XML Schema Definition. NoSQL generally, though, is regarded as schema-free, or as supporting variable schema.

✔ **Records**

- *Record:* A single atomic unit of data representation in the particular database being described.

  In an RDBMS, this would be a row, as it is in column stores. This could also be a value in a key-value store, a document in a document store, or a subject (not triple) in a triple store.

- *Row:* Atomic unit of record in an RDBMS or column store.

  Could be modeled as an element within a document store or as a map in a key-value store.

- *Field:* A single field within a record. A column in an RDBMS.

  May not be present in all records, but when present should be of the same type or structure.

- *Table:* A single class of record. In Bigtable, they are also called tables. In a triple store, they may be called subject RDF types or named be graphs, depending on the context. In a document store, they may be collections. I'm using record type generically to refer to this concept.

✔ **Record associations**

- *Primary key:* A guaranteed unique value in a particular table that can be used to always reference a record. A key in a key-value store, URI in a document store, or IRI in a triple or graph store.

- *Foreign key:* A data value that indicates a record is related to a record in a different table or record set. Has the same value as the primary key in the related table.

- *Relationship:* A link, or edge in graph theory, that indicates two records have a semantic link. The relationship can be between two records in the same or different tables.

  In RDBMS, it's normally other tables, whereas in a triple store it's common to relate subjects of the same type (people in a social graph, for example). Some databases, mainly graph stores, support adding metadata to the relationships.

✔ **Storage organization**

- *Server:* A single computer node within a cluster. Typically runs a single instance of a database server's code.

- *Cluster:* A physical grouping or servers that are managed together in the same data center to provide a single service. May replicate its databases to clusters in other data centers.

- *Normal form:* A method of normalizing, or minimizing duplication, in data in an RDBMS.

  NoSQL databases typically lead to a denormalized data structure in order to provide faster querying or data access.

✔ **Replication technology**

- *Disk replication:* Transparent replication of data between nodes in a single cluster to provide high-availability resilience in the case of a failure of a single node.

- *Database replication:* Replication between databases in different clusters. Replicates all data in update order from one cluster to another. Always unidirectional.

- *Flexible replication:* Provides application controlled replication of data between databases in different clusters. Updates may not arrive in the same order they were applied to the first database. Typically involves some custom processing, such as prioritization of data updates to be sent next. Can be bi-directional with appropriate update conflict resolution code.

✔ **Search tools**

- *Index:* An ordered list of values present in a particular record.

- *Reverse index:* An ordered list of values (terms), and a list of primary keys of records that use these terms.

  Provides for efficient unstructured text search and rapid aggregation functions and sorting when cached in memory.

- *Query:* A set of criteria that results in a list of records that match the query exactly, returned in order of particular field value(s).

- *Search:* A set of criteria that results in a relevancy-ordered list that match the query.

  The search criteria may not require an exact match, instead returning a relevancy calculation weighted by closeness of the match to the criteria. This is what Google does when you perform a search.

Applying Consistency Methods

The *consistency* property of a database means that once data is written to a database successfully, queries that follow are able to access the data and get a consistent view of the data. In practice, this means that if you write a record to a database and then immediately request that record, you're guaranteed to see it. It's particularly useful for things like Amazon orders and bank transfers.

Consistency is a sliding scale, though, and a subject too deep to cover here. However, in the NoSQL world, consistency generally falls into one of two camps:

- ✔ **ACID Consistency (ACID stands for *Atomicity, Consistency, Isolation, Durability*):** ACID means that once data is written, you have full consistency in reads.

- ✔ **Eventual Consistency (BASE):** BASE means that once data is written, it will eventually appear for reading.

A battle has been raging between people who believe strong consistency in a database isn't required and those who believe it absolutely is required (translate *people* to *NoSQL companies' marketing departments!*).

The reality is somewhere in between. Does it matter that a person's Facebook post isn't seen by all his friends for five minutes? No, probably not. Change "Facebook post" to "billion-dollar-financial transaction," though, and your attitude changes rapidly! Which consistency approach you pick depends on the situation. In my experience, though, strong consistency is always the choice in mission-critical enterprise system situations.

When you finish this book, one of the things I hope you take away is the difference between eventual consistency (BASE) and strong consistency (ACID), which I cover next.

ACID

ACID is a general set of principles for transactional systems, not something linked purely to relational systems, or even just databases, so it's well worth knowing about. ACID basically means, "*This database has facilities to stop you from corrupting or losing data,*" which isn't a given for all databases. In fact, the vast majority of NoSQL databases don't provide ACID guarantees.

Foundation DB, MarkLogic, and Neo4j are notable exceptions. Some NoSQL databases provide a lower-grade guarantee called *Check and Set* that verifies whether someone else has altered a document before allowing a transaction to complete. This behavior is usually limited because it tends to be implemented on a single-record basis.

MongoDB is a notable database that provides Check and Set capabilities. With MongoDB, an entire node-worth of data can be locked during an update, thereby preventing all read and all write operations until the operation completes. The company is working on removing this limitation, though.

How ACID works

ACID is a four-letter acronym, as explained here:

- **Atomicity:** Each operation affects the specified data, and no other data, in the database.

- **Consistency:** Each operation moves the database from one consistent state to another.

- **Isolation:** One operation in-flight does not affect the others.

- **Durability:** The database will not lose your data once the transaction reports success.

ACID transactional consistency can be provided various ways:

- In the locking model, you stop data from being read or written on the subset of information being accessed until the transaction is complete, which means that during longer-running transactions, the data won't be available until all of the update is committed.

- An alternative mechanism is multiversion concurrency control (MVCC), which bears no resemblance to *document versioning;* instead, it's a way of adding new data without read locking.

In MVCC, each record gets a creation and deletion timestamp. When a record is created, it's given a creation timestamp. When a new transaction starts that alters that record, a new record is created with different information — the original data isn't altered or locked.

This behavior means the original can still be read with all original values, even during a long-running transaction. Only when the transaction completes is the old record given a deletion timestamp.

The database shows only the latest undeleted record at the time you start your query. Therefore, transactions don't interfere with each other. MVCC provides for fully serializable transactions, which is a hard beast to implement!

The downside is that your database periodically needs a merge operation to remove deleted records, although this is usually managed automatically, so generally only a small storage price is paid for rapid ingestions or updates. This approach, however, does require that the database administrator plan for this occasional extra read and write load when sizing the hardware required for a particular NoSQL database application.

BASE

BASE means that rather than make ACID guarantees, the database has a tunable balance of consistency and data availability. This is typically the case when nodes in a given database cluster act as primary managers of a part of the database, and other nodes hold read-only replicas.

To ensure that every client sees all updates (that is, they have a consistent view of the data), a write to the primary node holding the data needs to lock until all read replicas are up to date. This is called a *two-phase commit* — the change is made locally but applied and confirmed to the client only when all other nodes are updated.

BASE relaxes this requirement, requiring only a subset of the nodes holding the same data to be updated in order for the transaction to succeed. Sometime after the transaction is committed, the read-only replica is updated.

The advantage of this approach is that transactions are committed faster. Having readable live replicas also means you can spread your data read load, making reading quicker.

The downside is that clients connecting to some of the read replicas may see out-of-date information for an unspecified period of time. In some scenarios, this state is fine. If you post a new message on Facebook and some of your friends don't see it for a couple of minutes, it's not a huge loss. If you send a payment order to your bank, though, you may want an immediate transaction.

An alternative approach to read-only replicas is to have a *shared-nothing* cluster in which only one node on a cluster always serves a particular part of the database.

Shared-nothing doesn't mean you lose replication, though. Databases that employ this method typically do replicate their data to a secondary area on another primary node or nodes — but only one node is the master for reads and writes at any time.

Shared-nothing clusters have the advantage of a simpler consistency model but require a two-phase commit to replicas. This fact means the transaction locks while all replicas are updated. (An internal lock plus locking for other nodes gives you two phases.)

This typically has less impact than shared data clusters with read-only replicas, though, because shared-nothing replica data areas don't receive read requests for that part of the database. Therefore, two-phase commits are faster on a shared-nothing cluster than on a cluster with readable replicas.

Choosing ACID or BASE?

As you might expect, much of the argument is because NoSQL vendors can differentiate themselves from their competitors by claiming a different, unique approach. It's interesting to note, however, the number of NoSQL vendors with ACID-compliance on their roadmap.

Some NoSQL databases have ACID-compliance on their roadmap, even though they are proponents of BASE, which shows how relevant ACID guarantees are to *enterprise*, *mission-critical* systems.

Many companies use BASE-consistency products when testing ideas because they are free but then migrate to an ACID-compliant paid-for database when they want to go live on a mission-critical system.

The easiest way to decide whether you need ACID is to consider the interactions people and other systems have with your data. For example, if you add or update data, is it important that the very next query is able to see the change? In other words, are important decisions hanging on the current state of the database? Would seeing slightly out-of-date data mean that those decisions could be fatally flawed?

In financial services, the need for consistency is obvious. Think of traders purchasing stock. They need to check the cash balance before trading to ensure that they have the money to cover the trade. If they don't see the correct balance, they will decide to spend money on another transaction. If the database they're querying is only eventually consistent, they may not see a lack of sufficient funds, thus exposing their organization to financial risk.

Similar cases can be built for ACID over BASE in health care, defense, intelligence, and other sectors. It all boils down to the data, though, and the importance of both timeliness and data security.

Availability approaches

Consistency is a sliding scale, not an absolute. Many NoSQL databases allow tuning between levels of consistency and availability, which relates to the *CAP theorem.*

The CAP theorem is a computer science conjecture, now proven, that shows the list of options as to how the balance between consistency, availability, and partitioning can be maintained in a BASE database system.

Eric Brewer has a lot to answer for! He came up with the CAP conjecture in 2000. It was later proved in 2002, and so is now a theorem. The CAP theorem in computer science is fundamental to how many NoSQL databases manage data.

CAP stands for *C*onsistency, *A*vailability, and *P*artitioning, which are aspects of data management in databases. Here are some questions to consider when considering a BASE and thus CAP approach:

- ✔ **Consistency:** Is the database fully (ACID) consistent, or eventually consistent, or without any consistency guarantees?

- ✔ **Availability:** During a partition, is all data still available (that is, can a partitioned node still successfully respond to requests)?

- ✔ **Partitioning:** If some parts of the same database cluster aren't communicating with each other, can the database still function separately and correct itself when communication is restored?

The CAP theorem states that you cannot have all features of all three at the same time. Most of the time, this is claimed to mean that you can have only two of the three. The reality is that each is a sliding scale. You may be able to trade off a little of one for more of another.

A traditional RDBMS typically provides strong consistency. Some clustered RDBMS also provide good availability, but they don't provide partitioning.

Availability in the CAP theorem is a different concept from high availability as used to describe services. In CAP, I'm talking about data availability.

Also, remember that the definition of consistency in ACID isn't the same definition as in CAP:

- ✔ In ACID, it means that the database is always in a consistent state.
- ✔ In CAP, it means that a single copy of the data has been updated.

Therefore, in CAP, a system that supports BASE can be consistent.

On the other hand, some NoSQL products, such as Cassandra, are partition-tolerant. Each part of the database continues to operate if one is not communicating with the rest of the nodes. This typically occurs because of networking outages rather than outright system failure.

When you allow part of a database to be updated when partitioned, you're saying that the other part of the database cannot see this update. Consequently, allowing partitioning means you always lose some consistency.

Typically, the tradeoff is between consistency and partitioning when you talk about cross data-center database replication use. A particular NoSQL database generally provides either

- ✔ CA (consistency and availability)
- ✔ AP (availability and partition tolerance)

A pragmatic approach to this problem is to allow a data center to operate at full consistency but to make the other data centers' replicas lag their primary stores, thus becoming eventually consistent. In the real world, this setup is the best you can hope for — even permanent fiber cables get dug up by humans!

Within a single data center, you can trade consistency and availability. Some NoSQL databases allow you to tune consistency, usually by adding read-only replicas of data on additional nodes. Replicas are updated outside the transaction boundary and, therefore, are eventually consistent. The upside to this approach is improved read performance and greater availability (at least for read, not write).

Some NoSQL databases don't relax the consistency model when performing this local disk replication between nodes. The MarkLogic NoSQL database, for example, updates its replicas in the local data center within a transaction boundary using a two-phase commit. This means the replicas are always consistent, so if an outage occurs that affects the primary node for data, the secondary node takes over and provides ACID consistency and availability for both write and read operations.

These replicas in MarkLogic are held on nodes that manage their own primary data. Other NoSQL databases' same data-center replicas are stored on nodes that are only for failover — they are read replicas only. As a result, more hardware is needed in these products, just in case of an outage.

It's worth taking into account how NoSQL databases provide local data replicas, as well as how (or if) they have data management or catalog nodes, particularly in terms of their support for high availability and also cost. In this case, you could have three primary nodes and two replicas for each, with a total of nine systems. In this way, you basically triple your computing costs! These are important points when comparing apparently low-cost options to other databases. Don't worry, though, in Parts II through VII, you find out about these and other *enterprise* issues you need to be aware of.

Developing applications on NoSQL

One of the most common conclusions about the emergence of NoSQL databases is that of *polyglot persistence.* Polyglot persistence means that, in order to write a single complete application, the application's developer must use multiple types of databases, each for its most appropriate data type.

I am a polyglot persistence sceptic because I think multiple databases are only required because hybrid NoSQL databases are in their infancy, which I'm not convinced will last; however, people are practicing implementing polyglot persistence now, and no discussion of NoSQL's relevance is complete without including this topic. Moreover, this discussion may influence decisions you make about which software to purchase over the next 5 to 25 years.

Martin Fowler (no relation to me, honest!) writes in his book with Pramod Sadalage, *NoSQL Distilled,* about the era of polyglot *persistence.* In this book he describes how he believes that polyglot persistence will be a long-term need in enterprise systems. Whatever the truth turns out to be, you need to be aware of the current limitations to data type handling in NoSQL databases.

Polyglot persistence

The database world has gone through a steady evolution over the last 40 years. When relational databases first became popular, developers wondered if they would replace mainframe systems and would require them to write applications using data from both types of systems, or replace them entirely.

Of course, mainframes still run many more financial transactions than relational databases do. These mainframes are generally hidden under corporate systems, away from the prying eyes of application developers. Both RDBMS and mainframe systems are used in modern systems such as online banking. The mainframe systems manage bank account balances whereas the RDBMS manage online banking user preferences and application form filling data.

Using both mainframe and RDBMS databases in the same application is what we term polyglot persistence.

On the other hand, you rarely see four or five different relational databases for the same application. Even when used together, they are typically hidden under a data access layer, so an application developer learns how to set up communication with, for example, two SOAP (Simple Object Access protocol) web services, not two different database systems.

Polyglot persistence explained

If you need to store a web of facts, a set of documents, and shopping cart datasets, you can't do so in one NoSQL database. Or when you can store them, it's hard to retrieve all data with a single query. Instead, you must use a single data access layer to handle the various data storage demands, and that's where polyglot persistence comes in.

Polyglot persistence is the idea that a single application that uses different types of data needs to use multiple databases behind that application. Nobody sat down and decided that polyglot persistence was the way forward. It's currently the case that no single database provides all the functionality of a column, key-value, document, or triple store.

Unlike the relational database world where the structural support hasn't changed much in years (except for XML field support), NoSQL databases are gradually crossing over and covering multiple data types. For example, the Elasticsearch search engine is positioning itself as a JSON document store. MongoDB, CouchDB, and MarkLogic have the concept of primary keys or URIs. In this way, they act as key-value stores — the value is just a document.

If you look closely at document NoSQL databases, you can see that they provide some or a majority of the functionality you expect from a column or key-value store.

- ✔ If you're considering a key-value store but some features are missing that handle specifics of the data, then consider a column store.
- ✔ If a column store can't handle a very complex structure in your application, then consider a document store.
- ✔ If you need to manage relationships or facts in your data, then you need features of a triple store, too.

MarkLogic and OrientDB are interesting because they work as a document store and also act as triple and key-value stores. Traditional relational database rows and modern NoSQL column families can be represented easily as a document (JSON or XML).

Column stores are very good at holding a lexicon of data for a field across all record instances. These lexicons can then be used to calculate aggregation values quickly — for example, statistical operations like mean average, standard deviation, or even just listing unique values and their counts.

Some document databases expose their internal field indexes for similar operations. MarkLogic, for example, allows a search to be executed with faceted results returned. These facets are normally just counts of the frequency of mentions of values within search results, and are used to power search applications. Custom user-defined functions (UDFs) and statistical aggregate operations are also supported, though, just as with column stores.

Document databases achieve fast aggregate operations by allowing you to index the structure (XML element or JSON property name and location) and the value of data within a document, which expands the database capabilities beyond just doing a search.

 These indexes may be held or cached in memory, making the speed of statistical operations equivalent to those in a column store. If you have data structures that could be held in a document store but that you want to perform calculations for, don't discount document databases without looking at their lexicon and index functions. You may find a single database to answer multiple business problems.

You can take this scenario even further. If you apply search engine technology over your indexes and provide a well-designed query planner, then you can limit your aggregate functions using query terms efficiently.

If these indexes and queries are handled across a cluster, then you have a very fast in-database MapReduce capability that is efficient for high-speed operational database workloads, as well as for analytic workloads.

NoSQL databases are progressively improving their internal search support. In this regard, document databases and search engines in particular are strongly linked technologies.

NoSQL vendors are trying to add all the preceding features to their products. MarkLogic, for example, already provides these functions within a single product.

I fully expect all NoSQL databases to follow suit. Once this happens, there will be little reason to use multiple databases for non-relational workloads. I predict that by 2017, polyglot persistence in NoSQL will largely be a thing of the past.

The death of the RDBMS?

It's tempting to think that once NoSQL databases evolve to handle more data and query types, the RDBMS will no longer be needed. Nothing could be further from the truth because NoSQL databases can't provide all the functionality of a relational database.

When I was just a glint in my father's eye, a lot of the world's data was stored on hierarchical mainframe systems. These days, you're forgiven if you think that all major systems use relational databases to store their data. Actually this isn't the case. The financial services industry is powered today by mainframe systems. They are the core of all banking transactions that happen today. They haven't been replaced by relational databases because mainframes are better suited for these particular loads.

The same will happen with relational databases. Those applications that are better served by using NoSQL will migrate to those databases. An RDBMS will still run structured, known data loads. Sales force management platforms like Siebel, Salesforce, and Sugar CRM are good examples. Each sales cycle has opportunities, accounts, deal teams, and product line items. There's no need for a schema agnostic approach in these systems. So why would people migrate from a relational database to a NoSQL database?

The answer is, they won't. The majority of today's applications will stay on relational databases. On the other hand, NoSQL databases can be used for the following:

✔ New business problems

✔ Data loads where the schema isn't known upfront or varies wildly

✔ Situations where existing relational databases aren't providing the performance required for the data being managed

Therefore, polyglot persistence's outlook is similar to the state of affairs for today's traditional applications. You may have polyglot persistence over mainframe, relational, and NoSQL systems, but you won't have multiple types of each database for each type of data store.

Some organizations do have legacy systems, though. So, they may have a corporate direction to use Oracle's relational database but still run IBM's DB2 as well. It's possible, therefore, that some applications do run polyglot persistence over the same type of database, which reflects the slow pace of data migrations, not the fact that each database is designed for a different data type.

Integrating Related Technologies

As I mentioned, NoSQL databases are adapting to support more data types. As this is happening, their capabilities around this data will also expand.

These trends will allow organizations to simplify their overall architectures. By analyzing their needs early, organizations can find a single product to meet all their needs, rather than use three products that they must glue together. For example, some current products may provide basic text-search functionality but not all the functionality, such as word stemming, that a full-fledged search engine provides. Understanding your own needs first allows you to select the correct product, or product set, for solving your business needs.

Nothing exists in a vacuum. Pizza needs cheese. Hardware needs software. NoSQL databases are no different. Consequently, in this section, I cover a few complementary technologies that you can consider using in NoSQL projects. I mention them here because they're fundamental to some of the NoSQL databases I discuss later in this book.

Search engine techniques

NoSQL databases are used to manage volumes of unstructured content. Be they long string fields, tweet content (all 140 characters), XML medical notes, or plain text and PDF files. As a result, search functionality is important. Whether the functionality is built in (for example, by embedding Lucene), developed through an optimized search engine, or provided by links to external search platforms (such as Solr or Elasticsearch) varies according to each NoSQL vendor's strategy.

People generally associate search engines only with full-text searches. However, there are many other uses for search engines.

MarkLogic, for example, comes with a built-in search engine developed specifically for the data it was designed to store — documents. The database indexes are the same as those used for full-text search. MarkLogic includes a *universal index*. As well as indexing text content, it indexes exact field values, XML and JSON elements, and attribute and property names, and it maintains document ID (URIs in MarkLogician-speak) and collection lexicons.

Range indexes can be added to this mix after data is loaded and explored. Range indexes enable you to take advantage of less-than and greater-than style queries with integers and times, as well as more complex mathematics such as geospatial searches.

Range index support enables MarkLogic to have one set of indexes to satisfy simple document metadata queries, full-text content queries, or complex search queries, including geospatial or bi-temporal queries.

Other NoSQL databases, though, are often linked to search engines. The most common reason to do so is for full-text search, so it's no surprise that search engines are often integrated to the document NoSQL databases.

Some NoSQL databases embed the common Apache Lucene engine to add full-text indexes for string fields. In some situations, this is enough; but in others, a full-featured distributed search engine is required to run alongside your distributed NoSQL database.

Solr is a distributed search platform that uses Lucene internally to do the indexes. Solr developers have applied many horizontal scalability tricks that NoSQL databases are known for.

Solr can also be used as a simple document store, saving and indexing JSON documents natively, similar to MarkLogic's database.

The lines will continue to be blurred between document NoSQL databases and distributed search platforms, which is why I include search engines alongside the core types of NoSQL search.

Business Intelligence, dashboarding, and reporting

Storing data is all very well and good, but it'd be nice to reuse it for strategic work as well as for operational workloads. In the RDBMS world, an entire second tier of databases is used to allow this type of historical analytics and reporting.

I'm speaking of course of *data warehouses*. These warehouses hold the same information as an operational system but in a structure that's more useful for reporting tools to query.

The problem with this approach is that the source system and the warehouse are never up to date. Typically, this report required an overnight batch update, but sometimes the update occurs only once a week. You might think this isn't a big deal. However, with today's fast pace, institutions are finding that even a 24-hour lag is too slow. Financial services, in particular, must answer questions from regulators on the same day, sometimes within five minutes of being asked!

So, there's a need to perform business intelligence-style queries of data held in operational data stores, showing the current real-time state of the database (for example, "What's my current risk exposure to Dodgy Banking, Incorporated?").

In NoSQL column stores, data is still held in tables, rows, and column families in a structure suited for the operational system, not a warehousing one. Column databases, though, often provide the capability to update aggregations on the fly.

Logging databases are a good example. Cassandra has been used to store log files from systems as events occur. These live events are aggregated automatically to provide hourly, daily, weekly, and monthly statistics.

Document NoSQL databases take a different approach. They store primary copies of data but allow data transformation on query and allow denormalizations to be computed on the fly (see Chapter 14 for more on providing alternative structures of data held in a document NoSQL database).

Regardless of the approach taken, NoSQL databases can be used simultaneously because both the operational data store and for warehousing workloads.

Naturally, you don't want 25 Business Intelligence (BI) reporting users retrieving vast copies of the data on an operational system. This use case can be achieved by using a BI tool that understands the internal NoSQL databases structure. Tableau, for example, has native connectors to several NoSQL databases.

Alternatively, you can create read-only replicas of your NoSQL database. You can allow your reporting users to query that database rather than the live one.

In many situations, though, reporting needs are a lot less complex than people might like to think. Many people simply want a solid operational view of the current state of the world — in other words, dashboards.

You can create dashboards by using aggregate functions over indexes of column or document stores. You can use search to restrict which data is aggregated — for example, just give aggregates of sales from the Pacific Northwest.

Having a NoSQL database with a rich REST (REpresentational State Transfer — a simple way of invoking networked services) API that you can rapidly plug into web widgets is advantageous when building out dashboarding apps, and it's even better if internal data structures (like search results, for example) are supported by a NoSQL vendors' JavaScript API. Using these API removes a lot of the plumbing code you will need to write to power a dashboard.

Batch processing with Hadoop Map/Reduce

Hadoop technology is designed for highly distributed data management and batch analysis. The batch analysis part is called *map/reduce*. The idea is that any operation, or chained operations, consists of two parts:

- ✔ The *map* phase fetches data stored in a record that matches a request.
- ✔ The *reduce* phase boils the data down to a single answer, which is done by distributing the query to all nodes that contain relevant data. Consequently, the work is massively parallelized.

Map/reduce is a way to spread workloads across nodes, assimilate them, and boil them down to unique data before passing it to the client.

In a database context, this means farming a query to all the nodes that hold data for that database and then merging data and removing duplicates when they arrive.

A lot of the time, though, these queries only extract a subset of the data to return as the answer to the caller or perform an aggregate match over the data. Examples are typically counts, sums, and averages of elements or values within each record (whether it's a Bigtable column or a document element).

Many NoSQL database vendors provide an in-database map/reduce-like capability for farming out queries within the cluster and performing similar analyses. In this way, they can take advantage of distributed querying without always having to process all the data on the servers; instead in-memory indexes are evaluated, making index-driven NoSQL databases faster than map/reduce process-driven HBase.

Hadoop HDFS

Hadoop uses a storage technology called the Hadoop Distributed File System (HDFS). This functionality is particularly applicable to NoSQL.

NoSQL databases are highly distributed operational data stores, usually with indexing. Hadoop is a highly distributed store, too, but currently is best suited to batch processing.

The HDFS file system is a great way to use distributed storage and is a cheaper alternative to SANs and NAS storage. You achieve a cost reduction by using commodity servers without expensive RAID disk arrays.

 RAID stands for *R*edundant *A*rray of *I*nexpensive *D*isks. It means data is distributed among disks such that if one disk fails, the system can continue to operate. True enough, the disks are inexpensive, but the RAID controller can be costly!

Although the HDFS approach is slower in terms of query-processing, for long-tail historical data, the tradeoff in cost of storage versus retrieval time may be acceptable.

A NoSQL database that supports automated data tiering based on values can help organizations manage the movement of information during its lifecycle, from being added, updated during use (say financial data in the same quarter), moved to low cost storage for historical low volume reporting, and deletion.).

NoSQL vendors are moving to support HDFS in order to provide operational databases to replace HBase. Accumulo, MongoDB, and MarkLogic are just three examples of these products.

The trend, therefore, is for NoSQL databases to support Hadoop HDFS as one of many types of storage tier while providing their own optimized query processing. As long as the query returns the data you ask for, you don't need to be concerned about whether it uses Hadoop map/reduce or a database's internal query engine — as long as it fast!

Semantics

Semantic technology is a pet love of mine. Weirdly, it predates NoSQL by years! Sir Tim Berners-Lee came up with the principles of the semantic web way back in 1998.

The concept models distributed data in such a way that computers can traverse links among datasets on the web much like users traverse hyperlinks among web pages.

Technologies like RDF and SPARQL are used to model and query shared data, respectively. Resource Description Framework (RDF) is a common mechanism for modeling assertions (known as triples). The query language SPARQL is designed to be to triples what Structured Query Language (SQL) is to relational databases. These triples are stored in a triple store or a graph store.

These technologies have particular relevance for NoSQL. In an RDBMS, people are used to querying across tables using relationships. NoSQL databases don't provide this construct.

However, triple stores provide relationships that can be dynamic, subclassed, and described in their own right, and where the relationships possible among records may not be known at the time a database is designed.

Triple stores, therefore, provide the flexibility in storing relationships that other NoSQL databases provide for the data itself — namely, schema agnosticism and the ability to store different data and relationships without schema definition up front.

So, graph and triple stores hold the promise of providing the answer to cross-record joins currently lacking in other NoSQL databases. A particularly good, albeit not widely used, example is OrientDB.

OrientDB allows you to define document attributes whose value may relate to another document. This is similar to the primary/foreign key relationships from the relational database world. What OrientDB does, though, is to automatically generate the triples to describe this relationship when it recognizes the data in documents.

Furthermore, OrientDB allows you to query this data and dynamically generate a merged document from the result of a set of relationships held in its triple store. It's a very cool approach that other NoSQL vendors are sure to begin applying to their own databases.

Semantic technology also holds the promise of providing more context around search. Rather than return documents that mention "Thatcher," you may want to say "Job Role: Thatcher" or "Politician (subclass of Person): Thatcher." This provides disambiguation of search terms.

Several products exist, including Temis, Smartlogic, and Open Calais, that use text analytics to extract entities (people, places, and so on) and generate semantic assertions so they can be stored in a triple store, linked to the source text it describes in the NoSQL database.

Public cloud

Something worth considering alongside adoption of NoSQL technology is the public cloud. Companies like Amazon and Microsoft offer flexible infrastructure that can be provisioned and shut down rapidly, on demand. A cloud approach aligns well with NoSQL because of NoSQL's ability to scale across many commodity systems.

Adopting NoSQL means you will have a database that naturally fits in a cloud environment. Many NoSQL database products can have nodes added and removed from a cluster dynamically with no down time, which means that during periods of peak usage, you can deploy the hardware dynamically using Amazon Web Services, for example, and also add extra database storage or query capacity on demand, too.

Although many NoSQL databases have their roots in open-source, enterprise features — including cloud management utilities — these database features though are available only as commercial add-ons.

Some databases may be able to scale to any number of nodes, but providing that extra capability may require the database to shut down, or at least negatively affect short-term performance.

These concerns and others are detailed alongside the products in Parts II through VII of this book.

Chapter 3

Evaluating NoSQL

So you've decided you need a NoSQL solution, but there are oh so many options out there. How to decide?

Well, you begin by writing a Request for Information (RFI) and send it to potential suppliers. You're not a NoSQL expert, but you know what you like! Unfortunately, you also know that the vendors' responses to all your questions will be, "Yes, we can do that!"

So, your job is to separate the wheat from the chaff, and that's the purpose of this chapter. My intention is to help you identify the differences among the many options and to make your post-RFI analysis much easier.

The Technical Evaluation

When performing a technical evaluation of products, it's tempting to create a one-size-fits-all matrix of features and functions against which you evaluate all products.

When assessing NoSQL options, though, this approach rapidly falls apart. NoSQL is too broad a category. With traditional relational database management systems, you can request things like "SQL support" or "Allows modifying the schema without system restart."

The range of NoSQL databases means one database may be strong in managing documents, whereas another is strong in query performance. You may determine that you need multiple products, rather than carrying out a simple one-size-fits-all box-ticking beauty pageant.

This section narrows your focus before embarking on the creation of a compliance matrix for your evaluations. By doing so, you can ask the right questions about the right products and do a high-value evaluation.

Table 3-1	NoSQL Data Management Use Cases
Data to Manage	***NoSQL Database***
Trade documents (FpML), Retail insurance policies (ACORD), healthcare messages, e-form data	Document database with XML support
Monthly data dumps in text delimited (CSV, TSV) files, or system/web log files	Bigtable clone for simple structures Document database for very complex structures
Office documents, emails, PowerPoint	Document database with binary document text and metadata extraction support
Web application persistent data (JavaScript Object Notation — JSON)	Document database with JSON support and a RESTful API
Metadata catalog of multiple other systems (for example, library systems)	Bigtable for simple list of related fields and values Document database for complex data structures or full text information
Uploaded images and documents for later retrieval by unique ID	Key-value store for simple store/retrieval Document store with binary text extraction and search for more complex requirements
RDF, N-Triples, N3, or other linked (open) data	Triple store to store and query facts (assertions) about subjects Graph store to query and analyze relationships between these subjects
Mix of data types in this table	Hybrid NoSQL database

Which type of NoSQL is for you?

The first question is what does your data look like? Unlike relational databases, where it's a given that the data model includes tables, rows, columns, and relationships, NoSQL databases can contain a wide variety of data types.

Table 3-1 matches data types with the NoSQL database you may want to consider.

Search features

You can narrow the field of databases if you consider how data is managed and how it's revealed to users and other systems.

Query versus search

An entire book can be filled on discussing query versus search. However, requirements tend to fit on a sliding scale of functionality from simple to complex:

- ✔ Any NoSQL database should be able to handle basic queries. Retrieving a record by an exact property, value, or ID match is the minimum functionality you need in a database. This is what key-value stores provide. These basic queries match exact values, such as

  - By the record's unique ID in the database

  - By a metadata property associated with the record

  - By a field within the record

- ✔ Comparison queries, also commonly called *range queries,* find a stored value within a range of desired values. This can include dates, numbers, and even 2D geospatial coordinates, such as searching:

  - By several matching fields, or fields within a range of values

  - By whether a record contains a particular field at all (query on structure)

  Comparison queries typically require a reverse index, where target values are stored in sequence, and record IDs are listed against them. This is called a Term List.

- ✔ Handling of free text, including more advanced handling such as language selection, stemming, and thesaurus queries, which are typically done by search engines. In the NoSQL world (especially document NoSQL databases), handling unstructured or poly-structured data is the norm, so this functionality is very desirable for such a use case, including support for searching:

- By a free text query

- By a stemmed free text query (both *cat* and *cats* stem to the word cat) or by a thesaurus

- By a complex query (for example, geospatial query) across multiple fields in a record

- By calculating a comparison with a query value and the value within a record's data (for example, calculated distance of five miles based on a point within a record, and the center of a City — Finding hotels in London.)

Some databases have these search functions built in, whereas others integrate an Apache Lucene-based search index or an engine such as Solr.

✔ In the world of analytics, you calculate summaries based on the data in matching records, and perhaps as compared to the search criteria. It's common to calculate relevancy based on distance from a point, instead of simply returning all records within a point and radius geospatial query. So, too, is returning a heat map of the data rather than all matching data. These tools are useful for complex searches such as the following:

- By calculating the above while returning a summary of all results (for example, heat map, facetted search navigation, co-occurrence of fields within records)

- By an arbitrarily complex set of AND / OR / NOT queries combining any of the previously mentioned query terms

- By including the above terms in a giant OR query, returning a higher relevancy calculation based on the number of matches and varying weights of query terms

✔ Facetted search navigation where you show, for example, the total number of records with a value of Sales in the Department field is also useful. This might be shown as "Department — Sales (17)" in a link within a user interface. Faceting is particularly useful when your result list has 10,000 items and you need to provide a way to visually narrow the results, rather than force the user to page through 10,000 records.

Timeliness

Search engines were originally developed to over time index changes of data sources that the search engine didn't control. Engines like Google aren't informed when every web page is updated, so they automatically index websites based on a schedule, for example:

- ✔ Rapidly changing and popular websites like BBC News and CNN may be indexed every few minutes.
- ✔ The index of an average person's blog may be updated weekly.

The timeliness of indexes' updates is very important for some organizations. Financial regulators, for example, now need a near-live view of banks' exposure to credit risks — an overnight update of this vital information is no longer sufficient.

If your information retrieval requirements are nearer the search end of the spectrum than the basic query end, then you need to seriously consider timeliness. If this describes you, I suggest considering two products:

- ✔ A NoSQL database for data
- ✔ A separate search engine like Solr or Elasticsearch for your search requirements

Having these two products installed separately may not be sufficient to guarantee timely access to new data. Even if you can use a NoSQL database distribution that comes with Solr integrated, the indexes may not be updated often enough for your needs. Be sure to check for this functionality when talking to vendors.

When timely updating of search indexes is required, consider a hybrid NoSQL solution that includes advanced search functionality, and definitely ACID compliance in a single product. Sometimes, this may be a case for using Solr built on Lucene as a document store, but many organizations need a full-blown commercial system like MarkLogic with both advanced data management and search capabilities built in.

ACID compliance means the database provides a consistent view over the data — so there's no lag between the time the data is saved and the time it's accessible. Without an ACID compliant fully consistent view, the search index can never be real time.

A NoSQL database with indexes that are used by both the database and the search functionality means that when a document is saved, the search indexes are already up to date, in real time.

RFI questions

The following sample questions identify key required features about information retrieval, ranging from simple to advanced query and search functionality.

In this chapter, I use some common conventions for vendor specification questions:

- ✔ I use these common abbreviations:
  - • TSSS = The System Should Support
  - • TSSP = The System Should Provide
  - • TSSE = The System Should Ensure
- ✔ I use the term "record," but you may change it to "document," "row," "subgraph" or "subject" when appropriate.

General data storage question examples:

- ✔ TSSS storing and retrieving a record by a unique key
- ✔ TSSS indexes over record fields for fast single-key retrieval of matching records
- ✔ TSSS not requiring additional compound indexes for retrieval of records by multiple keys

  Forcing the creation of additional compound indexes can adversely affect storage, and means you need to consider up front every possible query combination of fields.

- ✔ TSSS indexing a range of intrinsic field types (such as Boolean, text, integer, and date)
- ✔ TSSS word, stem, and phrase full-text searching across a record
- ✔ TSSS word, stem and phrase full-text searching limited to a set of fields in a record
- ✔ TSSS range queries, such as dates or integers within a particular range
- ✔ TSSS returning part of a record as a match (as an alternative to returning a complete, long record)
- ✔ TSSS queries including multiple query terms
- ✔ TSSS limiting a query (or query terms) to a specific subset of a record (normally for complex document NoSQL stores — for example, just the "patient summary" section)
- ✔ TSSS returning configurable text snippets along with matches of a query
- ✔ TSSS custom snippeting to return matching data segments, not limited to just text matches (for example, returning a three-minute partial

description of a five-hour video's metadata that matches the query, rather than returning the whole five hour video and forcing the user to find the segment manually)

✔ TSSS, a configurable Google-like grammar for searches beyond simple word queries (for example, `NoSQL AND author:Adam Fowler AND (publication GT 2013)`)

✔ TSSS queries with compound terms (terms containing multiple terms) down to an arbitrary depth

✔ TSSS geospatial queries for points held within records that match an area defined by a bounding box, point-radius, and arbitrarily complex polygon

For timeliness, include these questions:

✔ TSSE that search indexes are up to date within a guaranteed *x* minute window of time from the time a record is updated

✔ TSSE that search indexes are up to date at the same time as the record update transaction is reported as complete (that is, real-time indexing)

✔ TSSS updating multiple records within the boundary of a single ACID transaction

Be sure the vendor *guarantees* that all sizing and performance figures quoted are for systems that ensure ACID transactions and real-time indexing. Many vendors often ascertain their quotes with these features turned off, which leads to inaccurate estimates of performance for NoSQL databases on the web.

Scaling NoSQL

One common feature of NoSQL systems is their ability to scale across many commodity servers. These relatively cheap platforms mean that you can scale up databases by adding a new server rather than replace old hardware with new, more powerful hardware in a single shot.

There are high-volume use cases that will quickly force you to scale out. These include

✔ **You receive status reports and log messages from across an IT landscape.** This scenario requires fast ingest times, but it probably doesn't require advanced analysis support.

✔ **You want high-speed caching for complex queries.** Maybe you want to get the latest news stories on a website. Here, read caches take prominence over query or ingest speeds.

The one thing common to the performance of all NoSQL databases is that you can't rely on published data — none of it — to figure out what the performance is likely to be on your data, for your own use case.

You certainly can't rely on a particular database vendor's promise on performance! Many vendors quote high ingest speeds against an artificial use case that is not a realistic use of their database, as proof of their database's supremacy.

However, the problem is that these same studies may totally ignore query speed. What's the point in storing data if you never use it?

These studies may also be done on systems where key features are disabled. Security indexes may not be enabled, or perhaps ACID transaction support is turned off during the study so that data is stored quickly, but there's no guarantee that it's safe.

This all means that you must do your own testing, which is easy enough, but be sure that the test is as close to your final system as possible. For example, there's no point in testing a single server if you plan to scale to 20 servers. In particular, be sure to have an accurate mix of ingesting, modifying, and querying data.

Consider asking your NoSQL vendor these questions:

- Can you ensure that all sizing and performance figures quoted are for systems that ensure ACID transactions during ingest that support real-time indexing, and that include a realistic mix of ingest and read/query requests?
- Does your product provide features that make it easy to increase a server's capacity?
- Does your product provide features that make it easy to remove unused server capacity?
- Is your product's data query speed limited by the amount of information that has to be cached in RAM?
- Does your product use a memory map strategy that requires all indexes to be held in RAM for adequate performance (memory mapped means the maximum amount of data stored is the same as the amount of physical RAM installed)?
- Can your database maintain sub-second query response times while receiving high-frequency updates?
- Does the system ensure that no downtime is required to add or remove server capacity?
- Does the system ensure that information is immediately available for query after it is added to the database?

✔ Does the system ensure that security of data is maintained without adversely affecting query speed?

✔ Does the system ensure that the database's scale-out and scale-back capabilities are scriptable and that they will integrate to your chosen server provisioning software (for example, VMWare and Amazon Cloud Formation)?

Keeping data safe

As someone who has an interest in databases, I'm sure you're used to dealing with relational database management systems. So, you trust that your data is safe once the database tells you it's saved. You know about journal logs, redundant hard disks, disaster recovery log shipping, and backup and restore features.

However, in actuality, not all databases have such functionality in their basic versions, right out of the box. In fact, very few NoSQL databases do so in their basic versions. These functions tend to be reserved only for enterprise or commercial versions.

So, here are a few guidelines that can help you decide which flavor of a NoSQL database to use:

✔ If you choose open-source software, you'll be buying the enterprise version, which includes the preceding features, so you might as well compare it to commercial-only NoSQL databases.

✔ The total cost of these systems is potentially related more to their day-to-day manageability (in contrast to traditional relational database management systems) — for example, how many database administrators will you need? How many developers are required to build your app?

✔ You need to be very aware of how data is kept safe in these databases, and challenge all vendor claims to ensure that no surprises crop up during implementation.

The web is awash with stories from people who assumed NoSQL databases had all of these data safety features built in, only to find out the hard way that they didn't.

Sometimes the problems are simply misunderstandings or misconfigurations by people unfamiliar with a given NoSQL database. Other times, though, the database actually doesn't have the features needed to handle the workload and the system it's used on.

A common example relates to MongoDB's capability for high-speed data caching. Its default settings work well for this type of load. However, if you're running a mission-critical database on MongoDB, as with any database, you need to be sure that it's configured properly for the job, and thoroughly tested.

Here are some thoughts that can help you discover the data safety features in NoSQL databases:

- The vendor should ensure that all sizing and performance figures quoted are for systems that ensure strongly consistent (ACID) transactions during ingest, real time indexing, and a real-life mix between ingest and read/query requests.

- Vendor should provide information about cases in which the database is being used as the primary information store in a mission-critical system. This should *not* include case studies where a different database held the primary copy, or backup copy, of the data being managed.

- TSSE that, once the database confirms data is saved, it will be recoverable (not from backups) if the database server it's saved on fails in the next CPU clock cycle after the transaction is complete.

- Does the database ensure data is kept safe (for example, using journal logs or something similar)?

- Does the system support log shipping to an alternative DR site?

- TSSE that the DR site's database is kept up to date. How does your database ensure this? For example, is the DR site kept up to date synchronously or asynchronously? If asynchronously, what is the typical delay?

- TTSP audit trails so that both unauthorized access and system problems can be easily diagnosed and resolved.

- What level of transactional consistency does your database provide by default (for example, eventual consistency, check and set, repeatable read, fully serializable)?

- What other levels of transactional consistency can your database be configured to use (for example, eventual consistency, check and set, repeatable read, fully serializable)? Do they include only the vendor's officially supported configurations?

- What is the real cost of a mission-critical system?

  - Ask the vendor to denote which versions of its product fully support high availability, disaster recovery, strong transactional consistency, and backup and restore tools.

  - Ask the vendor to include the complete list price for each product version that achieves the preceding requirements for five physical Intel 64 bit servers with 16 cores, with each running on Red Hat Enterprise Linux. This provides an even playing field for comparing total cost of ownership.

Visualizing NoSQL

Storing and retrieving large amounts of data and doing so fast is great, and once you have your newly managed data in NoSQL, you can do great things, as I explain next.

Entity extraction and enrichment

You can use database triggers, alert actions, and external systems to analyze source data. Perhaps it's mostly free text but mentions known subjects. These triggers and alert actions could highlight the text as being a Person or Organization, effectively tagging the content itself, and the document it lays within.

A good example is the content in a news article. You can use a tool like Apache Stanbol or OpenCalais to identify key terms. These tools may see "President Putin" and decide this relates to a person called Vladimir Putin, who is Russian, and is the current president of the Russian Federation.

Other examples include disease and medication names, organizations, topics of conversation, products mentioned, and whether a comment was positive or negative.

These are all examples of *entity extraction* (which is the process of automatically extracting types of objects from their textual names). By identifying key terms, you can tag them or wrap them in an XML element, which helps you to search content more effectively.

Entity enrichment means adding information based on the original text in addition to identifying it. In the Putin example, you can turn the plain text word "Putin" into `<Person uid="Vladimir-Putin">President Putin</Person>`. Alternatively, you can turn "London" into `<Place lon="-0.15" lat="52.5">London</Place>`.

You can show this data in a user interface as highlighted text with a link to further information about each subject.

You can provide enrichment by using free-text search, alerting, database triggers, and integrations to external software such as TEMIS Luxid and SmartLogic.

Search and alerting

Once you store your information, you may want to search it. Free-text search is straightforward, but after performing entity extraction, you have more options. You can specifically search for a person named "Orange" (as in William of Orange) rather than search records that mention the term orange — which, of course, is also a color and a fruit.

Doing so results in a more granular search. It also allows faceted navigation. If you go to Amazon and search for Harry Potter, you'll see categories for books, movies, games, and so on. The *product category* is an example of a *facet,* which shows you an aspect of data within the search results — that is, the most common values of each facet across all search results, even those not on the current page.

User interfaces can support rich explorations into data (as well as basic Google-esque searches). Users can also utilize them to save and load previous searches.

You can set up saved search criteria so that alerts are activated when newly added records match that criteria. So, if a new record arrives that matches your search criteria, an action occurs. Perhaps "Putin" becomes <Person>Putin</Person, or perhaps an email lets you know a new scientific article has been published.

Not all search engines are capable of making every query term an alert. Some are limited to text fields; others can't do geospatial criteria. Be sure yours can handle the alerts you need to configure.

Aggregate functions

Once you find relevant information, you may want to dig deeper. Depending on the source, you might ask how many countries have a GDP of greater than $400 billion, or what's the average age of all the members in your family tree, or where do the most snake bites occur in Australia. These examples illustrate how analytics are performed over a set of search results. These are count, mean average, and geospatial heat map calculations, respectively.

Being able to make such calculations next to the data offers several advantages. The first advantage is that you can use the indexes to speed things up. Secondly, these indexes are likely to be cached in memory, making them even faster. Thirdly, in memory indexes are particularly useful for a NoSQL database using Hadoop File System (HDFS) storage. HDFS doesn't do native indexing or in-memory column stores for fast aggregation calculations itself — it requires a NoSQL database on top to do this.

Facetted navigation is an example of count-based aggregations over search results that show up in a user interface. The same is true for a timeline showing the number of records that mention a particular point in time. For example, do you want to show results from this year, this month, or this hour?

If you want this functionality, be sure your database has the ability to calculate aggregates efficiently next to the data. Most NoSQL databases do, but some don't.

Charting and business intelligence

The next obvious user-interface extension involves charting and viewing table summaries for live management information and historical business intelligence analysis.

Most NoSQL databases provide an easy-to-integrate REST API in their databases. This means you can plug in a range of application tiers, or even directly connect JavaScript applications to these databases. A variety of excellent charting libraries are available for JavaScript. You can even use the R Ecosystem to create charts based on data held in these databases, after installing an appropriate database connector.

Some NoSQL databases even provide an ODBC or JDBC relational database plug-in. Creating indexes within a given record and showing them as a relational view is a neat way to turn unstructured data in a NoSQL document database into data that can be analyzed with a business intelligence tool.

Check whether your NoSQL database vendor provides visualization tools or has business partners with tools than can connect to these databases. In vogue tools include Tableau Server, which is a modern shared business intelligence server that supports publishing interactive reports over data in a variety of databases, including NoSQL databases.

Extending your data layer

A database does one thing very well: It stores data. However, because all applications need additional software to be complete, it's worth ensuring that your selected NoSQL database has the tools and partner software that provide the extended functionality you require.

Not ensuring that extended functionality is supported will mean you will end up installing several NoSQL databases at your organization. This means additional cost in terms of support, training and infrastructure. It's better to be sure you select a NoSQL database that can meet the scope of your goals, either through its own features or through a limited number of partner software products.

The ability to extend NoSQL databases varies greatly. In fact, you might think that open-source software is easy to extend; however, just because its API is public, doesn't mean it's documented well enough to extend.

Whether you select open-source or commercial software, be sure the developer documentation and training are first rate. You may find, for example, that commercial software vendors have clearer and more detailed published API documentation, and well-documented partner applications from which you can buy compatible software and support.

These software extensions can be anything useful to your business, but typically they are on either the ingest side or the information analysis side of data management rather than purely about storage. For example, extract, transform, and load (ETL) tools from the relational database world are being slowly (slowly) updated for NoSQL databases. Also partner end user applications are emerging with native connectors. The Tableau Business Intelligence (BI) tool, for example, includes native connectors for NoSQL databases.

Ingestion connectors to take information from Twitter, SharePoint, virtual file systems, and combine this data may be useful. Your own organization's data can be combined with reference data from open data systems (for example, data. gov, data.gov.uk, geonames, and dbpedia websites). These systems typically use XML, JSON or RDF as open data formats, facilitating easier data sharing.

Integration with legacy apps is always a problem. How do you display your geospatially enriched documents within a GIS tool? It's tricky. Open standards are key to this integration and are already widely supported. Examples are GeoJSON, OGC WFS, and WMS mapping query connectors.

File-based applications are always a bit of a problem. It's a logical next step to present a document database as a file system. Many NoSQL databases support the old and clunky WebDAV protocol. Alas, as of yet, no file system driver has become prevalent. Some NoSQL databases are bound to go this way, though.

Ask your NoSQL vendors about their supported partner applications and extensions. These may cost less than building an extended solution yourself, or paying for vendors' professional services.

The Business Evaluation

Technical skills are very necessary in order for you to build a successful application. What is as important, but all too often given much lower priority, is the business evaluation.

Writing the code is one thing, but selecting a database which has a community of followers, proven mission critical success, and people and organizations to call on for help when you need it is just as important.

In this section, I describe some of the areas of the non-technical, or business evaluation, you should consider when evaluating NoSQL databases.

Developing skills

NoSQL is such a fast-growing area that the skills required to use it can't keep up, and with so many different systems, there aren't any open standards equivalent to those for SQL in the relational database world.

Therefore, it's a good idea to find and employ or contract, at the right price, those people who have expertise in the database you select. Also, be sure that you can find online or in-person training. In doing so, don't accept, outright, people's LinkedIn profiles in which experience with MongoDB is listed — sometimes it's listed only because it's a very popular database and the person is looking for a job when in fact they haven't any proven delivery experience with that database. So, you want to be sure they're actually skilled in the database you're using.

Getting value quickly

NoSQL databases make it easy to load data, and they can add immediate value. For example, if early on you solve a few high-value business cases, you may get financial and management backing for larger projects. With this background, you will be able to deploy new applications quickly — potentially stealing a march on your competitors and having fun with awesome new databases in the process!

So, start by identifying high-value solutions for a few difficult, well-scoped, business problems and perform some short-term research projects on them. Use a selection of NoSQL databases during the project's initial phases, and check whether vendor-specific extensions can help you achieve your aims. In NoSQL, vendor lock-in is a given because every product is so different — you may as well embrace the database that best fits your needs.

Having said this, the situation is improving. XML and JSON are the defacto information interchange formats now. In the semantic technology space standards like RDF and SPARQL are the predominant standards. Adopting these long term enables you to switch vendors, but at the moment the fragmented nature of implementation of some of these standards means you may well be better off adopting database specific extensions.

Finding help

With any software product, there comes a point where you need to ask for help. Finding answers on StackOverflow.com is one thing, but in a real-life project, you may come upon a knotty problem that's unique to your business.

In this situation, web searches probably can't help you. You need an expert on the database you're using. Before selecting a database, be sure you can get help when you need it. This could be from freelance consultants or NoSQL software vendors themselves.

Check the price tag, though, before selecting a database — some vendors are charging double the day rate of others for a consultant to be on site. By handing software out for free or very cheaply they have to make their money somewhere!

24 hour, 7 day, 365 day a year dedicated support is also a very good idea for mission critical solutions. "Follow the sun" problem resolution models will also help fix problems quickly. Some vendors' support staff are less technical IT support people, whereas other vendors use actually engineers able to take your problem through to resolution themselves. This is quicker than having to wait for the right time zone for a few third level support engineers to get to work in the morning.

Deciding on open-source versus commercial software

Many people are attracted to open-source software because of the price tag and the availability of online communities of expertise. I use open-source software every day in my job — it's essential for me, and it may well be essential for you, too.

The good news is that you can find a lot of open-source NoSQL vendors and commercial companies that sell support, services, and enterprise versions of their software.

Here are a few reasons to use open-source software in the first place:

- **Freely available software:** This kind of software has been downloaded and tried by others, so some developers are at least familiar with it; and people spend time contributing only to the development of software they consider valuable or are passionate about.

- **Sites like** `StackOverflow.com`: Sites like StackOverflow.com are full of fixes, and someone has probably approached these sites with problems you're likely to encounter.

- **Try before you buy:** With open-source software, you can become familiar with a free version of software before sinking your annual budget into purchasing an enterprise, fully supported version.

Conversely, there are several good reasons for buying and using commercial NoSQL databases instead:

- ✔ **Documentation:** Product documentation is usually much more complete and in-depth than open-source software.

- ✔ **Support:** These companies may offer global 24/7 support and will have trainers, consultants, and sales engineers that can travel to your office to show you how their software can help you — good for getting support for internal proof of concept and business cases.

- ✔ **Rationale:** These companies make money by selling software, not consulting services — their day rates may be lower than those selling add-ons and support for open source databases, which can reduce the cost of implementation.

- ✔ **Products:** Products usually have many more built-in enterprise features than open-source ones do, which means you need fewer add-on modules and services.

- ✔ **Freebies:** Because of the overwhelming number of open-source options, commercial companies now offer free or discounted training and free, downloadable versions of their products that you can use and evaluate.

Building versus buying

As I alluded to earlier, many open-source NoSQL vendors make their money by offering commercial support and services rather than by selling software.

Many open-source NoSQL products are also very new, so not all the features you may need are readily available in the software. As a result, you are likely to spend money on paying for services to add this functionality.

Many organizations have internal technical teams, especially in financial services companies and in some defense and media organizations. Because financial services companies take any advantage they can get to make a profit, so they hire very capable staff.

Your organization may also have a skilled staff. If so, "Congratulations," because you're the exception rather than the rule! If you're in this situation, you may be able to add the extra features yourself, rather than buy expensive services.

However, most organizations aren't in this position, so it's worth checking out the "additional" features in commercial software, even if they don't provide every single feature you want of the box, but allow you to build those features faster.

It's easy to burn money paying for software to be built to fix deficiencies in open source software. Consider the total cost of ownership of any future NoSQL database.

Evaluating vendor capabilities

Whom to trust? Trusting no one, like Fox Mulder (remember, *The X-Files*) only gets you so far. Eventually, you must take the plunge and choose a firm to help you in your endeavors.

Small companies may be local, independent consultancies or smaller NoSQL vendors. They offer a couple of advantages:

- ✔ Small vendors may be more tuned into your industry or geography. They're particularly useful in small countries or sectors where large commercial companies don't often venture.

- ✔ Small vendors tend to be flexible — because you're likely to be a major percentage of their annual income, as well as a useful addition to their portfolio.

Small vendors may be prone to financial troubles and downturns. Also, they may not have enough personnel to service and support your organization's expanded use of a NoSQL database.

Large (usually commercial) software companies typically have their own strengths:

- ✔ Large companies have a greater reach and more resources — both human and financial — to call on.

- ✔ If you have a problem that needs to be solved fast, these companies may be better placed to help you than smaller companies are.

  Large companies have broader experiences than smaller companies have, which means the bigger companies have probably dealt with unique edge cases. So, if you have a unique requirement, these companies may have people who've dealt with similar problems.

Finding support worldwide

You want to find out whether local support is available, as either service consultants or engineering and product support personnel. Be sure you can contact them in your time zone and that they speak your language fluently.

Perhaps you can request a meeting with their local support leader before signing a contract.

In government organizations, security is paramount. In some countries, a support person who's reviewing log files and handling support calls for public sector systems must have proper security clearance, and this is true even for unclassified civilian systems. Usually, these stringent requirements are due to government organizations having suffered data losses or theft in the past. Be sure these people are available if you work in the public sector.

Expanding to the cloud

Many organizations outsource the delivery and support of their IT services to a third party. When provisioning new hardware or applications, this process is typically ongoing. It can also prove costly.

NoSQL databases often are used to solve emerging problems rapidly. Agile development is the norm in delivering the solutions to these problems. This is particularly the case when systems need to go into production within six months or so.

Many organizations are now moving to the cloud for their provisioning and servicing needs in order to make delivery of new IT systems less expensive and more agile. Be sure your NoSQL database can be used in these environments.

Several NoSQL products have specific management features in a cloud environment. Their management APIs can be scripted and integrated with existing systems management tools. Ask your vendor what support it has with the cloud environment you choose.

Getting Support

All sophisticated IT systems have features that become acutely important if they're being used for business or mission-critical jobs. This section details many enterprise class features that you may want to consider if you're running business critical workloads.

Business or mission-critical features

If your organization's reputation or its financial situation will suffer if your system fails, then your system is, by definition, an enterprise class system.

A good example of such a system in the financial services world is a trade management system. Billions of dollars are traded in banks every day. In this case, if your system were to go down for a whole day, then the financial and reputational costs would be huge — and potentially fatal to your business.

The consequences of a failure in a government system might be politically embarrassing, to both executives and those implementing the systems! A possible and more serious side effect, though, might be the risk of life and limb. For example, take a military system monitoring advancing troops. If it were to fail for a day, troops might be put in harm's way.

In the civilian sphere, certainly in the UK and the European Union, primary healthcare systems manage critical information. In the UK, there are what's called Summary Care Records in which patient information is held and shared if needed — for example, information about allergies and medications. If a person is rushed to a hospital, this record is consulted. Without this information on hand, it's possible that improper care might be given.

Vendor claims

Often, people confuse a large *enterprise customer* with a large *enterprise system*. Amazon, for example, is definitely a large-enterprise organization. Everyone is familiar with this organization, so naturally vendors will mention Amazon in their marketing material if they have sold their software to Amazon. If this software is for printing labels on HR folders though, it's not a mission critical *enterprise system*. Treat vendor claims with suspicion unless you know exactly how these organizations are using the NoSQL databases you are considering.

It's worth reading the small print of these vendors' customer success stories:

- ✔ If a database is used to store customer orders and transactions, then it's a mission-critical enterprise system.
- ✔ If a database is used behind an internal staff car sharing wiki page, then it's most definitely not a mission-critical application.

Some systems fall in between the preceding definitions of enterprise and non-enterprise systems. Consider, for example, a database that caches thumbnail images of products on an e-commerce website. Technically, an e-commerce app is mission-critical. If the images weren't available for a full day, that company might well have a major problem. In this scenario, it doesn't take much to imagine that the retailer's reputation might be damaged.

But back to Amazon. If you're buying this book from Amazon (and please do), you probably don't care about thumbnail images. If the database storing just the thumbnail images were to fail, you would still be able to place orders; therefore, this aspect of the system isn't really mission-critical, unlike the preceding situation with the e-commerce retailer's system.

Vendors who mention a *minor system* and an *enterprise customer* in the same breath aren't trying to deceive you. It's perfectly natural for a software vendor to want to shout about a large enterprise customer from the rooftops . . . not that you'd listen! It's more an issue with the English language.

So, when selecting a NoSQL database, be aware of the difference between an enterprise customer and an enterprise system. Ask vendors exactly how their customers use their database software and how critical that part of the system is to the large enterprise's bottom line.

Enterprise system issues

When you're trying to figure out whether a database will work in a mission critical-system, certain issues are obvious — for example, when running a large cluster in which one server fails, the service as a whole is still available.

In this section, I cover these types of system maintenance issues along with disaster recovery and backups.

Perhaps less obvious enterprise issues are about how particular parts of the system work. Two main factors in an enterprise system are durability and security:

 ✔ *Durability* relates to a database's ability to avoid the loss of data. (You may think a database shouldn't be called a database unless it guarantees that you can't lose data, but in the NoSQL world durability isn't a given.)
 ✔ *Security* is essential to many customers. Think, here, about health records or military intelligence systems, as I mentioned earlier in the chapter.

This section treats these issues as being equally important with high availability and disaster recovery because they are as important, if not vital, for the organizations that need them. I include examples of databases which support these features in each subsection so you can decide which one might meet your requirements.

Security

Although security is a concern for all applications, it's a particular concern for certain types of applications. Earlier I talked about how a failed system can harm financial services and government entities; the same is true in terms of security for their databases.

When it comes to dealing with security-related issues, you can choose from a variety approaches. In this section, I cover issues and approaches related particularly to the security of NoSQL databases.

If you think that you can implement security in a layer of an application layer rather than in the database, you're right. However, why spend the time, effort, and money required to do so if you can purchase a database with built-in security features?

Doing otherwise will risk making security an afterthought, with programmers instead spending most of their time on end-user features rather than fundamental system architecture like ensuring security of data.

Given the amount of money you would spend writing in security features and the risks to your reputation and finances if you were to have a security breach, I recommend a *security in depth* approach. That is, buy a product with security features you need built in, rather than try to develop them yourself or rely on application developers to do so.

Role-based access control

One of the most common methods of securing data is to assign each record (or document or graph, depending on your database type) with a set of permissions linked to roles. This is role-based access control, or RBAC for short.

Consider a news release for a website that is being stored in a document (aggregate) NoSQL database. The editor role may have update permissions for the document, whereas a more public role may have only read permissions.

This use case requires assigning *role* permissions, not *user* permissions. Users can be assigned to one or more roles. Thus, users inherit permissions based on the sum of their roles.

Having to create a role in order to give a user permission to perform a particular function may seem like extra work, but this approach is very useful. Consider a user who moves to another department or who leaves entirely. You don't want to have to look manually for every document whose permissions mention this user and change or remove them. Instead just change that user's role assignments in a single operation. Using role-based access control (RBAC) is much easier for long-term maintenance of security permissions.

Watch how databases handle permissions and role inheritance. Consider underwriters in an insurance company, where there may be trainee, junior, and senior underwriters, each with increasing access to different types of information.

You could assign the junior underwriters the permissions the trainees are assigned, plus a few more. Then you could assign all the junior underwriters' permissions to senior underwriters, plus a few more, again. If you want to add extra permissions to all these roles, though, you have to make three identical changes.

If you have five levels of roles, that's five copies. Also, every system will have a multitude of roles like these. Personally, I'm far too lazy to perform the same mundane task over and over again. Plus, it wastes an employee's time and the organization's money.

There is a better way: Role inheritance.

Some systems include role inheritance. In this case, the JuniorUnderwriter role inherits from the TraineeUnderwriter role, and the SeniorUnderwriter role inherits from the JuniorUnderwiter role. Now all you need to do to add a permission to all roles is to add it to only the TraineeUnderwriter role (the lowest level of inheritance), and all roles will inherit the permission. Role inheritance is much easier to understand and maintain.

Role permission logic is generally implemented with OR logic. That is, if you assign three roles — RoleA, RoleB, and RoleC — to a record with a read permission, a user has this permission if he has RoleA OR RoleB, OR RoleC. If you don't assign role read permissions to a record, then no user has read permissions on that record (inheritance aside, of course).

Compartment security

For the vast majority of systems, OR logic is fine. There are some instances, however, where you want to use AND logic. In other words, a user must have all of the TopSecret, OperationBuyANoSQLDatabase and UKManagement roles in order to read a particular document.

This capability is variously referred to as *compartment security* (MarkLogic Server) or *cell level security* (Apache Accumulo).

In government systems, you may have several compartments. Examples include *classification, nationality, operation,* and *organizational unit.*

Each compartment has several roles. Classification, for example, may have *unclassified, confidential, secret* and *top secret* roles linked to this compartment.

A record is compartmentalized if it requires one or more roles that are members of a compartment to have a permission on the record. A record may have TopSecret:Read assigned to its permissions. Another record may have only British:Read assigned. A third record, though, may require both TopSecret:Read and British:Read.

Compartment security is different from normal RBAC permissions in that you must have both TopSecret and British roles to receive the read permission (AND logic). Normal RBAC requires only one of these roles (OR logic).

Although compartment security may sound like a very useful feature, and it's probably vital for military systems, many systems are implemented without requiring this feature.

Attribute-based access control (ABAC)

A useful pattern for security is to apply permissions based on data within a record rather than separately assign permissions to the record. This could be based on either metadata, individual column (Bigtable clones), or element (Aggregate NoSQL databases) values.

A good example is a customer name being mentioned within a document. You may want to restrict access to all the documents mentioning that customer to only those people with access to this customer's information. You can restrict access to these documents by processing the data within the document, and applying the relevant security permissions based on the value of that data.

No NoSQL databases provide this capability right out of the box. That's because permissions must be assigned to the record after the data is saved by the application but before it's available for retrieval by other applications or users. So, this permission assignment must occur within the transaction boundary.

Also, very few NoSQL databases support ACID-compliant transactions (MarkLogic, FoundationDB, and Neo4j, do for example). You can find examples of ACID compliant NoSQL databases in Chapters 4 and 21, where I provide a broader discussion about ACID compliance.

If a database doesn't support out-of-the-box assignment of permissions based on data within a document but does support ACID transactions and pre-commit triggers, then an easy workaround is possible.

It's generally easy to write a trigger that checks for the presence of a value within a record and to modify permissions based on its value. As long as a database supports doing so during the commit process, and not after the commit, then you know your data is made secure by using a simple pre-commit trigger.

As an example, MarkLogic Server supports fully serializable ACID transactions and pre-commit triggers. Following is a simple XML document that I want to support for attribute-based access control:

```
<MeetingReport>
    <SalesPerson>jbloggs</SalesPerson>
    <Customer>ACME</Customer>
    <Notes>Lorem Ipsum Dolar Sit Amet...</Notes>
</MeetingReport>
```

MarkLogic Server's triggers use the W3C XQuery language. The following XQuery example is a simple trigger that, when installed in MarkLogic, assigns read and write permissions:

```
xquery version "1.0-ml";
import module namespace
  trgr = 'http://marklogic.com/xdmp/triggers'
  at '/MarkLogic/triggers.xqy';
declare variable $trgr:uri as xs:string external;
declare variable $trgr:trigger as node() external;
if ("ACME" = fn:doc($trgr:uri)/MeetingReport/Customer)
then
  xdmp:document-set-permissions($trgr-uri,
    (xdmp:permission("seniorsales","update"),
     xdmp:permission("sales","read")
    )
  )
else ()
```

Once the trigger is installed in the file setperms.xqy in a MarkLogic Server Modules Database, execute the following code in the web coding application for MarkLogic - Query Console to enable the trigger. On a default MarkLogic Server installation, you can find the Query Console at the URL: http://localhost:8000/qconsole.

Here is code showing how to install the trigger using Query Console:

```
xquery version "1.0-ml";
import module namespace
  trgr='http://marklogic.com/xdmp/triggers'
  at '/MarkLogic/triggers.xqy';
trgr:create-trigger("setperms",
```

```
    "Set Sales Doc Permissions",
  trgr:trigger-data-event(
    trgr:collection-scope("meetingreports"),
    trgr:document-content("modify"),
    trgr:pre-commit()
  ), trgr:trigger-module(
    xdmp:database("Modules"), "/triggers/",
    "setperms.xqy"
  ), fn:true(),
  xdmp:default-permissions(),
  fn:false()
)
```

Identity and Access Management (IdAM)

Authorizing a user for access to information or database functionality is one thing, but before you can do that, you must be sure that the system "knows" that the user is who she says she is. This is where authentication comes in. Authentication can happen within a particular database, or it can be delegated to an external service — thus the term Identity and Access Management (IdAM).

When relational databases were introduced, there were only a few standards around authentication – that's why most relational databases are still used with internal database usernames and passwords. Most NoSQL databases take this approach, with only a few supporting external authentication standards.

The most common modern standard is the Lightweight Directory Access Protocol (LDAP). Interestingly, most LDAP systems are built on top of relational databases that hold the systems' information!

NoSQL databases are a modern invention. They appeared at a time when existing authentication and authorization mechanisms and standards exist, and so many have some way of integrating with them.

Where to start, though? Do you integrate your NoSQL database with just a single IdAM product, or do you try to write a lot of (potentially unused) security integrations, and risk doing them badly? It's tempting to expect NoSQL databases to be ahead of the curve here — but let's be realistic. No software developer can possibly support all the different security systems out there.

Instead, each NoSQL database has its own internal authentication scheme, and usually support for plugging in your own custom provider. NoSQL databases provide a plugin mechanism as a first step before using this mechanism to implement specific standards.

Although a lack of security system integrations is a weakness from the standpoint of a box-ticking exercise, providing a plugin mechanism actually allows these databases to be flexible enough to integrate with any security system you need.

Fortunately, LDAP is one of the first options that NoSQL vendors integrate. On the Java platform, this may be presented as support for the Java Authentication and Authorization Standard (JAAS). This is a pluggable architecture, and one of its commonly used plug-ins is LDAP directory server support.

When selecting a NoSQL database, don't get hung up that some don't support your exact authentication service. As long as the software can be adapted relatively quickly using the database's security plugin mechanism, that will be fine. The product's capabilities are more important, as long as they support security plug-ins.

This is where it's useful to have the resources of a commercial company supporting your NoSQL database — writing these security integrations yourself may take your software engineers longer, and they might even introduce security bugs. Commercial companies have the resources and experience of providing these integrations to customers.

External authentication and Single Sign-On

A NoSQL database supporting a pluggable architecture, rather than a limited set of prebuilt plug-ins for authentication and authorization, can sometimes be beneficial.

This is especially true in the world of Single Sign-On (SSO). SSO allows you to enter a single name and password in order to access any service you use on a corporate network. It means your computer or application session is recognized without you having to type in yet another password. Think of it as "authentication for the password-memory-challenged."

You're probably already familiar with such systems. For example, did you ever log on to Gmail, then visit YouTube and wonder why you're logged on there, too? It's because both services use a single, independent logon service — your Google account. Well, that's SSO at work.

SSO is an absolute joy on corporate networks. Most of us need access to many systems — in my case, dozens unfortunately — to do our daily jobs.

Explaining exactly how this works in detail is beyond the scope of this book, but typically when you first log on to a site, you receive a token. Rather than have your computer send your password to every single website (eek!), it passes this token. Alone, the token means nothing, so passing it along is not a security breach.

The token allows an application to ask the security system that created the token a question, usually something like this: "Is this token valid, and does this guy have access to use this service? If so, who is he and what roles does he have?" Basically, behind-the-scene services do the legwork, and not the user.

The most common SSO on corporate networks is one provided on Microsoft Windows machines and Microsoft Active Directory on the server-side that works automatically out of the box. Active Directory can issue Kerberos tokens to you when you log on at the start of your working day. After logging on, when you access any service that supports Kerberos SSO on the corporate network, you aren't prompted again for a username and password.

The downside is that not all software services support every type of SSO software, and they certainly don't do it automatically out of the box. If you're planning on building a set of applications that a single user may need access to using a NoSQL database then consider using an SSO product (who knows, you might prevent someone's meltdown).

Often, though, SSO token validation is handled by the application stack, not by the underlying database. If you're assigning roles and permissions for records held in a NoSQL databases, you can reduce hassles during development by having the database use the same tokens, too.

Needing SSO support is especially true of use cases involving document (aggregate) NoSQL databases. These types of records (documents) generally are the types that have a variety of permissions. Most relational- or table-based (for example, Bigtable) systems give the same role based access to all rows in a table. Documents tend to be a lot more fluid, though, changing from instance to instance, and even between minor revisions.

Having support for SSO in the database, or at least allowing external authentication security plug-ins to be added, is a good idea for document databases.

Security accreditations

The best yardstick for assessing any product — from databases to delivery companies — is this: "Where have you done this before?" In some instances, this information is commercially or security sensitive. The next best yardstick is, "Has anyone done due diligence on your product?"

When it comes to security, especially for government systems, organizations are very unwilling to share exact technical knowledge. Even within the same government! In this scenario, an independent assessment is the next best thing to talking with someone who previously implemented the product.

If software vendors have significant footprints in government agencies, their products will eventually be used in systems that require independent verification for either

- ✔ A particular implementation — for example, information assurance (IA) testing for a federal high-security system
- ✔ A reference implementation of the product, its documentation, code reviews, and security testing

Government agencies have their own standards for accreditation, and a variety of testing labs available to do this. In the U.S., a common standard to look for is accreditation to Common Criteria (CC). Products are tested against specific levels, depending on what they're used for. A good yardstick for the latest CC standard is EAL2 accreditation. This means that the software has been tested in accordance with accepted commercial best practices.

You can find a good introduction to Common Criteria assurance levels and their equivalents on the CESG website, the UK's IA Technical Authority for Information Assurance, at `www.cesg.gov.uk/servicecatalogue/Common-Criteria/Pages/Common-Criteria-Assurance-Levels.aspx`.

Generally, enterprise systems do their own security testing before going live. These days it's even commonplace for them to do so when handling material that has a relatively low-level classification, such as a database holding many confidential documents, even for civilian government departments.

If the release of information your system is holding could result in a great risk to reputation, financial stability, or life and limb, have your system independently accredited — no matter which database you're using — before it goes live.

Durability

It's tempting to assume that a database — that is, a system that's designed to hold data — always does so in a manner that maintains the integrity of the data. The problem is, data isn't either safe or unsafe; its durability is on a sliding scale.

Durability is absolutely vital to any mission-critical system. Specific requirements depend on a number of factors:

- ✔ Using a database that is ACID-compliant is necessary on mission-critical systems.
- ✔ Using an ACID-compliant database reduces development costs in the short-term and maintenance costs over the long-term.

✔ If many records need to be updated in a single batch (with only either All or Zero updates succeeding), then use a database that supports transactions across multiple updates. (These NoSQL databases are limited in number.)

Never use a database that reports a transaction is complete, when the data may not be safe or the transaction applied. Several databases' default consistency setting will allow you to send data to the database with it being held just in RAM, without guaranteeing it hits disk. This means if the server's motherboard fails in the next few seconds you run the risk of losing data.

Preparing for failure

The relational database management system revolution provided us with a very reliable system for storing information. In many ways, we take those management features for granted now.

For NoSQL databases, though, assume nothing! The vast majority of NoSQL databases have been around only since 2005 or later. The developers of these databases remain mostly concerned about building out data storage and query functionality, not about systems maintenance features.

Resilience is when commercial NoSQL vendors, or commercial companies offering an expanded enterprise version of an open-source NoSQL product, come into their own. These paid-for versions typically include more of the management niceties that system administrators are used to in large database systems. Weigh the cost of these enterprise editions against the ease of recovery from a backup, and don't reject commercial software out of hand, because the cost of a long outage could be much greater than the cost of a software license.

When selecting a NoSQL database that needs to be resilient to individual hardware failures, watch for the following features.

High availability (HA)

HA refers to the ability for a service to stay online if part of a system fails. In a NoSQL database, this typically means the ability for a database cluster to stay online, continuing to service all user requests if a single (or limited number of) database servers within a cluster fail. Some users may have to repeat their actions, but the entire service doesn't die.

Typically, HA requires either a shared storage system (like a NAS or a SAN) or stored replicas of the data. A Hadoop cluster, for example, stores all data locally but typically replicates data twice (resulting in three copies) so that, if the primary storage node fails, the data is still accessible. MarkLogic Server can operate using shared storage or local replicated storage. Some NoSQL databases that provide sharding don't replicate their data, or they replicate it just for read-only purposes. Therefore, losing a single node means some data can't be updated until the node is repaired.

Disaster recovery (DR)

DR is dramatically described as recovering from a nuke landing on your primary data center. More likely, though, an excavator driver just cut your data center's Internet cable in half.

No matter the cause, having a hot standby data center with up-to-date copies of your data ready to go within minutes is a must if your system is mission-critical. Typically, the second cluster is an exact replica of your primary data center cluster.

I've seen people specify fewer servers for a DR cluster than for their primary cluster. However, doing so increases your chance of a double failure! After all, if your primary service goes down for 20 minutes, when the cluster goes back online you'll probably have the normal daily usage *plus* a backlog of users ready to hit your DR cluster. So, specify equal or more hardware for a DR center — not less. The shorter the downtime (under a couple of minutes should be possible), the more likely you can use the exact configuration in your primary and DR sites.

Scaling up

NoSQL databases were designed with considerable scalability in mind. So, the vast majority of them implement clusters across many systems. Not all NoSQL databases are born equal, though, so you need to be aware of scalability issues beyond the basics.

In the following subsections, I promise to avoid really techie explanations (like the intricacies of particular cluster query processing algorithms) and discuss only issues about scalability that affect costs in time and money.

Query scalability

Some NoSQL databases are designed to focus more on query scalability than data scalability. By that, I mean they sacrifice the maximum amount of data that can be stored for quicker query processing. Graph databases are good examples.

A very complex graph query like "Find me the sub graphs of this graph that most closely match these subjects" requires comparing links between many stored data entities (or subjects in graph speak). Because the query needs data about the links between items, having this data stored across many nodes results in a lot of network traffic.

So, many graph databases store the entire graph on a single node. This makes queries fast but means that the only multiserver scalabilities you get are multiple read-only copies of the data to assist multiple querying systems.

Conversely, a document database like MongoDB or MarkLogic may hold documents on a variety of servers (or database nodes). Because a query returns a set of documents, and each document exists only on a single node (not including failover replicas, of course), it's easy to pass a query to each of the 20 database nodes and correlate the results together afterward with minimum networking communication.

Each document is self-contained and evaluated against the query by only the database node it's stored on. This is the same MapReduce distributed query pattern used by Hadoop MapReduce.

Storing your information at the right level means that the queries can be evaluated at speed. Storing information about a program that deals with its scheduling, genre, channel, series, and brand in a single document is easier to query than doing complex joins at query time.

This is the old "materialized views versus joins" argument from relational database theory reimagined in the NoSQL world.

In a document database, you can denormalize the individual documents around series, programs, channels, and genres into a single document per combination. So, you have a single document saying, for example, "Doctor Who Series 5, Episode 1 will be shown on BBC 1 at 2000 on the March 3, 2015," rather than a complex relational web of records with links that must be evaluated at query time.

For an Internet catchup TV service, querying the denormalized document set is as simple as saying "Return me all documents that mention 'Doctor Who' and 'Series 5' where the current time is after the airing time.'" No mention of joins, or going off and looking across multiple record (in this case document) boundaries.

Denormalization does, correctly, imply duplication. This is simply a tradeoff between storage and update speed versus query speed. It's the same tradeoff you're used to when creating views in relational databases, and it should be understood in the same way — that is, as a way to increase query performance, not a limitation of the database software itself.

Cluster scalability

What do you do if your data grows beyond expectation? What if you release a new product on a particular day, and your orders go through the roof? How do you respond to this unforeseen situation rapidly enough without going over the top and wasting resources?

Some NoSQL databases have scale-out and scale-back support. This is particularly useful for software as a service (SaaS) solutions on a public cloud like Amazon or Microsoft Azure.

Scale out is the ability to start up a new database instance and join it to a cluster automatically when a certain system metric is reached. An example might be CPU usage on query nodes going and staying above 80 percent for ten minutes.

Cluster horizontal scaling support should include automated features (rather than just alerts for system administrators) and integration to cloud management software like AWS. The database should also be capable of scaling on a live cluster without any system downtime.

Perhaps the hardest part of horizontal scaling is rebalancing data once the new node is started. Starting a new node doesn't get you very far with a query processing issue unless you share the data across all your nodes equally. If you don't rebalance data then the server with little or no data will be lightning fast and others will be slow. Support for auto-rebalancing data transparently while the system is in use solves this problem rapidly, and without administrator intervention.

Auto-rebalancing can be reliably implemented only on NoSQL databases with ACID compliance. If you implement it on a non-ACID-compliant database, you run the risk that your queries will detect duplicate records, or miss records entirely, while rebalancing is occurring.

So, now you've solved the high-usage issue and are running twice the amount of hardware as you were before. Your sale ends, along with the hype, and system usage reduces — but you're still paying for all that hardware!

Support for automatic scale-back helps. It can, for example, reduce the number of nodes when 20 percent of the CPU is being used across nodes in the cluster. This implies rebalancing support (to move data from nodes about to be shut down to those that will remain online). Having this feature greatly reduces costs on the public cloud.

Scale-back is a complex feature to implement and is still very rare. At the time of this writing, only MarkLogic Server can perform automatic scale-back on Amazon. MarkLogic Server also has an API that you can use to plug in scale-out/scale-back functionality with other public and private cloud management software.

Acceptance testing

News websites are frequently mentioning stories about large systems where an "update" caused major chaos. These happen in government and banking systems. When they do happen, they happen very publicly and to a great cost to the reputation of the organization at fault.

These issues can often be avoided through a significant investment in testing, particularly User Acceptance Testing (UAT), before going live. Even something that you may think is a minor update can irritate and alienate customers.

Don't be tempted to reduce your testing in order to meet deadlines. If anything, increase your testing. Missing development deadlines means the job was likely more complex than you originally thought. This means you should test even more, not less.

The Y2K bug deadline was one that absolutely could not be moved. The vast majority of systems, though, even important national systems, are given artificial timelines of when people want systems to be working, not when IT professionals are sure the systems will work.

Trust your IT professionals or the consultants you have brought in to work on a project. Delays happen for many reasons (often because IT professionals are trying to make things work better).

When it comes to testing, the old adage is true — you only get one chance to make a first impression.

Monitoring

Your system is built, and it's gone live. Now, we can all retire, right? Wrong! It may seem counterintuitive, but just like an old, decrepit body, software breaks down over time.

Perhaps an upgrade happens that makes a previously working subsystem unreliable. Maybe you fix a bug only to find an issue with performance after the patch goes live. Or even some system runs out of support and needs replacing entirely.

It all means extra work. You can spot problems in one of two ways:

✔ You get an angry phone call from a user or customer because something critical to them failed.

✔ Your own system monitoring software spots a potential issue before it becomes a critical one.

Monitoring comes in two broad forms:

✔ Systems monitoring watches components such as databases, storage, and network connectivity. This is the first form that you can enable without any database- or application-specific work.

✔ Application monitoring spots potential performance issues before they bring a system down.

As an example, a "simple bug fix" could test fine, but when put live, it may cause performance issues.

The only way to spot what is causing a performance issue in part of the database is to be monitoring the application. Perhaps the bug fix changed how a particular query was performed. Maybe what was one application query resulting in one database query is now generating five database queries for the same action.

This issue results in lower performance, but you can't link the performance issue with the bug fix if you don't know precisely where the faulty code is in the application. Diagnosing the issue will be impossible without some form of application monitoring.

Many NoSQL databases are still playing catchup when it comes to advanced application monitoring. Open-source NoSQL databases often have no features for this issue. To get these features, you have to buy expensive support from the commercial vendor that develops the software.

Ideally, you want at least a way to determine

✔ What queries or internal processes are taking the longest to complete

✔ What application or user asked for these queries or processes to be executed

Also ideally, a monitoring dashboard that allows you to tunnel down into particular application queries on particular database nodes is helpful. In this way, you may be able to list the queries in-flight on a single node of a highly distributed database. Viewing the process details (for example, the full query or trigger module being executed) at that point can greatly reduce live system debugging time.

Quick debugging results in your application team spotting potential issues and rolling back bad updates, for example, before your users give you a ring. In extreme cases, effective monitoring will keep a system that was performing well from grinding to a halt during peak periods.

Once you find an issue, to prevent a repeat situation, it's important to advise your testing team to incorporate a test for that issue in the next bug-fix testing cycle.

Over time, detailed monitoring pays for itself many times over, although putting an exact number on money saved is a hard thing to do, and you certainly can't really quantify this number upfront.

I've worked for a variety of software vendors and have seen many customers who didn't pay for monitoring or support until they had a major, and sometimes public, failure. However, from that point on, they all made sure they did so.

Part II
Key-Value Stores

Visit www.dummies.com/extras/nosql for great Dummies content online.

In this part . . .

- Segment your customers for better targeting.
- Know your customer segments better with personas.
- Find what value different customers bring to your company.
- Visit www.dummies.com/extras/nosql for great Dummies content online.

Chapter 4

Common Features of Key-Value Stores

Key-value stores are no frills stores that generally delegate all value-handling to the application code itself. Like other types of NoSQL databases, they are highly distributed across a cluster of commodity servers.

A particular benefit of key-value stores is their simplicity. Redis, for example, is only 20,000 lines of code! It can be embedded into an application easily and quickly.

Throughput is the name of the game. Many using a key-value store will sacrifice database features to gain better performance. Key-value stores lack secondary indexes, and many of them eschew synchronized updates (thus also eschewing guaranteed transactional consistency) to their data's replicas in order to maximize throughput.

In this chapter, I cover how to configure a key-value store to ensure that no matter what happens to the database servers in your cluster, your data is always available.

Key-value stores also place some constraints on how you model your data for storage. I talk about the best strategies for this, including information on setting appropriate keys for your data records, and indexing strategies.

Managing Availability

As with other NoSQL database types, with key-value stores, you can trade some consistency for some availability. Key-value stores typically provide a wide range of consistency and durability models — that is, between availability and partition tolerance and between consistent and partition tolerance.

Some key-value stores go much further on the consistency arm, abandoning BASE for full ACID transactional consistency support. Understanding where to draw the line can help you shorten the list of potential databases to consider for your use case.

Trading consistency

Key-value stores typically trade consistency in the data (that is, the ability to always read the latest copy of a value immediately after an update) in order to improve write times.

Voldemort, Riak, and Oracle NoSQL are all *eventually consistent* key-value stores. They use a method called *read repair*. Here are the two steps involved in *read repair*:

1. At the time of reading a record, determine which of several available values for a key is the latest and most valid one.

2. If the most recent value can't be decided, then the database client is presented with all value options and is left to decide for itself.

 Good examples for using eventually consistent key-value stores include sending social media posts and delivering advertisements to targeted users. If a tweet arrives late or a five-minute-old advertisement is shown, there's no catastrophic loss of data.

Implementing ACID support

Aerospike and Redis are notable exceptions to eventual consistency. Both use *shared-nothing* clusters, which means each key has the following:

- ✔ **A master node:** Only the masters provide answers for a single key, which ensures that you have the latest copy.

- ✔ **Multiple slave replica nodes:** These contain copies of all data on a master node. Aerospike provides full ACID transactional consistency by allowing modifications to be flushed immediately to disk before the transaction is flagged as complete to the database client.

Aerospike manages to do that at very high speeds (which refutes claims that having ACID decreases write speed). Aerospike natively handles raw SSDs for data-writing by bypassing slower operating systems' file system support.

Of course, more SSDs mean higher server costs. You may decide that using Redis (configured to flush all data to disk as it arrives) is fast enough and guarantees sufficient durability for your needs. The default setting in Redis is to flush data to disk every few seconds, leaving a small window of potential data loss if a server fails.

Here are some examples of when you may need an ACID-compliant key-value store:

- ✔ When receiving sensor data that you need for an experiment.

- ✔ In a messaging system where you must guarantee receipt.

  Redis, for example, provides a Publish/Subscribe mechanism that acts as a messaging server back end. This feature combined with ACID support allows for durable messaging.

Managing Keys

Key-value stores' fast read capabilities stem from their use of well-defined keys. These keys are typically hashed, which gives a key-value store a very predictable way of determining which partition (and thus server) data resides on. A particular server manages one or more partitions.

A good key enables you to uniquely identify the single record that answers a query without having to look at any values within that record. A bad key will require that your application code interprets your record to determine if it does, in fact, match the query.

If you don't design your key well, you may end up with one server having a disproportionately heavier load than the others, leading to poor performance. Using the current system-time as a key, for example, pushes all new data onto the last node in the cluster, which leads to a nightmare scenario of rebalancing. (Similar to what happens to me when I eat a burger. The more I place into the same large bucket — my mouth — the slower I get!)

Partitioning

Partition design is important because some key-value stores, such as Oracle NoSQL, do not allow the number of partitions to be modified once a cluster is created. Their distribution across servers, though, can be modified. So start with a large number of partitions that you can spread out in the future.

One example of partitioning is Voldemort's consistent hashing approach, as shown in Figure 4-1. Here you see the same partitions spread across three servers initially and then across four servers later. The number of partitions stays the same, but their allocation is different across servers. The same is true of their replicas.

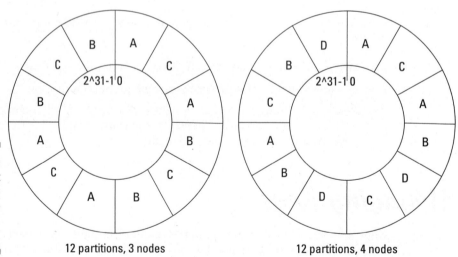

Figure 4-1: Consistent hashing partition allocation in Voldemort.

12 partitions, 3 nodes   12 partitions, 4 nodes

Accessing data on partitions

Key-value stores are highly distributed with no single point of failure. This means there's no need for a master coordinating node to keep track of servers within a cluster. Cluster management is done automatically by a chat protocol between nodes in the server.

You can use a trick in the client driver to squeeze maximum performance out of retrieving and storing keys and values — the client driver keeps track of which servers hold which range of keys. So the client driver always knows which server to talk to.

Most databases, NoSQL included, pass a request on to all members of a cluster. That cluster either accepts the write internally or passes it one under the hood to the correct node. This setup means an extra network trip between nodes is possible, which can add to latency.

In order to avoid discovery latency, most key-value stores' client drivers maintain a metadata list of the current nodes in a cluster and which partition key ranges each nod manages. In this way, the client driver can contact the correct server, which makes operations faster.

If a new node is added to a cluster and the metadata is out of date, the cluster informs the client driver, which then downloads the latest cluster metadata before resending the request to the correct node. This way maximum throughput is maintained with a minimum of overhead during development. Another side benefit is that there's no need for a load balancer to pass queries on to the next available, or least-busy, server — only one server (or read replica server) ever receives a client request, so there's no need for load balancing.

Managing Data

Once you manage the keys appropriately, you're ready to design how to store data and ensure that it's safe and always accessible for the work you need to do, which I explain in this section.

Data types in key-value stores

Key-value stores typically act as "buckets" for binary data. Some databases do provide strong internal data typing and even schema support. Others simply provide convenient helper functions in their client drivers for serializing common application data structures to a key-value store. Examples include maps, lists, and sorted sets.

Oracle NoSQL can operate in two modes:

✔ Simple binary store

✔ Highly structured Avro schema support

An Avro schema is akin to a relational database schema — enforcing a very stringent set of format rules on JavaScript Object Notation (JSON) data stored within the database, as illustrated here:

```
{username: "afowler", sessionid: 13452673, since: 1408318745, theme: "bluesky"}
```

You define an Avro schema using a JSON document. This is an example of the Avro schema for the stored data shown previously:

```
{"type": "record","namespace": "com.example","name": "UserSession","fields": [
  {"name": "username", "type": ["string","null"]},
  {"name": "sessionid", "type": "int"},
  {"name": "since", "type": "long"},
  {"name": "theme", "type": ["string","null"]}
]}
```

An Avro schema provides very strong typing in the database for when schema is important. In the preceding example, you see string data, a numeric session id, a date (milliseconds, since the Unix Time Epoch, as a long integer), and a personalization setting for the theme to use on the website.

Also notice that the type of username and theme has two options — string and null, which is how you instruct Oracle NoSQL that null values are allowed. I could have left theme as a string and provided an additional configuration parameter of "default": "bluesky".

Other NoSQL databases provide secondary indexes on any arbitrary property of a value that has JSON content. Riak, for example, provides secondary indexes based on *document partitioning* — basically, a known property within a JSON document is indexed with a type. This allows for range queries (less than or greater than) in addition to simple equal and not equal comparisons. Riak manages to provide range queries without a stringent schema — just simple index definition. If the data is there, it's added to the index.

Replicating data

Storing multiple copies of the same data in other servers, or even racks of servers, helps to ensure availability of data if one server fails. Server failure happens primarily in the same cluster.

You can operate replicas two main ways:

- ✔ **Master-slave:** All reads and writes happen to the master. Slaves take over and receive requests only if the master fails.

  Master-slave replication is typically used on ACID-compliant key-value stores. To enable maximum consistency, the primary store is written to and all replicas are updated before the transaction completes. This mechanism is called a *two-phase commit* and creates extra network and processing time on the replicas.

- ✔ **Master-master:** Reads and writes can happen on all nodes managing a key. There's no concept of a "primary" partition owner.

  Master-master replicas are typically eventually consistent, with the cluster performing an automatic operation to determine the latest value for a key and removing older, stale values.

  In most key-value stores, this happens slowly — at read time. Riak is the exception here because it has an anti-entropy service checking for consistency during normal operations.

Versioning data

In order to enable automatic conflict resolution, you need a mechanism to indicate the latest version of data. Eventually consistent key-value stores achieve conflict resolution in different ways.

Riak uses a vector-clock mechanism to predict which copy is the most recent one. Other key-value stores use simple timestamps to indicate staleness. When conflicts cannot be resolved automatically, both copies of data are sent to the client. Conflicting data being sent to the client can occur in the following situation:

1. Client 1 writes to replica A 'Adam: {likes: Cheese}'.

2. Replica A copies data to replica B.

3. Client 1 updates data on replica A to 'Adam: {likes: Cheese, hates: sunlight}'.

   At this point, replica A doesn't have enough time to copy the latest data to replica B.

4. Client 2 updates data on replica B to 'Adam: {likes: Dogs, hates: kangaroos}'.

   At this point, replica A and replica B are in conflict and the database cluster cannot automatically resolve the differences.

An alternative mechanism is to use time stamps and trust them to indicate the latest data. In such a situation, it's common sense for the application to check that the time stamps read the latest value before updating the value. They are checking for the *check and set* mechanism, which basically means *'If the latest version is still version 2, then save my version 3'*. This mechanism is sometimes referred to as *read match update (RMU)* or *read match write (RMW)*. This mechanism is the default mechanism employed by Oracle NoSQL, Redis, Riak, and Voldemort.

Chapter 5

Key-Value Stores in the Enterprise

● ●

In This Chapter

▶ Ensuring you have enough space for your data

▶ Achieving faster time to value in implementations

● ●

Key-value stores are all about fast storage and retrieval. If you need a key-value store, then by definition you need to scale out — massively — and ensure maximum performance of your database. This high speed comes at the cost of more-advanced database features — features that would add to each request's processing time.

Being designed for high speed means that key-value stores have a straightforward architecture that allows you to quickly create applications. Knowing some easy approaches can greatly reduce the time you spend deploying them. For large-scale enterprise systems these features are a must.

In this chapter, I cover how to ensure that not only is your key-value store fast, but that you can achieve productivity (and cost savings) quicker. I also mention how to do this while being frugal with resources, such as disk space.

Scaling

Scaling is important to ensure that as your application and business grows, you can handle the new users and data that come online. Some aspects of scaling are difficult to pull off at the same time — for example, the ability to handle high-speed data ingestion while simultaneously maximizing the speed of reading.

Key-value stores are great for high-speed data ingestion. If you have a known, predictable primary key, you can easily store and retrieve data with that key. It's even better if the key is designed to ensure an even distribution of new data across all servers in the cluster.

Avoid traditional approaches of an incremented number. Instead, use a Universal Unique Identifier (UUID). A UUID is a long alphanumeric string that is statistically unlikely to already be in use.

Using a UUID means that statistically the partitions you create over the key will each receive an even amount of new data. This approach evens out the ingestion load across a cluster. One partition will have keys starting with, for example, 0000 to 1999.

Unfortunately, the more records you have, the more likely your keys will clash, even when using UUIDs. This is where you can use a timestamp — concatenated to after the UUID — to help ensure uniqueness.

Without complex indexing or query features, key-value stores ensure the maximum ingestion speed of data. The databases needed to accomplish fast storage are relatively simple, but you need to consider hardware such as the following:

- ✔ **Memory:** Many databases write to an in-memory storage area first and only checkpoint data to disk every so often.

    Writing to RAM is fast, so it's a good idea to choose a database that does in-memory writing to provide more throughput.

- ✔ **SSD:** High-speed flash storage is great for storing large synchronous writes — for example, large in-memory chunks of new data that are offloaded to disk so that RAM can be reserved for new data. Using high-quality SSDs take advantage of this write speed advantage. Some databases, such as Aerospike, natively support SSD storage to provide maximum throughput.

- ✔ **Disk arrays:** It's always better to have more spindles (that is, more discs) with less capacity than one large disk. Use 10K RPM spinning discs as your final tier and consider a high-performance RAID card using RAID 10. RAID 10 allows newly written data to be split across many discs, maximizing throughput. It also has the handy benefit of keeping an extra copy of your data in case a hard disk fails.

Simple data model – fast retrieval

Storing all the data you need for an operation against a single key means that if you need the data, you have to perform only one read of the database. Minimizing the number of reads you need to perform a specific task reduces the load on your database cluster and speeds up your application.

If you need to retrieve data by its content, use an index bucket. Suppose you want to retrieve all orders dispatched from Warehouse 13. (Assuming, of course, you're not worried about the supernatural content of the package!)

Key-value stores aren't known for their secondary index capabilities. It's sometimes better to create your own "term list" store for these lookups. Using the warehouse ID as a key and a list containing order IDs as the value allows you to quickly look up all orders for a given warehouse.

In-memory caching

If you're offering all website visitors the current top-ten songs according to their sales, many of your queries will look the same. Moreover, choosing a database that has an in-memory value cache will improve repeated reading of the top-ten songs information.

Aerospike is notable for giving you the ability to dynamically reprioritize its use of memory, depending on whether you have a high ingest load or a high query load. If your load varies during the day, you may want to consider using Aerospike.

You can also use Redis or a similar key-value store as a secondary layer just for caching. Redis is used frequently in conjunction with NoSQL databases that don't provide their own high-speed read caching.

Having a cache in front of your primary database is generally good practice. If you suffer a distributed denial of service (DDoS) attack, the cache will be hit hard, but the underlying database will carry on as normal.

Reducing Time to Value

Time to value is the amount of time required from starting an IT project to being able to realize business benefit. This can be tangible benefits in cost reduction or the ability to transact new business, or intangible benefits like providing better customer service or products.

Key-value stores are the simplest NoSQL databases with regards to data model. So, you can quickly build applications, especially if you apply a few key principles, including reviewing how you manage data structures, which I cover next.

Using simple structures

Key-value stores are more flexible than relational databases in terms of the format of data. Use this flexibility to your advantage to maximize the rate of your application's throughput. For example, if you're storing map tiles, store them in hex format so that they can be rendered immediately in a browser.

In your application, store easy-to-use structures that don't require scores of processing time. These structures can be simple intrinsic types like integers, strings, and dates, or more sophisticated structures like lists, sorted sets, or even JSON documents stored as a string.

Because it can be interpreted directly by a JavaScript web application, use JSON for simple web app status or preference storage. If you're storing log data, store it in the format most appropriate for retrieval and analysis.

Use the most appropriate structure for your application, not your database administrator. Also consider the effects of time on your database. Will you want to modify data structures in the future to support new features?

Data structures change over time. A flexible JSON document is better than a CSV data file or fixed-width data file because JSON structures can easily vary over time without needing to consider new or deleted properties. Change a column in a CSV file stored in a key-value store, and you must update all of your application's code! This isn't the case with a JSON document, where older code simply ignores new properties.

Complex structure handling

If you have complex interrelated data sets, give careful thought to the data structures in your key-value store. My best advice is to store data sets in a way that allows easy retrieval. Rather than store eight items separately that will require eight reads, denormalize the data — write the data to the same record at ingestion time — so that only one read is needed later. This does mean some data will be stored multiple times. An example is storing customer name in an order document. Although this stores the customer name across many orders, it means when showing a summary of the order you don't have to discover that the value *customer_number=12* means *Mr A Fowler* — preventing an additional read request.

Denormalization consumes more disk space than relational databases' *normal form*, but greatly increases query throughput. It's the NoSQL equivalent of a materialized view in a relational database. You're sacrificing storage space for speed — the classic computer science tradeoff.

For computer scientists of my generation, it's considered heresy to keep multiple copies of the same data. It's simply inefficient. Our relational database lecturers would eat us for breakfast!

However, with the current low cost of storage and the increasing demands of modern applications, it's much better to sacrifice storage for speed in reading data. So, consider denormalization as a friend.

Chapter 6

Key-Value Use Cases

In This Chapter

▶ Handling transient user information

▶ Managing high-speed caching of your data

Key-value stores can scale prodigiously, and this capability is reflected in the various ways that they're used. Maybe you need to deliver hundreds of thousands of targeted web advertisements every second, perhaps to users in different countries, in different languages, and to different categories of websites. Speed is critical. You want your ads to appear as the web page appears so that the ad doesn't slow down the user's experience. When people visit a blog looking for information, they want to see the blog, not wait for the ads.

On the other hand, maybe you have a globally distributed web application and need to store session information or user preferences, but you don't want to clog up your transactional database systems with this data. Or perhaps your requirements are even simpler. You just need to cache data from another system but serve it at a very high speed.

Whatever your needs for high-speed retrieval, key-value NoSQL stores can help.

Managing User Information

There's mission-critical data, and there's supporting data. It's okay if your mission-critical data appears a little slowly because you want to be sure it's safe and properly managed. But you don't want the supporting data of your application to hinder overall transactions and user experiences. Although the supporting data may be lower in value, its need to scale up is great — typically by providing delivery of query responses in less than ten milliseconds. Much of this supporting data helps users access a system, tailor a service to their needs, or find other available services or products.

Delivering web advertisements

Although advertisements are critical to companies marketing their wares or services on the web, they aren't essential to many users' web-browsing experiences. However, the loading time of web pages is important to them, and as soon as a slowly delivered ad starts adding to a page's load time, users start moving to alternative, faster, websites.

Serving advertisements fast is, therefore, a key concern. Doing so isn't a simple business, though. Which advertisement is shown to which user depends on a very large number of factors, often determined by such factors as the user's tracked activity online, language, and location.

Companies that target their advertisements to the right customers receive more click-throughs, and thus more profit. However, the business of targeted advertising is increasingly scientific.

Key-value stores are used mainly by web advertisement companies. (You can find case studies about such usage on key-value NoSQL vendors' websites.) Utilizing their proprietary software, these companies use a combination of factors to determine what a user wants or is interested in so that they can target advertisements to that user effectively. You can think of this combination of factors as being a *key,* and it's this composite key that points to the most compelling advertisement. Everything that is needed to serve the advertisement is kept as the value within a key-value store.

If you need to serve data fast based on a set of known factors, then a key-value store is an excellent match. All you need to do is set up the key effectively.

To set up the key, perform some offline analysis of which advertisements will be relevant to each combined profile of people. If the information you have on the visiting user is country, language, and favorite category of purchases on Amazon, then perhaps an appropriate key would be UK-english-guitars.

This prevents having to do any complex queries at ad serving time — just instead concatenate these fields together to form a key and ask for the value of that key.

Handling user sessions

You can spend all the money you want on a state-of-the-art datacenter for your transactional data, but if your website is slow, people will say that your entire service is slow. In fact, when companies and governments launch new online services that can't handle the load placed on them, the press eats them for breakfast.

Typically, the problem isn't that a primary processing system goes down; rather, it's because the users' identities or sessions are handled poorly. Perhaps the username isn't cached, or every request requires opening a new session from the application server instead of than caching this information between requests.

A user session may track how a user walks through an application, adding data on each page. The data can then be saved at the end of this journey in a single hit to the database, rather than in a sequence of small requests across many page requests. Users often don't mind waiting a couple of seconds after clicking a save button. Providing an effective user session on a website that has low latency has a couple of benefits:

✔ The user (soon to be customer!) receives good service.

✔ Partially complete data doesn't get saved to your main back-end transactional database.

Websites use a cookie to track the user's interaction with a website. A cookie is a small file linked to a unique ID, just like a record in a key-value store. The server uses these cookies to identify that it already knows a user on their second or subsequent requests, so the server needs to fetch a session using this data quickly. In this way, when users log in, the websites recognize who they are, which pages they visit, and what information they're looking for.

This unique ID is typically a random number, perhaps our old friend, the Universally Unique Identifier (UUID). The website may need to store various types of data. Typically, this data is short-lived — the length of a user's session, perhaps just a few minutes.

Key-value stores are, therefore, ideal for storing and retrieving session data at high speeds. The ability to *tombstone* (that is delete) data once a time-stamp is exceeded is also useful. In this way, the application doesn't need to check the timestamp of the session on each request — if the session isn't in the database, it's been tombstoned. So the session is no longer valid, which removes some of the application programmer's administrative burden.

Supporting personalization

Similar to the user-session requirement, but longer-lived, is the concept of *user service personalization.* This is where the front-end application is configured by users for their specific needs.

Again, this is a front-end secondary type of data, not the primary transactional data within a system. For example, imagine that you have a primary database showing the work levels for all your team, the current case files they're working on, and all the related data. This is the primary data of the application. Perhaps it's stored in an Oracle relational database or a MarkLogic NoSQL document database.

Use of the data can vary. For instance, one user may want to view a summary of only his team's workload, whereas a manager might want to track all employees on a team.

These users are receiving different personalized views of the same data. These view preferences need to be saved somewhere. You probably don't want to overload your case database with this personalization data; it's specific to the front-end application, not the core case-management system.

Using a key-value store with a composite key containing user id (not session id) and the service name allows you to store the personalization settings as a value, which makes lookups very quick and prevents the performance of your primary systems from being negatively affected.

High-Speed Data Caching

Imagine you are a bank teller with three other colleagues working. You each have a line of people to be served. One of the customers, though, keeps getting in line to ask if his check has been cashed yet and the amount credited to his account. When you answer him, instead of leaving he joins the back of the line again.

This small query repeating increases your workload, and so the line keeps increasing in size, until all customers are unhappy about the amount of time they are waiting around for their query.

The same analogy is true of NoSQL databases. Imagine each bank teller is instead a partition of data within a NoSQL database cluster. Asking the same question over and over again — whether the data exists or not — stresses systems as much as the re-queuing customer. Better instead for him to check his internet banking on his phone. The application cashes the customer's recent bank balance and transactions processed, taking load off of the tellers and the core banking systems.

High-speed in-memory caching provides this caching capability without the need for a separate application level caching layer. This reduces total cost of ownership and makes developing well-performing applications quicker and easier.

Lowering latency in financial services

Many complex financial transaction processing systems are built on top of mainframe or relational databases. Banks that operate proprietary mainframes are usually charged for the amount of processing they do, so they must watch their total processing, particularly if they're using a mainframe system. By caching all general responses to common queries, the impact and cost of mainframe use is minimized.

Consider a list of the latest interest rates calculated by the banks for interbank lending. Caching these rates with a staleness timeout — or tombstone — of one minute means they're deleted when stale. If a system has thousands of transactions per minute, this approach may cut the primary system's processing by 99 percent. That's a lot less mainframe instructions processed, or fewer expensive Oracle server licenses required.

Using the same information you use in a Structured Query Language "where" clause as the key allows fast access. If the information isn't present, then query the back-end database and cache the result for a minute.

So, in the relational database application, if you have

```
select ExchangeRate from ExchangeRateTable where
   FromCurrency="GBP" and ToCurrency="EUR";
```

you can model it with a key-value model of

```
Bucket: ExchangeRateTable
Key: GBP:EUR, Value: 1.8
```

In this case, secondary indexes and complex "where" clauses aren't required; you're simply fetching a single unique key value from a single bucket.

Chapter 7

Key-Value Store Products

*S*ome applications require storage of information at high speeds for later analysis or access. Others are all about responding as quickly as possible to requests for data. Whatever your use case, when speed is key, key-value stores reign. Their simple processing and data models adapt to a range of use cases.

You can find many NoSQL key-value stores, each with its own niche. Understanding these niches and the unique benefits of each option is the path to selecting the best solution for your particular business problem.

In this chapter, I introduce the main vendors in the key-value NoSQL database space by describing use cases they are each uniquely useful for. This contrasts against the general use cases in the previous chapter that all key-value stores can address.

The Amazon Dynamo paper

Amazon came up with the modern concept of a NoSQL key-value store when it created the Dynamo DB. This database, and its accompanying published paper, introduced the world to highly scalable distributed key-value stores.

Dynamo incorporated the ideas of storing all information by a single primary key, using consistent hashing to spread data throughout a cluster and using object versioning to manage consistency.

Dynamo introduced a gossip intercommunication protocol between key-value servers and replication techniques between servers, all with a simple data access API. Dynamo was designed to allow tradeoffs between consistency, availability, and cost-effectiveness of a data store.

These have all since become standard features of key-value stores.

High-Speed Key Access

Key-value stores are all about speed. You can use various techniques to maximize that speed, from caching data, to having multiple copies of data, or using the most appropriate storage structures.

Caching data in memory

Because data is easily accessed when it's stored in random access memory (RAM), choosing a key-value store that caches data in RAM can significantly speed up your access to data, albeit at the price of higher server costs.

Often, though, this tradeoff is worth making. You can easily calculate what percentage of your stored data is requested frequently. If you know five percent is generally requested every few minutes, then take five percent of your data size and add that number as spare RAM space across your database servers.

Bear in mind that the operating system, other applications, and the database server have memory requirements, too.

Replicating data to slaves

In key-value stores, a particular key is stored on one of the servers in the cluster. This process is called *key partitioning*. This means that, if this key is constantly requested, this node will receive the bulk of requests. This node, therefore, will be slower than your average request speed, potentially affecting the quality of service to your users.

To avoid this situation, some key-value stores support adding read-only replicas, also referred to as slaves. Redis, Riak, and Aerospike are good examples. Replication allows the key to be stored multiple times across several servers, which increases response speed but at the cost of more hardware.

Some key-value stores guarantee that the replicas of the key will always have the same value as the master. This guarantee is called being fully consistent. If an update happens on the master server holding the key, all the replicas are guaranteed to be up to date. Not all key-value stores guarantee this status (Riak, for example), so if it's important to be up to date to the milli-second, then choose a database whose replicas are fully consistent (such as Aerospike).

Data modeling in key-value stores

Many key-value stores support only basic structures for their value types, leaving the application programmer with the job of interpreting the data. Simple data type support typically includes strings, integers, JSON, and binary values.

For many use cases, this works well, but sometimes a slightly more granular access to data is useful. Redis, for example, supports the following data value types:

✔ String

✔ List

✔ Set

✔ Sorted set

✔ Hash maps

✔ Bit arrays

✔ Hyperlog logs

Sorted sets can be queried for matching ranges of values — much like querying an index of values sorted by date, which is very useful for searching for a subset of typed data.

Operating on data

Redis includes operations to increment and decrement key values directly, without having to do a read-modify-update (RMU) set of steps. You can do so within a single transaction to ensure that no other application changes the value during an update. These data-type specific operations include adding and removing items to lists and sets, too.

You can even provide autocomplete functionality on an application's user interface by using the Redis ZRANGEBYLEX command. This command retrieves a set of keys which partially matches a string. So, if you were to type "NoSQL for" in the search bar of an application built on Redis, you would see the suggestion "NoSQL For Dummies."

Evaluating Redis

Redis prides itself on being a very lightweight but blazingly fast key-value store. It was originally designed to be an in-memory key-value store, but now boasts disk-based data storage.

You can use Redis to safeguard data by enabling AOF (append only file) mode and instructing Redis to force data to disk on each query (known as forced *fsync flushing*). AOF does slow down writes, of course, but it provides a higher level of durability for data. Be aware, though, that it's still possible to lose up to one second of commands.

Also, Redis only recently added support for clustering. In fact, at the time of this writing, Redis's clustering support is in the beta testing phase. Fortunately, Redis uses a shared-nothing cluster model, with masters for particular keys and slaves that are never directly written to by a client; only the master does so. Providing shared-nothing clustering should make it easier for Redis to implement reliable clustering than it is for databases that allow writes to all replicas.

If you want a very high-speed, in-memory caching layer in front of another database — MongoDB or Riak are commonly used with Redis — then evaluate Redis as an option. As support for clustering and data durability evolves, perhaps Redis can overtake other back-end databases.

Taking Advantage of Flash

When you need incredibly fast writes, flash storage is called for (as opposed to calling for Flash Gordon). This comes at the cost of using RAM space, of course. Writing to RAM will get you, well, about as far as the size of your RAM. So having a very high-speed storage option immediately behind your server's RAM is a good idea. This way, when a checkpoint operation to flush the data to disk is done, it clears space in RAM as quickly as possible.

Spending money for speed

Flash is expensive — more so than traditional spinning disk and RAM. It's possible to make do without flash by using RAID 10 spinning disk arrays, but these will get you only so far.

A logical approach is to look at how fast data streams into your database. Perhaps provisioning 100 percent of the size of your store data for a spinning disk, 10 percent for flash, and one percent for RAM. These figures will vary depending on your application's data access profile, and how often that same data is accessed.

Of course, if you're in an industry where data ages quickly and you absolutely need to guarantee write throughput, then an expensive all-flash infrastructure could be for you.

To give you an idea about the possible scale achievable in a key-value store that supports native flash, Aerospike claims that, with native flash for data and RAM for indexes, 99.9 percent of reads and writes are completed within one millisecond.

Context computing

Aerospike espouses a concept called *context-aware computing*. Context-aware computing is where you have a very short window of time to respond to a request, and the correct response is dictated by some properties of the user, such as age or products purchased. These properties could include:

✔ **Identity:** Session IDs, cookies, IP addresses

✔ **Attributes:** Demographic or geographic

✔ **Behavior:** Presence (swipe, search, share), channels (web, phone), services (frequency, sophistication)

> ✔ **Segments:** Attitudes, values, lifestyle, history
>
> ✔ **Transactions:** Payments, campaigns

The general idea is to mine data from a transactional system to determine the most appropriate advertisement or recommendation for a customer based on various factors. You can do so by using a Hadoop map/reduce job, for example, on a transactional Oracle relational database.

The outputs are then stored in Aerospike so that when a particular customer arrives on your website and they have a mixture of the preceding list of factors (modeled as a composite key), the appropriate advertisement or recommendation is immediately given to the customer.

Evaluating Aerospike

Aerospike is the king of flash support. Rather than use the operating system's file system support on top of flash, as other databases do (that is, they basically treat a flash disk as any other hard disk), Aerospike natively accesses the flash.

This behavior provides Aerospike with maximum throughput, because it doesn't have to wait for operating system function calls to be completed; it simply accesses the raw flash blocks directly. Moreover, Aerospike can take advantage of the physical attributes of flash storage in order to eke out every last bit of performance.

Aerospike is one of my favorite NoSQL databases. I was very close to using it in this book as the primary example of key-value stores, instead of Riak. However, I didn't because Riak is currently more prevalent (and I wanted to sell books).

I fully expect Aerospike to start overtaking Riak in large enterprises and mission-critical use cases, though. It has *enterprise-level* features lacking in other databases, including the following:

> ✔ **Full ACID consistency:** Ensures data is safe and consistent.
>
> ✔ **Shared-nothing cluster:** Has synchronous replication to keep data consistent.
>
> ✔ **Automatic rebalancing:** Automatically moves some data to new nodes, evening out read times and allowing for scale out and scale back in a cluster.
>
> ✔ **Support for UDFs and Hadoop:** User defined functions can run next to the data for aggregation queries, and Hadoop Map/Reduce is supported for more complex requirements.

✔ **Secondary indexes:** Adds indexes on data value fields for fast querying.

✔ **Large data types:** Supports custom and large data types; allows for complex data models and use cases.

✔ **Automatic storage tier flushing on writes:** Flushes RAM to flash storage (SSDs) and disk when space on the faster tier is nearly exhausted.

Whether or not you need blazing-fast flash support, these other features should really interest people with mission-critical use cases. If you're evaluating Riak for a mission-critical system, definitely evaluate Aerospike as well.

Using Pluggable Storage

There are times when you want to provide key-value style high speed access to data held in a relational database. This database could be, for example, Berkeley DB (Java Edition for Voldemort) or MySQL.

Providing key-value like access to data requires a key-value store to be layered directly over one of these other databases. Basically, you use another database as the storage layer, rather than a combination of a file system for storage and an ingestion pipeline for copying data from a relational database.

This process simplifies providing a high speed key-value store while using a traditional relational database for storage.

Changing storage engines

Different workloads require different storage engines and performance characteristics. Aerospike is great for high ingest; Redis is great for high numbers of reads. Each is built around a specific use case.

Voldemort takes a different approach. Rather than treating the key-value store as a separate tier of data management, Voldemort treats the key-value store as an API and adds an in-memory caching layer, which means that you can plug into the back end that makes the most sense for your particular needs. If you want a straightforward disk storage tier, you can use the Berkeley DB Java Edition storage engine. If instead you want to store relational data, you can use MySQL as a back-end to Voldemort.

This capability combined with custom data types allows you to use a key-value store's simple store/retrieve API to effectively pull back and directly cache information in a different back-end store.

This approach contrasts with the usual approach of having separate databases — one in, say, Oracle for transactional data and another in your key-value store (Riak, for example). With this two-tier approach, you have to develop code to move data from one tier to the other for caching. With Voldemort, there is one combined tier — your data tier — so the extra code is redundant.

Caching data in memory

Voldemort has a built-in in-memory cache, which decreases the load on the storage engine and increases query performance. No need to use a separate caching layer such as Redis or Oracle's Coherence Java application data caching product on top.

The capability to provide high-speed storage tiering with caching is why LinkedIn uses Voldemort for certain high-performance use cases.

With Voldemort, you get the best of both worlds — a storage engine for your exact data requirements and a high-speed in-memory cache to reduce the load on that engine. You also get simple key-value store store/retrieve semantics on top of your storage engine.

Evaluating Voldemort

In the *Harry Potter* books Lord Voldemort held a lot of magic in him, both good and bad, although he used it for terrorizing muggles. The Voldemort database, as it turns out, can also store vast amounts of data, but can be used for good by data magicians everywhere!

Voldemort is still a product in development. Many pieces are still missing, so it doesn't support the variety of storage engines you might expect. This focus for Voldemort's development community is likely because Voldemort is built in the Java programming language, which requires a Java Native Interface (JNI) connector to be built for integration to most C or C++ based databases.

Voldemort has good integration with serialization frameworks, though. Supported frameworks include Java serialization, Avro, Thrift, and Protocol Buffers. This means that the provided API wrappers match the familiar serialization method of each programming language, making the development of applications intuitive.

Voldemort doesn't handle consistency as well as other systems do. Voldemort uses the *read repair* approach, where inconsistent version numbers for the same record are fixed at read time, rather than being kept consistent at write time.

There is also no secondary indexing or query support; Voldemort expects you to use the facilities of the underlying storage engine to cope with that use case. Also, Voldemort doesn't have native database triggers or an alerting or event processing framework with which to build one.

If you do need a key-value store that is highly available, is partition-tolerant, runs in Java, and uses different storage back ends, then Voldemort may be for you.

Separating Data Storage and Distribution

Oracle Corporation is the dominant player in the relational database world. It's no surprise then that it's at least dabbling in the NoSQL space.

Oracle's approach is to plug the gaps in its current offerings. It has a highly trusted, *enterprise-level* relational database product, which is what it's famous for. However, this approach doesn't fit every single data problem. For certain classes of data problems, you need a different way of storing things — that's why I wrote this book!

Oracle has a data-caching approach in Coherence. It also inherited the Berkeley DB code. Oracle chose to use Berkeley DB to produce a distributed key-value NoSQL database.

Using Berkeley DB for single node storage

Berkeley DB, as the name suggests, is an open-source project that started at the University of California, Berkeley, between 1986 and 1994. It was maintained by Sleepycat Software, which was later acquired by Oracle.

The idea behind Berkeley DB was to create a hash table store with the best performance possible. Berkeley DB stores a set of keys, where each key points to a value stored on disk that can be read and updated using a simple key-value API.

Berkeley DB was originally used by the Netscape browser but can now be found in a variety of embedded systems. Now you can use it for almost every coding platform and language. An SQL query layer is available for Berkeley DB, too, opening it up to yet another use case.

Berkeley DB comes in three versions:

- ✔ The Berkeley DB version written in C is the one that's usually embedded in UNIX systems.
- ✔ The Java Edition is also commonly embedded, including in the Voldemort key-value store.
- ✔ A C++ edition is available to handle the storage of XML data.

Berkeley DB typically acts as a single-node database.

Distributing data

Oracle built a set of data distribution and high-availability code using NoSQL design ideas on top of Berkeley DB. This approach makes Oracle NoSQL a highly distributed key-value store that uses many copies of the tried-and-true Berkeley DB code as the primary storage system.

Oracle NoSQL is most commonly used alongside the Oracle relational database management systems (RDBMS) and Oracle Coherence.

Oracle Coherence is a mid-tier caching layer, which means it lives in the application server with application business code. Applications can offload the storage of data to Coherence, which in turn distributes the data across the applications' server clusters. Coherence works purely as a cache.

Oracle Coherence can use Oracle NoSQL as a cache storage engine, providing persistence beneath Oracle Coherence and allowing some of the data to be offloaded from RAM to disk when needed.

Oracle Coherence is commonly used to store data that may have been originally from an Oracle RDBMS, to decrease the operational load on the RDBMS. Using Oracle NoSQL with Coherence or directly in your application mid-tier, you can achieve a similar caching capability.

Evaluating Oracle NoSQL

Despite claims that Oracle NoSQL is an ACID database product, by default, it's an eventually consistent — non-ACID — database. This means data read from read replica nodes can potentially be stale.

The client driver can alleviate this situation by requesting only the absolute latest data, which not surprisingly is called absolute consistency mode. This setting reads only data from the master node for a particular key. Doing so for all requests effectively means that the read replicas are never actually read from — they're just there for high availability, taking over if the master should crash.

It's also worth noting that in the default mode (eventually consistent), because of the lack of a consistency guarantee, application developers must perform a *check-and-set* (CAS) or *read-modify-update* (RMU) set of steps to ensure that an update to data is applied properly.

In addition, unlike Oracle's RDBMS product, Oracle NoSQL doesn't have a write Journal. Most databases write data to RAM, but write the description of the change to a Journal file on disk. Journal writes are much smaller than writing the entire change to stored data, allowing higher throughput; and because the journal is written to disk, data isn't lost if the system crashes and loses the data stored in RAM.

If there's a system failure and data held in RAM is lost, this journal can be replayed on the data store. Oracle NoSQL doesn't have this feature, which means either that you run the risk of losing data or that you slow down your writes by always flushing to disk on every update. Although small, this write penalty is worth testing before going live or purchasing a license.

Oracle is plugging Oracle NoSQL into its other products. Oracle NoSQL provides a highly scalable layer for Oracle Coherence. Many financial services firms, though, are looking at other NoSQL options to replace Coherence.

Another product that may be useful in the future is RDF Graph for Oracle NoSQL. This product will provide an RDF (Resource Description Format — triple data, as discussed in Chapter 19) persistence and query layer on top of Oracle NoSQL and will use the open-source Apache Jena APIs for graph query and persistence operations.

The concept of major and minor keys is one of my favorite Oracle NoSQL features. These keys provide more of a two-layer tree model than a single layer key-value model. So, I could store adam:age=33 and adam:nationality=uk. I could pull back all the information on Adam using the "adam" major key, or just the age using the adam:age key. This is quite useful and avoids the need to use denormalization or migrating to a NoSQL document database if your application has simple requirements.

Oracle NoSQL is also the only key-value store in this book that allows you to actively enforce a schema. You can provide an Avro schema document, which is a JSON document with particular elements, to restrict what keys, values, and types are allowed in your Oracle NoSQL database.

If you want a key-value store that works with Oracle Coherence or want to fine-tune availability and consistency guarantees, then Oracle NoSQL may be for you. Oracle's marketing messaging is a little hard to navigate — because so many products can be used in combination. So, it's probably better to chat with an Oracle sales representative for details on whether Oracle NoSQL is for you. One commercial note of interest is that Oracle sells support for the Community (free) Edition — that is, you don't have to buy the Enterprise Edition to get Oracle support. If cost is an issue, you may want to consider the Community Edition.

Handling Partitions

The word partition is used for two different concepts in NoSQL land. A *data partition* is a mechanism for ensuring that data is evenly distributed across a cluster. On the other hand, a *network partition* occurs when two parts of the same database cluster cannot communicate. Here, I talk about network partitions.

On very large clustered systems, it's increasingly likely that a failure of one piece of equipment will happen. If a network switch between servers in a cluster fails, a phenomenon referred to as (in computer jargon) *split brain* occurs. In this case, individual servers are still receiving requests, but they can't communicate with each other. This scenario can lead to inconsistency of data or simply to reduced capacity in data storage, as the network partition with the least servers is removed from the cluster (or "voted off" in true Big Brother fashion).

Tolerating partitions

You have two choices when a network partition happens:

- ✔ Continue, at some level, to service read and write operations.
- ✔ "Vote off" one part of the partition and decide to fix the data later when both parts can communicate. This usually involves the cluster voting a read replica as the new master for each missing master partition node.

Riak allows you to determine how many times data is replicated (three copies, by default — that is, n=3) and how many servers must be queried in order for a read to succeed. This means that, if the primary master of a key is on the wrong side of a network partition, read operations can still succeed if the other two servers are available (that is, r=2 read availability).

Riak handles writes when the primary partition server goes down by using a system called *hinted handoff*. When data is originally replicated, the first node for a particular key partition is written to, along with (by default) two of the following neighbor nodes.

If the primary can't be written to, the next node in the ring is written to. These writes are effectively handed off to the next node. When the primary server comes back up, the writes are replayed to that node before it takes over primary write operations again.

In both of these operations, versioning inconsistencies can happen because different replicas may be in different version states, even if only for a few milliseconds.

Riak employs yet another system called *active anti-entropy* to alleviate this problem. This system trawls through updated values and ensures that replicas are updated at some point, preferably sooner rather than later. This helps to avoid conflicts on read while maintaining a high ingestion speed, which avoids a two-phase commit used by other NoSQL databases with master-slave, shared-nothing clustering support.

If a conflict on read does happen, Riak uses *read repair* to attempt to return only the latest data. Eventually though, and depending on the consistency and availability settings you use, the client application may be presented with multiple versions and asked to decide for itself.

In some situations, this tradeoff is desirable, and many applications may intuitively know, based on the data presented, which version to use and which version to discard.

Secondary indexing

Secondary indexes are indexes on specific data within a value. Most key-value stores leave this indexing up to the application. However, Riak is different, employing a scheme called *document-based partitioning* that allows for secondary indexing.

Document-based partitioning assumes that you're writing JSON structures to the Riak database. You can then set up indexes on particular named properties within this JSON structure, as shown in Listing 7-1.

Listing 7-1:   JSON Order Structure

```
{
  "order-id": 5001,
  "customer-id": 1429857,
  "order-date": "2014-09-24",
  "total": 134.24
}
```

If you have an application that's showing a customer's orders for the previous month, then you want to query all the records, as shown in Listing 7-1, where the customer id is a fixed value (1429857) and the order-date is within a particular range (the beginning and end of the month).

In most key-value stores, you create another bucket whose key is the combined customer number and month and the value is a list of order ids. However, in Riak, you simply add a secondary index on both customer-id (integer) and order-date (date), which does take up extra storage space but has the advantage of being transparent to the application developer.

These indexes are also updated live — meaning there's no lag between updating a document value in Riak and the indexes being up to date. This live access to data is more difficult to pull off than it seems. After all, if the indexes are inconsistent, you'll never find the consistently held data!

Evaluating Riak

Basho, the commercial entity behind Riak, says that its upcoming version 2.0 NoSQL database always has strong consistency, a claim that other NoSQL vendors make. The claim by NoSQL vendors to always have strong consistency is like claiming to be a strong vegetarian . . . except on Sundays when you have roast beef.

Riak is not an ACID-compliant database. Its configuration cannot be altered such that it runs in ACID compliance mode. Clients can get inconsistent data during normal operations or during network partitions. Riak trades absolute consistency for increased availability and partition tolerance.

Running Riak in strong consistency mode means that its read replicas are updated at the same time as the primary master. This involves a two-phase commit — basically, the master node writing to the other nodes before it confirms that the write is complete.

At the time of this writing, Riak's strong consistency mode doesn't support secondary indexes or complex data types (for example, JSON). Hopefully, Basho will fix this issue in upcoming releases of the database.

Riak Search (a rebranded and integrated Apache Solr search engine uses an eventually consistent update model) may produce false positives when using strong consistency. This situation occurs because data may be written and then the transaction abandoned, but the data is still used for indexing — leaving a "false positive" search result — the result isn't actually any longer valid for the search query.

Riak also uses a separate *sentinel process* to determine which node becomes a master in failover conditions. This process, however, isn't highly available, which means that for a few seconds, it's possible that, while a new copy of the *sentinel process* is brought online, a new node cannot be added or a new master elected. You need to be aware of this possibility in high-stress failover conditions.

Riak does have some nice features for application developers, such as secondary indexing and built-in JSON value support. Database replication for disaster recovery to other datacenters is available only in the paid for version, whose price can be found on their website (rental prices shown, perpetual license prices given on application only).

The Riak Control cluster monitoring tool also isn't highly regarded because of its lag time when monitoring clusters. Riak holds a lot of promise, and I hope that Basho will add more *enterprise-level* cluster-management facilities in future versions. It will become a best-in-class product if it does.

Chapter 8

Riak and Basho

Riak is the highest praised and most-used NoSQL key-value store. Its customers range from public health services in Europe to web advertisement agencies the world over.

Basho Technologies, the makers of Riak, has offices worldwide and is the go-to place for support, which it offers 24/7.

In this chapter, I talk about issues you need to consider when selecting a key-value store. These include finding support for your key-value store based development efforts.

Choosing a Key-Value Store

As I've mentioned in Chapter 2, key-value stores are relatively simple database designs. The operations they provide are largely the same, with only a few providing extra features for application developers.

Most of the choices relate to whether you want an ACID-compliant database, one with secondary indexes, or one that supports a very specific, niche feature, such as native support for flash storage.

Being able to create well-built applications also means you need to find well-trained personnel and support services. You'll also need to consider integrating the key-value store with existing complementary technology, and how to handle storage of the data formats required by your application.

Ensuring skill availability

Skill availability is a major reason for using key-value stores. Being able to construct keys effectively and use special buckets to mimic indexes are very specific skills. Finding people who have proven these skills in the field rather than merely downloaded and ran through a tutorial for the database is a good idea!

Each key-value store also has different client libraries, each with a difference in feature support. Many are straightforward and use common semantics. Each, for instance, provides a *store*, *get*, and *delete* operation for keys. Ensure your developers are not only familiar with the database, but also conversant in the programming language API chosen for your project.

The application programming model of key-value stores is pretty straightforward. Application developers still may need to do some work on indexing and deserialization of the value returned by a key-value store, especially when the chosen NoSQL database doesn't support secondary indexes natively.

People who are familiar with an organization's programming language should be able to understand these semantics quickly. It's much easier to learn key-value semantics than it is to learn the Structured Query Language (SQL) of relational database systems.

Integrating with Hadoop Map/Reduce

Normally in a Hadoop Map/Reduce job, the Hadoop Distributed File System (HDFS) is the input source and output destination of an operation's data. It's possible, though, to use Riak as input, or output, or both.

Using Riak as an input means that you can specify a set of keys, a secondary index query, or a Riak Search query to execute which returns a list of keys for the records that Hadoop needs to process. When Hadoop requests these records by key, Riak fetches each of them, iterating through all the matching records.

When Riak is used as an output destination for map/reduce jobs, Riak's Java client library uses annotations to determine how to best store the output generated. You need, of course, to specify which bucket the output goes into. This Hadoop output mechanism supports secondary index tags, links, and metadata.

Using Riak as an output may be particularly useful when you're implementing context computing, which I describe in Chapter 7. For example, say that you write the output as "If you see a customer with these attributes, then serve this advertisement." The web application then uses the fast Riak key-value store to quickly determine which advertisement to show.

Meanwhile, map/reduce can batch-process customer information overnight to determine the best advertisements to show, updating Riak as an output data storage destination each day with the latest analysis.

Using JSON

JSON is short for JavaScript Object Notation. JavaScript programmers "discovered" this format. They realized that a subset of JavaScript object definition features could be used to store and pass data. Now, it's used extensively behind web applications for data serialization.

The following code shows an order modeled as a JSON document:

```
{
  "order-id": 5001,
  "customer": {
    "customer-id": 1429857,
    "name": "Adam Fowler",
    "address": {
      "line1": "some house",
      "line2": "some place",
      "city": "some city"
    }
  },
  "order-date": "2014-09-24",
  "total": 134.24,
  "items": [
    {"item-id": 567, "quantity": 5, "unit-price": 3.60},
    {"item-id": 643, "quantity": 1, "unit-price": 116.23}
  ]
}
```

Key-value stores don't tend to operate on complex values. (After all, document NoSQL databases are about dealing with documents.) A JSON order document, such as the preceding one, is a complex treelike structure. You can see that the JSON object includes a customer object, which in turn includes an address object.

Riak, however, can handle JSON documents natively. For example, in the preceding code, you can add secondary indexes to customer-id, item-id, and `order-date`. Doing so enables fast querying for a variety of order records. A good example is providing a summary of a customer's orders for a particular month.

Riak supports its own internal map/reduce engine, which is not the same as Hadoop Map/Reduce. The difference is that Riak uses JavaScript as the processing language and allows for processing data across Riak nodes without the need for a full Hadoop Map/Reduce installation.

Riak Search is a Solr-based (see Chapter 27) add-on that allows for full text searches. Note that, even though it's tightly integrated with Riak, unlike Riak's built-in secondary indexes, Riak Search's indexes aren't updated in real time. However, if you need free text search for Riak-held data (which is especially useful if you're storing JSON documents containing lots of free text), then Riak Search may be a good option.

Riak also supports multi-datacenter replication, which you can purchase from Basho. This feature allows asynchronous updates from a master cluster to one or more secondary (read-only) clusters. These updates are typically configured to occur as soon as possible, but are asynchronous so as not to affect the speed of operations on the primary datacenter.

Finding Riak Support (Basho)

A key aspect to selecting a vendor to bet a mission-critical application on is ensuring you have expert support when you need to. Perhaps you need support for a major live system outage, or maybe just best practice guidance when developing an application or sizing a cluster.

Basho was founded in 2008, and as I mentioned earlier, is the maker of Riak. This worldwide company is the primary consultant for Riak, and the contributions to Riak's code come primarily from Basho employees.

Enabling cloud service

Basho provides a rental option for cloud services known as Riak CS (Basho publishes the latest price on its website). Basho also sells the Enterprise version of Riak on a perpetual license basis — that is, with an upfront fee followed by a smaller annual maintenance and support. The price of this fee is available only upon application to Basho's sales team.

This cloud service supports Amazon S3 storage, a simple distributed storage API at affordable pricing. Riak CS also supports OpenStack and the Keystone authentication service.

Having Riak available on Amazon is particularly helpful if you need rapid scale out or scale back of the cluster. These services are typically seasonal and peak a few weeks out of each year, especially during the Christmas and tax-filing seasons.

Handling disasters

To ensure that your data remains available when an entire datacenter goes down (often caused by workers mechanically digging up network cables!), you need to have a second datacenter with the latest possible information.

You can do so with Riak by purchasing Basho's Riak Enterprise. This edition supports asynchronous or timed replication of data from a primary master site to one or more secondary replica sites. If the primary site goes down, you can switch your customers and applications to one of the replica sites. Because replication is asynchronous, it's still possible to lose some data, but this is the typical replication method used between datacenters across all types of database software. Asynchronous cluster-to-cluster replication provides the best tradeoff between primary cluster performance and data durability and consistency.

Evaluating Basho

Basho also offers expert consultation services for the Riak database. In the UK, Basho offers perpetual licenses, support, and consultation on the UK government's G-Cloud store, and you can find the government's prices online by searching for Riak at `https://www.digitalmarketplace.service.gov.uk`.

Basho also claims to have several high-profile customers, including Best Buy, the Braintree payments service, Comcast, and Google (in its Bump service). Various media and advertisement companies, including Rovio Entertainment, creator of Angry Birds, are customers, too.

At the time of this writing, Basho has offices in Washington, D.C., London, and Tokyo.

Part III
Bigtable Clones

In this part . . .

✔ Managing data.

✔ Building for reliability.

✔ Storing data in columns.

✔ Examining Bigtable products.

✔ Visit www.dummies.com/extras/nosql for great Dummies content online.

Chapter 9

Common Features of Bigtables

*I*n previous chapters, I've focused on RDBMS features. Now, I want to talk about the useful features provided by Bigtables and how to improve the performance of your Bigtable applications.

Bigtables clones are a type of NoSQL database that emerged from Google's seminal Bigtable paper. Bigtables are a highly distributed way to manage tabular data. These tables of data are not related to each other like they would be in a traditional Relational Database Management System (RDBMS).

Bigtables encourage the use of *denormalisation* — copying summary data in to several records — for fast read speed, rather than using relationships that require CPU-costly data reconstitution work at query time.

In Chapter 11, I cover the use of Bigtables; however, to make the best use of them, you first need to understand how they organize data and how to structure data for its optimal use. That's the purpose of this chapter.

In this chapter, I describe how Bigtable clones based on Google's original Bigtable are different from RDBMS technology. I also discuss the mindset needed to understand and best use Bigtable NoSQL databases.

Storing Data in Bigtables

A Bigtable has tables just like an RDBMS does, but unlike an RDBMS, a Bigtable tables generally don't have relationships with other tables. Instead, complex data is grouped into a single table.

A table in a Bigtable consists of groups of columns, called *column families,* and a row key. These together enable fast lookup of a single record of data held in a Bigtable. I discuss these elements and the data they allow to be stored in the following sections.

Using row keys

Every row needs to be uniquely identified. This is where a row key comes in. A row key is a unique string used to reference a single record in a Bigtable. You can think of them as being akin to a primary key or like a social security number for Bigtables.

Many Bigtables don't provide good secondary indexes (indexes over column values themselves), so designing a row key that enables fast lookup of records is crucial to ensuring good performance.

A well-designed row key allows a record to be located without having to have your application read and check the applicability of each record yourself. It's faster for the database to do this.

Row keys are also used by most Bigtables to evenly distribute records between servers. A poorly designed row key will lead to one server in your database cluster receiving more load (requests) than the other servers, slowing user-visible performance of your whole database service.

Creating column families

A column family is a logical grouping of columns. Although Bigtables allow you to vary the number of columns supported in any table definition at run-time, you must specify the allowed column families up front. These typically can't be modified without taking the server offline. As an example, an address book application may use one family for Home Address. This could contain the columns Address Line 1, Address Line 2, Area, City, County, State, Country, and Zip Code.

Not all addresses will have data in all the fields. For example, Address Line 2, Area, and County may often be blank. On the other hand, you may have data only in Address Line 1 and Zip Code. These two examples are both fine in the same Home Address column family.

Having varying numbers of columns has its drawbacks. If you want to HBase, for example, to list all columns within a particular family, you must iterate over all rows to get the complete list of columns! So, you need to keep track of your data model in your application with a Bigtable clone to avoid this performance penalty.

Using timestamps

Each value within a column can typically store different versions. These versions are referenced by using a timestamp value.

Values are never modified — a different value is added with a different time-stamp. To delete a value, you add a tombstone marker to the value, which basically is flagging that the value is deleted at a particular point in time.

All values for the same row key and column family are stored together, which means that all lookups or version decisions are taken in a single place where all the relevant data resides.

Handling binary values

In Bigtables, values are simply byte arrays. For example, they can be text, numbers, or even images. What you store in them is up to you.

Only a few Bigtable clones support value-typing. Hypertable, for example, allows you to set types and add secondary indexes to values. Cassandra also allows you to define types for values, but its range-query indexes (less-than and greater-than operations for each data type) are limited to speeding up key lookup operations, not value comparison operations.

Working with Data

NoSQL databases are designed to hold terabytes and petabytes of information. You can use several techniques to handle this amount of information efficiently.

Such a large store of information places unique problems on your database server infrastructure and applications:

✔ Effectively splitting data among several servers to ensure even ingestion (adding of data) and query load

✔ Handling failure of individual servers in your cluster

✔ Ensuring fast data retrieval in your application without traditional RDBMS query joins

This section looks at these issues in detail.

Partitioning your database

Each table in a Bigtable is divided into ordered sets of contiguous rows, which are handled by different servers within the cluster. In order to distribute data effectively across all servers, you need to pick a row key strategy that ensures a good spread of query load.

A good example of doing this is to use a random number as the start of your partition key. As each tablet server (a single server in a Bigtable cluster) will hold a specific range of keys, using a randomized start to a partition key ensures even data distribution across servers.

A bad example of doing this can be found in a financial transaction database or log file management database. Using the timestamp as a row key means that new rows are added to the last tablet in the cluster — on a single machine. This means one server becomes the bottleneck for writes of new data.

Also, it's possible most of your client applications query recent data more often than historic data. If this is the case, then the same server will become a bottleneck for reads because it holds the most up-to-date data.

Use some other mechanism to ensure that data is distributed evenly across servers for both reads and writes. A good random number mechanism is to use Universally Unique Identifiers (UUIDs). Many programming languages come with a UUID class to assist with this. Using a Java application with HBase, for example, means you have access to the Java UUID class to create unique IDs for your rows.

Clustering

NoSQL databases are well suited to very large datasets. Bigtable clones like HBase are no exception. You'll likely want to use several inexpensive commodity servers in a single cluster rather than one very powerful machine. This is because you can get overall better performance per dollar by using many commodity servers, rather than a vastly more costly single, powerful server.

In addition to being able to scale up quickly, inexpensive commodity servers can also make your database service more resilient and thus help avoid hardware failures. This is because you have other servers to take over the service if a single server's motherboard fails. This is not the case with a single large server.

Figure 9-1 shows a highly available HBase configuration with an example of data split among servers.

The diagram in Figure 9-1 shows two nodes (HRegionServers, which I talk about in the upcoming section "Using tablets") in a highly available setup, each acting as a backup for the other.

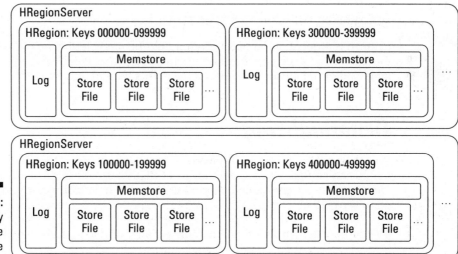

Figure 9-1:
Highly
available
HBase
setup.

In many production setups, you may want at least three nodes for high availability to ensure two server failures close in time to one another can be handled. This isn't as rare as you'd think! Advice varies per Bigtable; for example, HBase recommends five nodes as a minimum for a cluster:

✔ Each region server manages its own set of keys.

   Designing a row key-allocation strategy is important because it dictates how the load is spread across the cluster.

✔ Each region maintains its own write log and in-memory store.

   In HBase, all data is written to an in-memory store, and later this store is flushed to disk. On disk, these stores are called *store files.*

   HBase interprets store files as single files, but in reality, they're distributed in chunks across a Hadoop Distributed File System (HDFS). This provides for high ingest and retrieval speed because all large I/O operations are spread across many machines.

To maximize data availability, by default, Hadoop maintains three copies of each data file. Large installations have

✔ A primary copy

✔ A replica within the same rack

✔ Another replica in a different rack

Prior to Hadoop 2.0, Namenodes could not be made highly available. These maintained a list of all active servers in the cluster. They were, therefore, a single point of failure. Since Hadoop 2.0, this limit no longer exists.

Denormalizing

Rows in a particular table consist of several column families. Each column family can contain many columns. What Bigtables cannot do is store multiple values as a list in the same column for a row, which means that you must choose to either

✔ Store a list within the value (and serialize and load it yourself in code).

✔ Use a composite value for the column name, such as email|work and email|home.

Rather than normalize your data by having multiple tables that require joining to get a picture of a person, you may want to use a single record with multiple values copied (coalesced) in to a single record. This capability is called denormalization. Application developers find this approach easier to deal with because they can store an entire object as a row.

A good example is an e-commerce order. You may have a column family for billing information, a column family for delivery information, and a column family for items within the order. Many order items are in a single order. Applying denormalization means you can operate on all data about an order as a single entity.

There are several benefits to this approach in a NoSQL database:

- ✔ Application developers can work with an entire order as a single entity or object.
- ✔ Read operations don't need to do complex joins, as in SQL, on a relational DBMS.
- ✔ Write operations don't require shredding of data (taking an aggregate structure and spreading it across many tables), just writing of a single aggregate structure to a single record.

Bigtables like HBase have alternative mechanisms to denormalization:

- ✔ Use a version of a value to store each actual value.

  The number of retained versions is set at the time a column family is created, which means the number of items per order is limited.
- ✔ Store the Order Items object as an aggregate, perhaps in JSON or XML.
- ✔ Flatten some of the model keys and use composite row keys.

  This is similar to the way you'd store data with a relational database with joins, but it enables fast scanning of all the data in an order.

For a full discussion of this modeling scenario, go to the online HBase documentation, which you can find at `http://hbase.apache.org/book.html#schema.casestudies.custorder`.

If you find yourself storing many data values as JSON or XML "dumb" binary columns, consider a document database that supports secondary indexes. These document NoSQL databases are a much better fit for tree data models.

Managing Data

Once data is written to a database, you need to be able to manage it efficiently and ensure that it's always in a consistent, known state. You also need to be able to alter the storage structure over time as data needs to be rebalanced across a cluster.

There are several techniques available to manage data within Bigtable clones, and I discuss those next.

Locking data

Row locking means a record cannot have any field accessed while another process is accessing it. Row locking is an apt feature for a record that may be updated. Consider a situation where two clients are trying to update information at the same time. Without a row lock, one client could successfully write information that is immediately overwritten by the second process before the next read.

In this situation, a read-modify-update (RMU) sequence is helpful. This process requires that the database lock an entire row for edits until the first editing process is complete. However, doing so is particularly tricky if you need to either update or create a row but your application doesn't yet know if that row already exists. Should you create or update a row? The good news is that databases like HBase allow locking on any row key, including those that don't yet exist.

Using tablets

A *tablet server* is a server within a Bigtable cluster that can manage one or more tablets. HBase calls these *HRegionServers.* You use these servers to store rows of data that belong to a particular subset of a table. These subsets are contiguous rows as judged by their row key values.

A typical tablet server can store from 10 to 1,000 tablets. In turn, these tablets hold a number of rows within a particular table. Tablets, therefore, hold a group of records (called rows in Bigtables) for a single table within a single database.

A tablet is managed by a particular tablet server. If that server goes down, another tablet server is assigned to manage that tablet's data. Thus, a tablet is the unit of persistence within a Bigtable.

Alternative names for this mechanism exist across different Bigtable clones. HBase, for example, supports multiple regions per region server and multiple stores per region.

Configuring replication

Replication is an overloaded term in NoSQL land. It can mean one of several things:

- ✔ Copying data between multiple servers in case of disk failure.
- ✔ Ensuring that read replicas have copies of the latest data.
- ✔ Keeping a disaster recovery cluster up to date with the live primary cluster.

  This definition is the one that most people will recognize as replication. I call this *disaster recovery (DR) replication* to avoid confusion.

All DR functionality works on the premise that you don't want to block data writes on the primary site in order to keep the DR site up to date. So, DR replication is asynchronous. However, the changes are applied in order so that the database can replay the edit logs in the correct sequence. As a result, it's possible to lose some data if the primary site goes down before the DR site is updated.

This state of affairs applies to all traditional relational DBMS DR replication. The advantage, on the other hand, is very fast writes in the primary cluster.

Waiting for another server to confirm that it's updated before the client is told that the transaction is complete is called a *two-phase commit*. It's considered two phases because the local commit and all configured remote commits must happen before the client is informed of a transaction's success.

Replication means that data changes are sent from a primary site to a secondary site. You can configure replication to send changes to multiple secondary sites, too.

Replication happens between tablets or regions, not at the database level. This means that updates happen quickly and that the load is spread across both the primary and secondary clusters.

Improving Performance

Depending on how they're used, you must tweak the configuration of databases to ensure that they perform as needed. In this section, I talk about some common options to keep in mind when you're tuning a Bigtable clone.

Compressing data

All of the Bigtable clones that I looked at in detail for this book — HBase, Hypertable, Accumulo, and Cassandra — support *block compression,* which keeps data values in a compressed state to reduce the amount of disk space used. Because, in general, Bigtables don't store typed values, this compression is simple binary compression.

Several algorithms are typically supported, usually at least gzip and LZO compression. HBase and Cassandra, in particular, support several algorithms.

Cassandra stores its data in the SSTable format, which is the same format as Google's original Bigtable. This format has the advantage of using an append-only model. So, rather than update data in place — which requires uncompressing the current data, modifying it, and recompressing — data can simply be appended to the SSTable. This single compression activity makes updates fast.

Caching data

NoSQL databases generally use an append-only model to increase the performance of write operations. New data is added to the storage structure, and old data is marked for later deletion. Over time, merges happen to remove old data. *Compaction* is another word for this process.

For write-heavy systems, this model can lead to a lot of merges, increasing the CPU load and lowering data write speed. Some Bigtable systems, such as Hypertable, provide an in-memory write cache, which allows some of the merges to happen in RAM, reducing the load on the disk and ensuring better performance for write operations.

For read-heavy systems, reading the same data from disk repeatedly is expensive in terms of disk access (seek) times. Hypertable provides a read cache to mitigate this problem. Under heavy loads, Hypertable automatically expands this cache to use more of a system's RAM.

Filtering data

Retrieving all records where a value is in a particular range comes at the expense of data reading bandwidth. Typically, a hashing mechanism on the row key is used to avoid reading a lot of data just to filter it, you instead search just a smaller portion of the database. Searching this value space is I/O-intensive as data increases to billions of records.

Because "billions of records" isn't an unusual case in NoSQL, a different approach is required. One of the most common techniques is called a *Bloom filter,* named after Burton Howard Bloom who first proposed this technique in 1970.

A Bloom filter uses a predictable and small index space while greatly reducing requirements for disk access. This state is achieved because a Bloom filter is probabilistic; that is, it returns either *Value may be in set* or *Value is definitely not in set*, rather than a traditional *Value is definitely in set.*

Exact value matches can then be calculated based on the results from the Bloom filter — a much reduced key space to search. The disk I/O is still greatly reduced, as compared to a traditional simple hashing mechanism that scans the entire table.

HBase, Accumulo, Cassandra, and Hypertable all support Bloom filters.

Chapter 10

Bigtable in the Enterprise

In This Chapter

▶ Protecting your data when a server crashes

▶ Predicting reliability of your database service's components

▶ Growing your database service as your business grows

*B*usinesses are risk-adverse operations, and mission-critical systems rely on safeguard after safeguard, along with plan B and plan C, in case disaster strikes.

Distributed Bigtable-like databases are no exception, which requires Bigtable enthusiasts to prove that this newfangled way of managing data is reliable for high-speed and mission-critical workloads.

Thankfully, the people working on Bigtable clones are also intimately familiar with how relational database management systems (RDBMS) provide mission-critical data storage. They've been busily applying these lessons to Bigtables.

In this chapter, I talk about the issues that large enterprises will encounter when installing, configuring, and maintaining a mission-critical Bigtable database service.

Managing Multiple Data Centers

If all goes horribly, horribly wrong — or someone accidentally turns off all the lights in a city — you'll need an entire backup data center, which is referred to as a *disaster recovery site*.

In this section, I talk about the features commonly available in Bigtable clones that help guarantee a second data center backup in case of disaster.

Active-active clustering

Perhaps your organization does "live" business in many locations in the world. If so, you need high-speed local writes to your nearest data center — so all data centers must be writable. In this scenario, all data centers are primary active data centers for their own information.

Active-active clustering writes can happen at any location. All data centers are live all the time. Data is replicated between active sites, too, in order to provide for traditional disaster recovery.

However, if the same data record is overwritten in multiple locations, you may be faced with having to choose between two options:

✔ Wait for the site to write this data to all data centers, slowing down your transaction times.

This option is shown in part A of Figure 10-1.

✔ Replicate this data asynchronously, potentially losing some of the latest data if it wasn't replicated before an outage at one site.

✔ This option is shown in part B of Figure 10-1.

In my experience, it's unusual to have a situation where the same record must be updated from multiple data centers. Normally, writing a new record locally and pushing that to the other sites asynchronously is sufficient. In this model, each site does accept writes, but only for a fixed number of partitions (primary keys). This still allows a global view to be generated locally, with a small chance of inconsistency only with the remote replicated data. This option is show in part C of Figure 10-1.

When you absolutely need fast local data center writes across the world, a globally distributed database that supports full active-active clustering is needed. Cassandra is a Bigtable database that supports global active-active clusters while preserving as much speed as possible on ingest.

Managing time

Many Bigtable databases rely on identifying the latest record by a timestamp. Of course, time is different across the world, and coming up with a reliable, globally synchronized clock is incredibly difficult. Most computer systems are accurate individually to the millisecond, with synchronization lag of a few milliseconds. For most systems this is fine, but for very large systems a more accurate time stamp mechanism is required.

A. Full cross-data center consistency through 2 phase commit remotely

1. Write arrives   2. Not acknowledged until both local and remote replicas are updated

Data Center 1 ┊ Data Center 2

B. 2 phase commit locally, asynchronous eventually consistent replication remotely

1. Write arrives   3. Data replicated to remote cluster

2. Local replica updated
before acknowledgement

Data Center 1 ┊ Data Center 2

C. Local and remote replicas updated asynchronously, always eventually consistent

1. Write arrives   2. Acknowledged immediately. Replicas only updated sometime later

Data Center 1 ┊ Data Center 2

Figure 10-1:
Cross-data
center
replication
mecha-
nisms.

An out-of-sync clock means that one site thinks it has the latest version of a record, whereas in fact another site somewhere in the world wrote an update just after the local write. Only a very few applications, though, are affected by this time difference to the extent that data becomes inconsistent. Most records are updated by the same application, process, or local team of people that wrote it in the first place. Where this isn't the case (like in global financial services where trades can be processed anywhere), synchronization is an issue.

Google recently came up with a mechanism for a reliable global timestamp called the Google TrueTime API, and it's at the heart of the Spanner NewSQL relational database, which stores its data in the Bigtable NoSQL columnar database.

This API depicts the concept of uncertainty in terms of current time. It uses a time interval that's guaranteed to include the time at which an operation happened. This approach better clarifies when an operation definitely or may have happened. The time synchronization uses atomic clocks or GPS signals.

Many Bigtable databases, except Google Bigtable itself, support the concept of a record timestamp. These time stamps don't rise quite to the level of science that Google's TrueTime API does, but they provide a close approximation that may suffice in your particular use case. Notably, Accumulo has its own distributed time API within a cluster.

Reliability

Reliability refers to a service that's available and can respond to your requests. It means you're able to access the service and your data, no matter what's going on internally in a cluster.

Conversely, if you can't communicate with the server in the cluster and can't access the data in the server, your database needs to handle the lack of communication.

The database also needs to handle failures. What happens if the disk drive dies? How about a single server's motherboard? How about the network switch covering a quarter of your database cluster? These are the kinds of things that keep database administrators up at night (and employed, come to think of it).

In this section, I discuss how Bigtable databases provide features that alleviate database cluster reliability issues.

Being Google

In Google's Bigtable paper, which I introduced in Chapter 1, its authors discuss their observations on running a large distributed database. Bigtable powers Google Analytics, Google Earth, Google Finance, Orkut, and Personalized Search. These are large systems, and Googles' observations regarding such systems are interesting. In particular, they spotted various causes for system problems, as shown here:

- **Memory corruption:** Where a system's memory state becomes invalid
- **Network corruption:** Where data is modified while in transit
- **Large clock skew:** Where servers disagree on the "current" time
- **Hung machines:** Where some machines don't respond while others do
- **Extended and asymmetric network partitions:** Where long network lags occur, and also "split brains," which is where a cluster of nodes is divided into two (or more) clusters unevenly, each receiving requests as if the whole cluster was still operational and communicative
- **Bugs in other systems Google used:** For example, dependent services like the distributed Chubby file-lock mechanism

✔ **Overflow of GFS quotas:** Effectively running out of disk space

✔ **Planned and unplanned hardware maintenance:** Where workloads in the cluster are affected

These problems affect a wide variety of distributed databases, and when assessing a particular database for its reliability in enterprise applications, you need to find out how they handle the preceding situations.

With this information, you can identify higher-risk areas of your system, including whether a single point of failure (SPoF) needs to be addressed. SPoFs are the main cause of catastrophic service unavailability, so I spend a lot of time throughout this book identifying them. I recommend you address each one I talk about for a live production service.

Ensuring availability

A table in a Bigtable database is not a physical object. Instead, data is held within tablets. These tablets are all tagged as being associated with a table name. Tablets are distributed across many servers.

If a server managing a tablet fails, then this needs to be managed. Typically, in Bigtable clones, another tablet server is elected to take over as the primary master for the tablets on the failed server. These tablets are shared between the remaining servers to prevent a single server from becoming overloaded.

How these secondary servers are selected and how long it takes them to take over operations on those tablets are important issues because they can affect data and service availability, as shown here:

✔ Some Bigtable clones have a master process that monitors tablet servers and then reallocates their tablets if the tablets fail or become unresponsive. These masters are also responsible for database changes like adding or removing tables, so these masters also respond to limited client requests.

✔ On some databases (for example, Hypertable), these master processes aren't highly available, which means that, if the master also dies, you might have a problem. Usually, you can start another master within seconds, but it's important to understand this needs to be done to guarantee availability.

✔ Other Bigtable clones (HBase, Accumulo) will have standby master processes running, with failover happening immediately and without the client knowing. Accumulo even goes so far as to have a feature — called FATE, amusingly enough — that guarantees and replays any database structure altering requests if the master fails during a modification. This prevents schema corruption of the database.

✔ Other databases (Cassandra) use a chatter protocol between all members of the cluster, avoiding a master process altogether. This gives Cassandra the minimum number of components, and allows every server in the cluster to look the same, all of which makes administration and setup easier, while helping guarantee availability, too.

Scalability

Anyone can create a database that looks fast on a single machine while loading and querying a handful of records. However, scaling to petabytes requires a lot of work. In this section, therefore, I highlight features that can help you scale read and write workloads.

The features covered in this chapter are specific to Bigtable clones mentioned in this book. Many other strategies are possible to achieve scalability, including:

✔ **Use distributed file storage.** Shares load across physical disks/servers, which can be done in one of the following ways:

- A local RAID (Redundant Array of Inexpensive Disk) array
- A shared storage system such as HDFS (Hadoop File System)

✔ **Go native.** Using a compiled programming language next to an operating system like C++ is always faster than a bytecode or interpreted language like Java.

Most Bigtable clones are implemented on top of Java, with Hypertable being the notable C++ exception.

✔ **Utilize fast networks.** Use at least 10-Gbps switches for high-speed operations, especially if you're using shared network storage.

✔ **Set up separate networks.** Sometimes it's useful to keep client-to-database network loads separate from database-to-storage or database intra-node chatter. On larger clusters, intra-node chatter can also start flooding a data network if the network is shared. On very large clusters, it's best to have a secondary net for intra-server communication to avoid this problem.

✔ **Write to memory with journaling.** Some databases can receive writes in memory, which is very fast, while also writing a small record of the changes, called a Journal, to disk to ensure that the data is durable if the server fails. This Journal is smaller, and thus faster to save, than applying the change itself to all the database structures on disk.

Ingesting data in parallel

When writing large amounts of data to a database, spread the load. There's no point having a 2-petabyte database spread across 100 servers if 99 percent of the new data is landing on only one of those servers, and doing so can easily lead to poor performance when data is being ingested.

Bigtable databases solve this problem by spreading data based on its *row key* (sometimes called a *partition key*). Adjacent row key values are kept near each other in the same tablets.

To ensure that new data is spread across servers, choose a *row key* that guarantees new records aren't located on the same tablet on a single server, but instead are stored on many tablets spread across all servers.

✔ Accumulo allows you to plug in your own balancer implementations, which enables you to specify that rows can be kept together or spread across a cluster, depending on your needs.

✔ Accumulo and HBase also support *locality groups,* which keep particular columns for the same row together. This is particularly useful for guaranteeing fast read speeds. Hypertable supports locality groups, too, with a feature called *access groups.*

In-memory caching

A database system can experience extreme input and output load, as described here:

✔ In many systems, the same data is often requested. Consider a news site that shows the latest news stories across a range of segments. In this case, it's important to keep the latest stories cached, rather than go back to disk to access them each time they're requested.

✔ When high-speed writes are needed, the most efficient way to handle them is to write all the data to an in-memory database file, and just write the journal (a short description of the changes) to disk, which increases throughput while maintaining durability in the event of a system failure.

It's best to have a system that can cope with managing both high-speed writes and read caching natively and automatically. Hypertable is one such database that proactively caches data, watching how the system is used and changing memory priorities automatically.

Indexing

Like key-value stores, Bigtable clones are very good at keeping track of a large number of keys across many, if not hundreds, of database servers. Client drivers for these databases cache these key range assignments in order to minimize the lag between finding where the key is stored and requesting its value from the tablet server.

Rather than store one value, a Bigtable stores multiple values, each in a column, with columns grouped into column families. This arrangement makes Bigtable clones more like a traditional database, where the database manages stored fields.

However, Bigtables, like key-value stores, don't generally look at or use the data type of their values. No Bigtable database in this book supports — out of the box — data types for values, though Cassandra allows secondary indexes for values. However, these secondary indexes simply allow the column value to be used for comparison in a "where" clause; they don't speed up query times like a traditional index does.

You can apply the same workaround to indexing used in key-value stores to Bigtables. Figure 10-2 shows single and compound indexes.

The shown indexing method is limited, though, because you need to know in advance what combinations of fields are required in order to build an index table for each combination of query terms. The indexes are also consistent only if the Bigtable database supports transactions, or real time updates of the indexes during a write operation.

If the database doesn't support automatic index table updates within a transaction boundary, then for a split second, the database will hold data but have no index for it. Databases with transactions can update both the data table and index table(s) in a single atomic transaction, ensuring consistency in your database indexes. This is especially critical if the server you're writing to dies after writing the value, but before writing the index — the row value may never be searchable! In this case, you must check for data inconsistencies manually on server failover.

A. Single Product index linking to all orders

Row Key	Column family:name	Column family:name	Column family:name
Product-1234	"":Order-34 value: "-"		
Product-435	"":Order-34 value: "-"		"":Order-93 value: "-"
Product-9342		"":Order-78 value: "-"	

B. Compound index on Product and County purchaser resided in

Row Key	Column family:name	Column family:name	Column family:name
Product-1234_County:Derbyshire	"":Order-34 value: "-"		
Product-435_County:Derbyshire	"":Order-34 value: "-"		
Product-435_County:Norfolk			"":Order-93 value: "-"
Product-9342_County:Suffolk		"":Order-78 value: "-"	

Figure 10-2:
Secondary index tables in a Bigtable database.

Hypertable is a notable exception because it does provide limited key qualifier indexes (used to check whether a column exists for a given row) and value indexes (used for equals, starts with, and regular expression matches). These indexes do not support ranged less-than or greater-than queries, though.

Other general-purpose indexing schemes are available for use with Bigtable clones. One such project is Culvert (`https://github.com/booz-allen-hamilton/culvert`). This project aimed to produce a general-purpose secondary indexing approach for multiple Bigtable implementations over HDFS. HBase and Accumulo are supported.

This project has been dormant since January 2012, but the code still works. In the future it may no longer work with the latest databases, requiring organizations to build their own version. This means knowing about Culvert's approach could help you design your own indexing strategy.

Commercial support vendors, such as Sqrrl Enterprise for Accumulo, provide their own proprietary secondary indexing implementations. If you need this type of indexing, do consider those products. Similarly, the Solr search engine has also been used on top of Bigtable clones.

Using an additional search engine tier takes up much more storage (field values are stored twice) and may not be transactionally consistent if it's updated outside of a database transaction. Cassandra, which ensures consistent Solr index updates, is the notable exception in the DataStax Enterprise version.

Solr is a useful option for full-text indexing of JSON documents stored as values in Bigtables. But if you're storing documents, it's better to consider a document store.

Aggregating data

In transactional database systems, individual rows are created and updated, whereas in analytical systems, they're queried in batches and have calculations applied over them.

If you need to provide high-speed analytics for large amounts of data, then you need a different approach. Ideally, you want the ability to run aggregation calculations close to the data itself, rather than send tons of information over the network to the client application to process.

All Bigtable clones in this book support HDFS for storage and Hadoop Map/Reduce for batch processing. Accumulo is prominent because it includes a native extension mechanism that, in practice, may prove more efficient for batch processing than Hadoop Map/Reduce.

Accumulo iterators are plug-in Java extensions that you can write yourself and use to implement a variety of low-level query functionality. You can use them to:

✔ Shard data across tablet servers.

✔ Sort data (for storing the most recent data first).

✔ Filter data (used for attribute-based access control).

✔ Aggregate data (sum, mean average, and so on).

HBase coprocessors introduced recently in HBase 0.92 also allow similar functionality as Accumulo offers. They also will eventually allow HBase to have similar security (visibility iterator) functionality as Accumulo.

Configuring dynamic clusters

After you parallelize your data as much as possible, you may discover that you need to add more servers to your cluster in order to handle the load. This requires rebalancing the data across a cluster in order to even out the query and ingest loads. This rebalancing is particularly important when you need to increase the size of your cluster to take on larger application loads.

You can support cluster elasticity in Bigtable clones by adding more servers and then instructing the master, or entire cluster for master-less Bigtable clones like Cassandra, to redistribute the tablets across all instances. This operation is similar to server failover in most Bigtable implementations.

The control of the HDFS area is moved to a new server, which then may have to replay the journal (often called the write ahead log — WAL) if the changes haven't been flushed to HDFS. On some databases, like HBase, this process can take ten minutes to finish.

Once you've scaled out, you may decide you want to scale back, especially if during peak periods of data ingestion, you added more servers only to receive more parallel information. This is common for systems where information is submitted by a particular well known deadline, like for government tax-return deadlines. Again, this requires redistribution of the tablets, reversing the preceding scale out process.

Configuring and starting this process is in many cases a manual exercise. You can't join a Bigtable to a cluster and have that cluster magically reassign tablets without issuing a command to the cluster. Some commercial enterprise versions, such as DataStax Enterprise, do automate this process.

Chapter 11

Bigtable Use Cases

*B*igtable is used to manage very large amounts of data across many servers, up to petabytes of data and hundreds, if not thousands, of servers.

If you're using relational databases but having issues with them, you might think that Bigtable clones are the natural place to start looking for help. After all, they're tables, so they must be similar to relational databases, right? Unfortunately, that's not the case.

Bigtable clones handle some issues well that relational database don't solve — for example, with *sparse data* problems, where datasets contain many different types of values, but only a handful of those values are used. Bigtable clones are also able to analyze data while it's in-flight, rather than in overnight batches in a separate data warehouse.

This chapter shows how managing data in relational database differs from managing the same data in a Bigtable. I also talk about how to store data effectively for later analysis, and for providing historic summaries of data analyzed.

Handling Sparse Data

At times, a relational database management system (RDBMS) may have a table design (a schema) in which the columns don't have a value. An example is a social media site where someone hasn't provided their photo yet.

Using an RDBMS to store sparse data

Null values(as opposed to empty strings) in relational databases typically consume a couple of bytes, which is fine normally because the field isn't filled — which when filled would be more like a 20-byte string for, say, storing an uploaded a picture. Two bytes is better than 20 bytes.

In some situations, though, these two bytes per blank field can be a significant amount of wasted space. Consider a contacts application that supports usernames and phone numbers for every type of network — cell, home, and office phone — and social networks like Twitter, Facebook, and Baidu, with a column for each of the hundreds of options and addresses. This means hundreds of bytes wasted per record.

If you're anything like me, each contact consumes a minimum of three fields (see Figure 11-1). If you provide a contact management service, you may be storing 297 null fields for the 300 fields you support. Scale this up to a shared global application, and you're looking at terabytes of wasted space.

Author: So you can't scale up from global to worldwide, because they mean the same thing — so the scale is the same.

That's even before you consider doing a query on a single contact and pulling back 300 columns, many of which are null. Those null columns 2 bytes markers are costly in space on the result set when being sent over the network and processed at the client.

Using a Bigtable to manage sparse data instead of a relational database alleviates this storage issue.

	Contact ID	Email1	Email2	CellPhone	HomePhone	Twitter
	1234	a@a.org	NULL	NULL	555-4567	NULL
Figure 11-1: Sparse contacts table in an RDBMS.	5428	NULL	NULL	NULL	NULL	@somedude
	2353	b@c.com	u@v.net	NULL	NULL	NULL
	9724	NULL	NULL	NULL	NULL	NULL

Using a Bigtable

In a Bigtable, you can model the same contacts application with a column family for each type of network (phone, social media, email, snail mail) and a column for each one defined (home phone, cell phone, office phone).

Bigtable stores only the columns you indicate on each record instance. If you indicate three columns — email, home phone, and cell phone — then Bigtable stores exactly those three column values. No nulls, and no wasted space, as illustrated in Figure 11-2.

If you need to find all contacts with a phone number — say, at least one column in the phone column family — then you need to consider that factor. This scenario can happen if you're viewing all contacts in a phone in order to make a call; there's no point in showing contacts without phone numbers here!

In this case, the database must support a *column exists* query for the column family and column names. Some databases, such as Hypertable, allow you to set up special *qualifier indexes* to ensure that these types of existential queries will operate quickly over large datasets.

Also, keep in mind that some Bigtable clones don't provide advanced matching functions for values but store them instead as "dumb" binary data that cannot be compared with data-type specific operations — for example, searching for all contact names (a string field) starting with "Adam F". This is a *starts with* query that processes a string value. Most Bigtable clones provide *exact match* functionality, but don't natively support partial match or data-type-specific range queries (less than and greater than).

Row Key	Column Values	
1234	email:1 = a@a.org	phone:home = 555-4567
5428	social:twitter = @somedude	
2353	email:1 = b@c.com	email:2 = u@v.net
9724		

Figure 11-2:
Sparse data in a Bigtable clone.

Hypertable's value indexes do support exact match, starts with, and regular expression matches. If you need this functionality regularly, Hypertable may be for you.

Bigtable clones also don't support relationships, preferring to store multiple copies of data to minimize read-time processing. This is a process called denormalization. Although, in some situations, this approach consumes more disk space, it enables very efficient reads with higher throughput than most relational databases can provide.

Analyzing Log Files

Log files are very common across a range of systems and applications. Being able to record these files for later analysis is a valuable feature.

Log-file recording and analysis is a very complex business. It's not unusual for every system-to-system call in mission-critical Enterprise applications to include tracking code. This code enables the app to check for errors, invalid values, and security breaches, as well as the duration of each action.

This vast information is collected from hundreds of servers. It's then analyzed in nearly real time in order to ensure that a system's tracking capabilities and condition are up to date. In this way, problems are discovered before services to users are interrupted.

Analyzing data in-flight

The traditional relational database approach to analyzing data is to store it during the day and then at regular intervals (normally overnight) to create a different structure of that data in a data warehouse for analyzing the next day.

For your company's current Enterprise software sales, daily data summaries may be enough. On the other hand, in countries with highly regulated financial services, this information needs to be less than five minutes old. The same can be said for system monitoring. There's no point in having a view that's 24 hours or more out of date; you need summaries as soon as they're available.

Bigtable clones are great for collecting this information. They can have flexible columns, so if a particular log entry doesn't have data for a field, it simply can't be stored. (See Figure 11-3 for an example of a log entry.) Bigtable clones also allow you to store data in multiple structures.

A. Typical log file data

Host	Process	Timestamp	Type	Function	Duration
server1	jboss	2014-09-05T09:04:32	Java RPC	getCreditScore	12.3

B. Log file data modeled in a Bigtable clone

Row Key	Column Values					
34BD7E44	host:name server1	host:process jboss	event:time 2014-09-05 T09:04:32	event:type Java RPC	java:function getCreditScore	event:duration 12.3

Figure 11-3: A typical log file entry.

To build a quick picture of a day in five minute, one-hour, one-day chunks, you can store the same data in alternative structures at the same time. This is an application of the denormalization pattern commonly used in NoSQL systems, as shown in Figure 11-4.

A. 5 minute log index

Row Key	Column family:name
2014-09-05T09:05:00	Event-34BD7E44:duration 12.3

B. Hourly log index

Row Key	Column family:name	Column family:name
2014-09-05T10:00:00	Event-34BD7E44:duration 12.3	Event-72B45D43:duration 69.4

Figure 11-4: The same log entry indexed for different time periods.

The preceding denormalization approach enables quick searching for data in different systems at different time intervals, which is useful for ad-hoc querying and also for building data summaries, which I discuss next.

Building data summaries

Having extra index tables allows a daemon program to regularly and efficiently recalculate the last five minutes, hour, and daily summaries.

Instead of requiring a range index or scanning all data rows to find the last five minutes of data, you instead merely round the current time up to a five-minute interval and query for all data with that interval in your log summary table.

Using specialized system iterators (as Accumulo does) or stored procedures allows this calculation to happen within the database very efficiently. (See Figure 11-5, which shows a summary table being updated.)

Figure 11-5:
Calculated
summary
table.

Row Key	Column family:name	Column family:name
2014-09-05T10:00:00	duration:mean 40.85	duration:samples 2

Chapter 12

Bigtable Products

*R*ight now, I bet you're feeling like a kid in a candy store, knowing that he can have only one kind of candy — but *which one* is the question! You've seen the future, and you know you want a Bigtable NoSQL database, because, as the name implies, they're big, and they're tabular; and whether your thing is ridiculously large datasets, government grade security, high performance with data consistency, or global distribution of your data — there's a Bigtable out there for you!

In this chapter, I discuss each of these different use cases, to help you determine which Bigtable fits your needs.

History of Google Bigtable

Google published its Bigtable paper in 2006. This paper described for the first time a set of related technologies that Google had been using to store and manage data under its services.

Of particular interest was the design decision to avoid joins between tables, preferring instead a denormalization approach — that is, to keep copies of certain data for different uses, such as a summary record and a detail record both having "patient name" columns.

Google's Bigtable was designed to be flexible enough to use for a variety of Google's services. As a result, Bigtable is a general-purpose database, potentially applicable to a wide range of use cases, much like its relational database forebears.

Bigtable was built on a number of building blocks. The first was the distributed file system called GFS — Google File System. This file system is complemented by a distributed locking mechanism called *Chubby*, which ensures that writes and reads to a single file are atomic.

(continued)

(continued)

Today this design is applied in the open-source Hadoop Distributed File System (HDFS). The SSTable file format for storing data is also used. A number of today's Bigtable clones share this capability.

A variety of architectural and mathematical techniques are applied to Bigtable, too:

✔ Data compression

✔ Sharding parts of a table (tablets) between multiple servers

✔ Bloom filters

Bloom filters are special "space-efficient" indexes that tell you either "this key definitely doesn't exist" or "this key may exist" in the database. Their use reduces disk I/O operations when you're looking up keys that may not exist.

Bigtable has inspired (sometimes along with Dynamo in the key-value world) many open source software developers to implement highly scalable wide-column stores. These column stores are highly tolerant of patchy sparse data and operate at extreme scale.

Managing Tabular Big Data

Many best practices, tricks, and tips are available for working with big data and Bigtables. I've highlighted just a few, but forums are full of other options, too.

The term *big data* is overhyped. It refers to the management of very fast, large, variable, or complex datasets, typically involving billions of records (data) that are spread across many machines, and changing the structure of that data, in order to store it.

Designing a row key

HBase and Cassandra distribute data by row key. Each region server manages a different key space. This means that data distribution — and therefore, ingest and query performance — depends on the key you choose.

Consider an application that manages log files. You may be tempted to use the date and time of a message as the start of the row key. However, doing so means that the latest information will reside on the single server managing the highest row-key values.

All of your newly ingested data will hit this single server, slowing ingest performance. It's even worse if a set of monitoring dashboards are all querying for the last five minutes worth of data, because this single server will also have the highest query load. Performance suffers — and somebody may shout at you!

Instead, make the row key something that distributes well across machines. A unique key with random values across the spectrum of possible values is a good start. Java includes a Universally Unique Identifier (UUID) class to generate such an ID. Some Bigtables have this built-in capability, too.

Instead, model your key values that are used as lookups for column names rather than row keys (you find more on this topic in the following section).

You need to be careful, though, because different key strategies create different read and write tradeoffs in terms of performance. The more random the key, the less likely adjacent rows will be stored together.

Using a very random key means you will have a faster write speed, but slower read speed — as the database scans many partitions for related data in your application. This may or may not be an issue depending on how interrelated your rows are.

By using secondary indexes, you can alleviate this issue, because indexed fields are stored outside the storage key, which gives you the best of both worlds.

Key and value inversion

In a relational database, if you want to perform a quick lookup of table values, you add a column index. This index keeps a list of which records have which values, ordered by the value itself. This approach makes range queries (less-than and greater-than) much quicker than scanning the entire database.

Most Bigtables — with the exception of Hypertable — don't have such value indexes. Instead, all indexes are performed on keys — be they row keys or column keys (column names). This means you must get used to modeling your data differently. You may also have to create your own index tables for fast lookups. Consider the traditional relational database schema shown in Figure 12-1.

	Employee ID	Forename	Surname	SSN	TaxPercent	Department
Figure 12-1: Relational employee department table schema.	**1234**	Adam	Fowler	123-444422	80	Sales
	5428	Junior	Banker	146-236563	20	Investments
	2353	Kelly	Homeworker	834-125323	0	Engineering

In this schema, adding an index in the department column allows you to perform quick lookups. On Bigtable clones, this generally isn't possible. Some Bigtable clones provide secondary indexing that don't speed up queries, instead they just mark columns as being queriable. Apache Cassandra has these sorts of indexes. Other Bigtables, like Hypertable, have true secondary indexes which speed up queries, like their RDBMS relations.

Instead, you need an employee department index table, where you store the department values as row keys and the employee numbers using one of two methods:

✔ **Column names with blank values:** This is where you use the column name as a "flag" on the record.

✔ **Column families, with summary details in name and id:** Allows a summary to be shown with no further lookups. Figure 12-2 shows an example of denormalization.

A. Employee Table

Row Key	Column Values		
34BD7E44	person:forename Adam	person:surname Fowler	tax:SSN 123-444422
	employee:department Sales	employee:id 1234	tax:percent 80
27458BC8	person:forename Junior	person:surname Banker	tax:SSN 146-236563
	employee:department Investments	employee:id 5428	tax:percent 20
185CE732	person:forename Kelly	person:surname Homeworker	tax:SSN 834-125323
	employee:department Engineering	employee:id 1253	tax:percent 0

B. Department Index Table, with denormalized summary information

Row Key	Column Values	
Sales	34BD7E44:name Adam Fowler	34BD7E44:id 1234
Engineering	185CE732:name Kelly Homeworker	185CE732:id 1253

Figure 12-2:
Bigtable employee department and employee implementation.

This works because the keys are automatically indexed, and all data under a row key for a particular column family are kept local to each other, making lookups fast.

As an additional benefit, if an employee is in multiple departments, then this model still works. The same cannot be said of the default relational model in Figure 12-1.

Denormalization with Bigtables

A basic key-value inversion example leaves you with two tables in a database that don't support joins. So you have to execute two database requests to fetch all employee information for those employees in departments.

If you often perform lookups in this manner, you may want to consider another approach. For example, you always show a summary of the employees when looking up via department. In this scenario, copy some summary data from the employee details table into the employee department table. This is called denormalization and is shown in section B of Figure 12-2.

Some Bigtable clones, such as Cassandra, provide automatic column name ordering. In Figure 12-2, I use the employee's full name in a column name, which means that I don't have to sort the resulting data. (I kept the row key in case there are multiple John Smiths in the company!) In the application, I split the column name by semicolon when showing the name in the user interface.

In my application, I can now provide very fast lookups of employees by department and show a list of employees with summary information without significant processing or application side sorting. The only cost is a slight increase on storing this information in two ways in the same record (an example of trading disk space for higher speed read operations).

Scanning large key sets — Bloom filters

Bigtable clones, like their key-value store brethren, store data by managing a set of keys. These keys are usually hashed to balance data across a cluster.

When querying for a list of records where the key is of a particular value, you have to pass the query off to all nodes. If each node manages millions of records, then so can take some time.

This is where Bloom filters come in. You can add a Bloom filter onto column names in all Bigtable products. Rather than exhaustively scanning the whole database to answer the question "which rows have keys equaling this name," a Bloom filter tells you "this row may be in the results" or "this row definitely isn't in the results." This minimizes the key space that needs to be thoroughly searched, reducing disc I/O operations and query time.

Bloom filters use up memory storage space, but they are tunable. You can tune the chance that a row matches. An incorrect match is called a false-positive match. Changing the match weight from 0.01 to 0.1 could save you half the RAM in the filter — so doing so is worth considering. In HBase, this setting is `io.hfile.bloom.error.rate`, which defaults to 0.1. You can also tune Cassandra by using the `bloom_filter_fp_chance` parameter to the decimal value desired.

Distributing data with HDFS

So you have a fantastic HBase installation that's distributing data evenly across the whole cluster. Good work!

Now, turn your attention to data durability. What happens if a disk fails? How do you continually manage replicas? How do you perform fast appends to internal table structures?

This is where HDFS comes in. HDFS (the Hadoop Distributed File System) is based on the original Google File System. HDFS is great for ingesting very large files and spreading data across a cluster of servers.

Also, by default, HDFS maintains three copies of your data, providing redundancy across machines, and even racks of machines, in a data center.

What HDFS doesn't do is maintain indexes or pointers to data stored within those very large files. HDFS also doesn't allow alteration of specific parts of files stored on it. To provide indexing and support updates of data, you will need a NoSQL database running on top of HDFS. Figure 12-3 shows how an HBase cluster stores information on multiple Hadoop HDFS partitions spread across a Hadoop cluster.

Rather than store many small table files, HBase stores fewer, very large files one per row. New data is appended to these files. Changes are also appended, so you don't have to modify earlier parts of an existing table file. This process fits well with the HDFS storage mechanism.

HBase provides HDFS with a way to index and find appropriate small records within very large datasets. Hadoop provides HBase with a tried and true, highly parallel, distributed file system in HDFS, as well as batch processing through MapReduce.

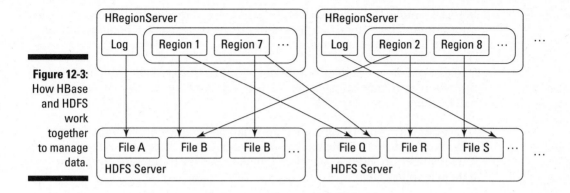

Figure 12-3:
How HBase
and HDFS
work
together
to manage
data.

Batch processing Bigtable data

There are two types of database queries:

✔ The result needs to be known as soon as possible.

These are data analysis use cases like users searching or listing records in a database.

✔ The result will take time to calculate.

These are long-running aggregations or analysis and reporting jobs.

These longer running jobs typically don't involve a user sitting in front of a screen waiting for an answer.

Answer sets may need to be processed, too, in order to generate a result, and this process requires a different way of scheduling and managing jobs. Thankfully, Hadoop MapReduce provides this functionality.

A simple Map/Reduce job typically consists of two operations:

1. The map task scans through a dataset and collates matching data in a required format.

2. The reduce task takes this data and produces an answer for the query. A reduce task's output can also form the input of a map task, allowing for chained analysis.

An example of a simple MapReduce job is analyzing citizen detail records in a HBase database, producing the average height of citizens, grouped by age.

In this example, the map function returns a set of records with height and age information. The reduce function tallies these by age and calculates a mean average using the sum and count.

You can run more complex MapReduce jobs to feed a result from one operation as an input to another. In this way, sophisticated chains of analysis can be built.

HBase provides special table-oriented map and reduce operations. Guess what they're called? TableMapper and TableReducer, of course! The TableMapper provides a row object, making it easy to operate on tabular data in MapReduce.

The downside to MapReduce for simple operations such as count, sum, and average is that a lot of data is shunted around to the querying MapReduce Java code. Ideally, you want these results to be calculated right next to the data, in the HBase runtime itself.

Coprocessors

HBase 0.92 introduced a coprocessors feature, which will allow HBase to eventually include built-in features like complex filtering and access control.

For now, though, you can implement pre-calculation routines with coprocessors. Rather than execute aggregate operations at query time, coprocessors provide observer instances that execute when data is read or saved. This effectively allows pre-calculation of results prior to querying. Think of them as akin to a relational database's triggers. A variety of observation points are provided, including

✔ `preGet, postGet`: Called before and after a Get request.

✔ `preExists, postExists`: Called before and after an existence check via a Get request.

✔ `prePut, postPut`: Called before and after saving client data.

✔ `preDelete, postDelete`: Called before and after a client deletes values.

Once these aggregates are calculated, HBase needs a way to allow clients to request their values. Custom endpoints can be created to provide this data. *Endpoints* can communicate with any *Observer* instance, which allows endpoints to access pre-calculated aggregates.

Endpoints can be thought of as the equivalent of stored procedures from the relational database world. They are similar to client-side code that actually runs on the server and can be called by a range of clients.

Endpoints and *Observers* can perform any operation within HBase, so be sure you know what your code is doing before you deploy it! Coprocessors should provide a way to extend the inner workings of HBase in the future.

Assessing HBase

HBase is the original and best-known Bigtable clone in the NoSQL space today, and it's tightly linked to Hadoop, which makes it an obvious NoSQL database candidate for any organization with a large Hadoop deployment.

However, if you're thinking about using HBase, you need to consider several points. For example, HBase is written in Java, so it isn't as fast as a database implemented in C++.

Moreover, HBase isn't transactionally consistent, so it may not be suitable for some mission-critical workloads as a primary master store of data. Also, the fact that HBase requires HDFS storage is a barrier for organizations that don't use Hadoop, so HBase adds more complexity to an application architecture, and requires extra knowledge to deploy it.

Not all of the issues from the relational database world have been solved in Bigtables. In a Bigtable, your data is still in a table structure, requiring at least some up-front schema design for fast operation, and it takes time to design this schema and get it right; making data fit in to a table storage model also forces you to write "plumbing" code to convert data when reading and writing to the database.

For example, HBase must be taken completely offline in order to create a new column family or new tables. This is a major barrier to ongoing agile development.

No dedicated commercial entity backs HBase. Cloudera is the only commercial company you could say offers extensive HBase support, but it's currently selling support for three NoSQL databases on top of its Hadoop distribution. The three are Accumulo, MongoDB, and HBase. On its website, Cloudera is positioning HBase as an entry-level database for Hadoop.

Be sure that HBase has all the features you need and that you can find the right level of support and development expertise for your rollout. You'll likely want more of this support in-house with HBase, and be sure to confirm your designs up front during rounds of proof of concept testing.

Securing Your Data

Once the excitement of getting data in and out of a system has passed — and it passes rapidly — you want to turn your attention to protecting your data.

One of the ways to protect it is to secure access to it based on specific user roles or privileges — for data such as medical records, employee addresses, and billing details.

Some industry standards require that you protect records. Credit card handling, for example, requires that after the entire card number is entered, only the last four digits are shown on screens that follow (the full card number is hidden in the application).

Cell-level security

Traditional approaches to security require that an application's code handles security, including authenticating users, discovering their roles, and ensuring that they access only the records they're supposed to. This has been the case with relational database management systems for years. The same is true for many Bigtable clones, too.

Where this model breaks down is in the accreditation of the database itself, with the likes of the DoD and regulators, and in the lack of a built-in permissions model.

Accreditation and certification for public groups such as defense and sensitive government agencies provide assurance to both the organizations and to the public that best practice with regards writing secure code has been followed. If security is implemented at the application level, then the application and database are accredited together as a single system. This may not be a problem for some, but if you're trying to justify the creation of a new application built on a secure database, having an accredited database is useful for providing information security assurances to the business.

Building a security model into your own code is not an easy task. You first have to build a set of security plug-ins that allow you to authenticate users and look up their roles in one or more existing corporate systems. Then you need a way to assign privileges for particular records to users. None of this is easy to build, maintain, or protect against intrusion.

Take the following summary care record example with individual user access in which I assume data is secured at the record level. This is an *anti-pattern* — a pattern you should not apply on a real system. It is an anti-pattern because it is incomplete, as I will discuss next when we build a complete security model for health data.

```
Patient: Name: Leo Fowler, Address: 12 Swansea, DoB: 06/March/2014
Permissions: Dr Dye: read+write
```

A summary care record is the minimum personal healthcare information required to provide emergency room care to a patient. In the UK National Health Service (NHS) this summary care record is accessible through a combination of surname, birth date, and first line of an address. It can be accessed by any emergency medical worker.

Role based access control

There are clear benefits to using a system that comes with built-in authentication, authorization, and support for role based access control (RBAC). RBAC allows privileges to be assigned not to users, but to roles, for actions on a particular record.

Using roles is easier to manage than individual user access — for example, if someone moves from one department to another. All you do is update a single user-role list in your corporate security system rather than all permissions attached to a single user. Your RBAC-based database then automatically reflects the new roles when the user next accesses it. Listing 12-1 shows a summary care record with Roles attached.

Listing 12-1:   Summary Care Record (SCR) Information and RBAC Read/ Write Privileges

```
Patient: Name: Leo Fowler, Address: 12 Swansea, DoB: 06/March/2014
Permissions: Doctor: read+write, Nurse: read

External Directory System
Role Nurse: Nurse Ratchett
Role Doctor: Dr Dye, Dr A Trainee
```

This shows that a user with at least one of the doctor or nurse roles can read the summary care record. This is OR Boolean logic between roles, and it's the default RBAC mechanism used by most security systems.

The problem with such an approach is that any doctor can see the information. The roles are too wide. You can further refine them to make them more specific. As you see in Listing 12-2, now only the general practice surgery doctors can see the information.

Listing 12-2:   SCR with RBAC Privileges for Two ER Doctors

```
Patient: Name: Leo Fowler, Address: 12 Swansea, DoB: 06/March/2014
Permissions: BrimingtonSurgeryDoctor: read+write

External Directory System
Role BrimingtonSurgeryDoctor: Dr Dye, Dr A Trainee
```

Now you have the opposite problem — being too specific. Now only local doctors have access. You want ER doctors to have access, too. You need a way to define exactly who has access to the record.

Compartment security

Ideally, you want to use Boolean logic as shown in Listing 12-3.

This use of AND logic on roles is typically managed through named compartments. In Listing 12-3, you have a job role compartment and a department compartment.

Listing 12-3: Doctor AND EmergencyRoom: read

```
Patient: Name: Leo Fowler, Address: 12 Swansea, DoB: 06/March/2014
Permissions: EmergencyRoom AND Doctor: read
             BrimingtonSurgery AND Doctor: read+write

External Directory System
Role EmergencyRoom: Dr Kerse, Dr Shelby, Dr Death
Role Doctor: Dr Dye, Dr A Trainee, Dr Kerse, Dr Shelby, Dr Death
Role BrimingtonSurgery: Dr Dye, Dr A Trainee
```

Forcing all role assignments to use AND logic is very restrictive, so systems instead use this logic: If any assigned roles are within a compartment, then ensure that the user has ALL compartment roles; otherwise, ensure that the user has ANY of the non-compartmentalized assigned roles.

Table 12-1 shows the roles needed in this scenario when using compartment security. Here Jane the Junior Doctor who works in the Children's Ward is trying to access (read) documents.

Table 12-1   Roles Required When Using Compartment Security

Record	General Roles	Department Compartment	Job Role Compartment	Result
HR Policy	Employee	-	-	Read allowed
Charlie Child's Ward Notes	Employee	-	Doctor	Read allowed
Children's Ward Procedures	Employee	Children's Ward	-	Read allowed
John Doe's SCR	Employee	Emergency Room	Doctor	Read denied

This role assignment works well. When any role assignment includes one with a compartment, roles are required — restricting who can read the records. Where multiple compartments are mentioned, AND logic is forced — the user must have both roles to access the summary care record.

Cell-level security in Accumulo

There may be situations where you don't have a summary record — just the main patient record. In this situation, you want to provide a summary care record filter. This filter prevents certain fields — rather than entire records — from being viewed by an unauthorized user.

Accumulo includes an extra field as part of its key. Along with the row key, column family, and column name, Accumulo includes a visibility key. This is a Boolean expression that you can use to limit visibility to certain roles defined within the system.

This invisible key is for read security only. It's possible, unless security settings are configured properly, for a user who cannot see a particular value to overwrite it. Thus the lack of visibility doesn't prevent a user overwriting a value. To ensure this doesn't happen, be sure to correctly define table visibility settings as well as cell value visibility.

Assessing Accumulo

Accumulo was originally created by the U.S. National Security Agency, so the security system is pretty flexible. Of course, you need to manage that flexibility to ensure there aren't any gaping holes.

In particular, you can use a variety of plug-ins to link Accumulo to existing or custom authentication and authorization technologies. Having these plugins built into the database layer simplifies a system's design and makes the overall architecture easier to accredit from a security standpoint.

Unless it has a good reason not to, the U.S. Department of Defense is mandated to use Accumulo for Bigtable workloads — not for all NoSQL use cases (such as document, triple store, or key-value), contrary to popular belief — although the NSA has been required to contribute its security and other enhancements to other open-source projects, including HBase and Cassandra.

Accumulo can also use HDFS storage, like HBase can, which fits the bill when HBase-like functionality is needed in a more security-conscious setting.

Like HBase, though, there are no larger companies providing dedicated support. Cloudera again provides support for Accumulo as a higher-end alternative to HBase.

Cloudera provides HBase, Accumulo, and MongoDB for its Hadoop offerings. Be sure that your local Cloudera team understands and has implemented Accumulo in similar organizations in the past, and where it should be used, rather than MongoDB and HBase. There are advantages and disadvantages to each database.

High-Performing Bigtables

In many situations that require high performance, moving to a Bigtable solution provides the desired result. There are always extremes, though. Sometimes you need to squeeze every last ounce of performance out of a potential implementation.

Perhaps this is to reduce the hardware required, perhaps you're cataloging the stars in the universe, or perhaps you simply want to get the most for your money. Whatever the reason, there are options to assess.

Using a native Bigtable

Java is a great language, but it's simply not as fast as C++. HBase, Accumulo, and Cassandra are all built as Java applications. Java is the defacto language for enterprise systems, so its status isn't surprising.

Using C++ and operating system-provided APIs directly allows you to access lower-level, higher-performing services than the Java tier. Hypertable is a Bigtable database written in C++ from the ground up, and it provides a high performance Bigtable implementation.

Indexing data

You've already seen that Bigtable clones index keys like key-value stores and treat values as binary data. In some situations, though, you do in fact have to index the values themselves. Or perhaps you're just too familiar with relational databases and want your typed columns back!

Having a database that provides strong typing on column values gives you the ability to index values and to perform other typed operations, such as sums and averages.

Hypertable provides secondary indexing for values and the column name qualifiers. These indexes allow exact match or "starts with" matches. The indexes are implemented internally by Hypertable automatically creating a table with the same name, but preceded by a caret ^ symbol.

This approach is more convenient than updating index values yourself, and ensures that index updates are transactionally consistent with the data these indexes link to, but this approach does have limitations. You're limited to Just three operations:

- ✔ Checking a column exists
- ✔ Checking exact value matches
- ✔ Checking prefix (starts with) matches

You can't do data-specific range queries like finding all orders with an item with a quantity greater than five. This limitation is potentially a big one if you need to perform substantial analytics over the data. Still, some indexing is always better than no indexing!

Ensuring data consistency

For mission-critical applications, it's vital to ensure that, once written, data remains durable. If you're using a Bigtable as the primary store of mission-critical and high-value business information, then you need an ACID compliant database.

Ensuring that data is durable, that writes are applied in the correct order, and that information is replicated in the same order that it was updated in the source database cluster are just a few of the desirable features in such a system. Also, such systems need to ensure that your database supports strong consistency or is ACID-compliant. So, be sure to ask your vendor how its database ensures the safety of your data. Specifically, ask if it's *fully* ACID-compliant.

Some vendors use the term "strong consistency" because their products aren't capable of providing ACID compliance. However, there's a big difference between the two.

Hypertable is an ACID-compliant database for atomic operations. The only thing it lacks is the ability to group multiple atomic operations in a single transaction. In this case, if you need to modify several rows, perhaps one in a data table and another in an index table, then your update will not be ACID-compliant — each update occurs in its own window.

Assessing Hypertable

Right out of the box, Hypertable provides richer value indexing than other Bigtable clones do. Hypertable also supports HDFS as well as other file systems, including locally attached storage. Local disk storage is attractive when you want a Bigtable NoSQL database but don't want to manage a large Hadoop cluster.

In my experience, many NoSQL implementations actually consist of three to five servers. In such an environment, a large HDFS array is overkill. Not everyone uses NoSQL to manage gazillions of bytes of information. Often, they want the schema flexibility, speed of deployment, and cost savings associated with using commodity hardware rather than traditional relational database management systems like Oracle and Microsoft SQL Server.

Hypertable allows access group definition. Access groups tell the database to group column families from the same rows together on the same server. Consider a summary page that needs information from two or three column families. Configuring an access group on these families allows them to be retrieved quickly from the database.

Column families in Hypertable are optional, so you can ignore family names, as you can in Cassandra. Or, when they're required, you can use them like you can in HBase. Better still, you can mix and match approaches in the same table definition!

I really like the approach Hypertable has taken. It provides a pragmatic set of features that application programmers want in databases, without sticking to the dogma that "values are just binary objects."

One of my favorite features is adaptive memory allocation:

✔ When Hypertable detects a heavy write load, more RAM is used as an in-memory region. This speeds up reads because many are written to RAM rather than to disk.

✔ When a significant amount of reads is detected, Hypertable automatically switches to using RAM so that more RAM is used as a read cache, which, again, minimizes disk access for reads.

Hypertable isn't as widely used as HBase, Accumulo, or Cassandra, though. If you want the features of Hypertable, be sure you can find local expert support and developers who are experienced with Bigtable clones like Hypertable.

I have a couple of concerns about Hypertable:

✔ Region servers in Hypertable are highly available, with the Hypertable master reallocating regions to another server when one goes down. However, the master service isn't highly available; it only has a standby.

This is similar to a disaster recovery approach, which means that it's possible for a master to go down, followed promptly by a region server that isn't replaced for a few seconds. This window of time is short, but one you need be aware of, and prior to going live with the application, you need to test failover. Data could become inaccessible if both the master and the region server are on the same rack in a data center, and the network fails on that rack.

✔ Hypertable is available under the more restrictive GPL version 3 license. Although an open-source license, the GPL prevents Hypertable from being embedded within a commercial product. If you want to create "black box" software that embeds Hypertable and sell it, you must obtain a commercial license from Hypertable, Inc.

The GPL is potentially restrictive. If you are a software development firm with Hypertable experts, then you may not want or need to pay for commercial support.

The GPL licensing issue is likely to affect only a few use cases, mainly OEM partners. This licensing doesn't stop organizations from building and selling access to services that use Hypertable for storage.

Distributing Data Globally

If, like me, you have a vast collection of data spread over the world then you would appreciate features in your database to perform this data distribution for you, rather than having to code it in your application yourself. Writing this code for several database clusters creates a lot of manual work.

In my case, I use replication for my enormous collection of food recipes, but the need for replication can also happen in a variety of other situations:

✔ Financial transactions being done in several countries at the same time — London, New York and Singapore, for example

✔ International shop orders being placed in more local warehouses

✔ A globally distributed social network or email service with local servers, but with globally shared contacts

Substituting a key-value store

Bigtable clones can be thought of as a specific subclass of key-value stores. You can quite happily run key-value workloads on a Bigtable clone, too. If you already have a Bigtable, then you may well want to consider doing so.

If you need blazing fast writes — in the order of 100,000 writes per second or more — then a key-value store performs more quickly. In most situations, though, you probably have lighter loads, and if this is the case and you need Bigtable features only occasionally, then Cassandra may be for you. Cassandra prides itself on having features of both Bigtable and key-value stores, and takes its inspiration from both Amazon's Dynamo and Google's Bigtable papers. Figure 12-4 shows the differences between the two models.

In a key-value store, you have to design your key carefully in order to ensure evenly distributed data in a cluster and that lookups are fast. Bigtables have these key hierarchies built in with its concept of column families and column names.

Consider that you're using a key-value store to hold data pulled from a website for later search indexing. You may want to store and retrieve data by the website domain, page URL, and the timestamp you stored it.

In a key-value store, you can design a key like this:

```
Key: AB28C4F2-com.wiley.www-/index.html
```

Figure 12-4:
Traditional key-value store versus using a Bigtable as a key-value store.

Key-value store

Key		Timestamp	Value

Bigtable clone

Row Key	Column Family	Column Name	Timestamp	Value

This uses a GUID or similar random string as the first part of the key to ensure that, during ingest, the data is distributed across a cluster. This key also uses a timestamp qualifier for the time the page was indexed.

Whereas, in a Bigtable, you could use the column family and name fields, too:

```
Key: AB28C4F2 Column Family: com.wiley.www Name: /index.html
```

This key allows you to be more flexible when querying, because you can easily pull back all web pages for a domain or a specific page in a domain, which you can do quickly because a query is based only on the exact value of a key. This approach eliminates you having to trawl all keys for lexicographic (partial string) matches.

Cassandra doesn't support column family names. Instead, you merge the preceding column family and page name or use two columns (the domain with a blank value). Cassandra does, however, allow you to specify an index of keys across values. So, in the preceding example, you could set up an index over key, domain, and page name.

I can ensure that entire domain content lookups are quick because the first key is the partition key in Cassandra, which keeps all data together for all pages in the same domain.

Inserting data fast

Cassandra manages its own storage, rather than farm it off to HDFS, like HBase does. As a result Cassandra offers some advantages, with the first being that it can manage and throttle compactions. A compaction, also called a *merge,* occurs every so often as Cassandra appends data to its database files and marks data for deletion. This deleted data builds up over time, requiring compaction. The benefit is higher ingest rates. Another advantage is that Cassandra doesn't need to go over the network to access data storage.

With Cassandra, you also have the advantage of using local SSDs, perhaps by writing the journal to an SSD and writing data to RAM and flushing it to a spinning disk later. This, too, aids the speed of ingestion.

You can also run Cassandra with both spinning disk HDDs and SSD disks for the same database. Perhaps some data is read more often and other data less often. This differently accessed data may even be columns on the same record. Storing these individual often-read columns on SSDs and the rest on a spinning disk boosts speed, without you having to replace every disk with an expensive SSD.

Replicating data globally

Cassandra is unique in allowing a cluster to be defined across geographic boundaries and providing tolerance of network partitions to ensure data is available worldwide when needed.

A Cassandra *ring* is a list of servers across server racks and data centers. You can configure Cassandra so that a replica is on the same rack, another on a different rack (in case that rack's network goes down), and maybe even another two copies in other data centers.

This enables maximum replication and ensures that data can always be accessed. However, note that all these replicated copies — whether in the same data center or another one — are replicated synchronously. This means it's possible for the replicas to disagree on the current value of a data item.

Consistency is guaranteed by configuring the client driver accessing Cassandra. By using a setting of ONE, you indicate you don't care about consistency; you're happy with any copy.

By using a setting of LOCAL_QUARUM, you're saying you want the value agreed on and returned by, for example, two out of three servers within just the local cluster. Specifying ALL requires that all servers in the cluster that contain a copy of that value are in agreement.

There are a variety of other settings to consider. A full list of the consistency settings their meaning can be found on the Apache Cassandra website: `http://cassandra.apache.org`

Assessing Cassandra

Cassandra allows partitioning and writing data when its primary master is unavailable. It's, therefore, not an ACID-compliant database, so in some cases, the data will be inconsistent or replicas will disagree on the correct value.

You need to be aware of this issue when building an application on Cassandra. A read repair feature is available to help with this issue, but when you use it, there's a potential ten-percent loss in performance. However, this may well be a good tradeoff for your purposes.

Global master-master replication is a great feature to have, but given that it can be used asynchronously, it doesn't provide a true "always consistent" master-master replication that you may be familiar with in the relational database world. Ensuring that the client uses full consistency leads to slower usage times.

Cassandra also doesn't support column families. This gives it a data model somewhere in between a key-value store and a Bigtable. This may or may not be an issue in your applications.

Cassandra's CQL query language will be familiar to most people who are familiar with the relational database and SQL world, which helps lower barriers to entry for existing database developers.

Cassandra does manage local storage very well. SSDs are recommended for at least part of the data managed. Using local SSD storage will always provide faster storage and retrieval in comparison to delegating file system management to a separate tier like HDFS.

Also, with no single points of failure anywhere in the architecture, Cassandra is easy to install and maintain, and it's capable of being very fast.

In Chapter 13, I discuss Apache Cassandra and the commercial company DataStax that provides support for Cassandra.

Chapter 13

Cassandra and DataStax

· ·

In This Chapter

▶ Creating high-speed key access to data

▶ Supporting Cassandra development

· ·

Cassandra is the leading NoSQL Bigtable clone. Its popularity is based on its speed and SQL-like query language for relational database type people, and the fact it takes the best technological advances from the Dynamo and Bigtable papers.

DataStax is the primary commercial company offering support and Enterprise extensions for the Cassandra open-source Bigtable clone. DataStax is one of the largest NoSQL companies in the world, having received more than $106 million in investor funding in September 2014, and $84 million during mid-2013.

In this chapter, I discuss both the Cassandra Bigtable NoSQL database and the support that can be found from DataStax, its commercial backer.

Designing a Modern Bigtable

The Cassandra design team took the best bits from Amazon's Dynamo paper on key-value store design and Google's Bigtable paper on wide column store (also called extensible record store) design.

Cassandra, therefore, provides high-speed key access to data while also providing flexible columns and a schema-free, join-free, wide column store. Developers who have used the Structured Query Language (SQL) in relational database management systems should find the Cassandra Query Language (CQL) familiar.

Clustering

The ability for a single ring (a Cassandra cluster) of Cassandra servers to be spread across servers, racks of servers, and geographically dispersed datacenters is a unique characteristic of Cassandra. Cassandra manages eventually consistent, asynchronous replicas of data automatically across each of these types of boundaries. Different datacenters can even differ in the number of replicas for each data set, which is useful for different scales at each site.

This treatment of every server holding the same data as a single dispersed cluster, rather than independent but connected sets of clusters, takes a bit of getting used to. It's unique to the databases in this book.

Scaling a cluster out to add one-third more capacity may require some thought, because you need to consider its position in the ring and how adding capacity may affect the automatically managed replicas.

You configure your physical Cassandra architecture by using a Gossiping Property File Snitch, which has nothing to do with Harry Potter's Quidditch, unfortunately. This is a configuration file that defines what servers are in which racks and datacenters. This configuration mechanism is recommended because it allows Cassandra to make the best use of the available physical infrastructure.

Tuning consistency

Data consistency in Cassandra is *tunable;* that is, it doesn't need to always be eventually consistent across all replicas. The settings used are up to the client API, though, and not the server.

By writing data using the ALL setting, you can be sure that all replicas will have the same value of the data being saved. For mission-critical financial systems, for example, this is the approach to take.

If you use the ALL setting for write consistency, be aware that a network partition anywhere in your global cluster will cause the whole system to be unavailable for writes!

Other settings are available — 11, in fact, for writes. These settings range from ALL to ANY. ANY means that data will try to write to any of the replicas. If no replicas for that key are online, Cassandra will use *hinted-handoff,* which is to say that it will save the write on a node adjacent to a replica node that is currently unavailable. This provides the highest service availability for the lowest consistency guarantees.

This flexibility is great if you need a single Bigtable implementation that provides a range of consistency and availability guarantees for different applications. You can use the same technology for all of these applications, rather than having to resort to a different database for only a small number of use cases.

Similarly, ten different read-consistency settings are available in the client API. These settings mirror the write levels, with the missing setting being ANY, because ONE means the same thing as ANY for a read operation.

Analyzing data

Cassandra provides a great foundation for high-speed analytics based on near-live data. This is how DataStax produced an entire integrated analytics platform as an extension to Cassandra.

Datastax's analytics extension enables rapid analysis in several situations, including detection of fraud, monitoring of social media and communications services, and analysis of advertisement campaigns, all running in real time next to the data.

Batch analytics is also supported by integrating Hadoop Map/Reduce with Cassandra. Cassandra uses its own local file system. DataStax provides a CFS alternative to HDFS to work around the historic single points of failure in the Hadoop ecosystem. This file system is compatible with Hadoop, and is accessible directly by other Hadoop applications.

CFS is a Java subclass of the *HadoopFileSystem* class, providing the same low-level interface, making it interchangeable with HDFS for Hadoop applications.

Searching data

With Cassandra, you can create indexes for values, which are implemented as an internal table in Cassandra. In this way, you don't have to maintain your own manually created index tables.

A default Cassandra index will not help you in several situations:

- ✔ **Typed range queries or partial matches:** Indexes are only for exact matches.

- ✔ **Unique Values:** Where each unique value isn't used more than once — results in a very large read scan of the index, hitting query performance

✔ **A frequently updated column:** Cassandra has a limit of 100,000 time-stamped versions of each record, so more than this number of updates causes the index to fail.

✔ **For queries across an entire partition:** This requires communication with every server holding data. It's best to limit data queried with another field (for example, record owner ID).

For more complex situations, DataStax offers an enhanced search capability based on Apache Solr. Unlike other NoSQL vendors' implementations of Solr, though, DataStax has overcome several general issues:

✔ Search indexes are updated in real time, rather than asynchronously like most Solr integrations are.

✔ Data is protected. Lucene indexes (the underlying index layer of Solr) can become corrupted. DataStax uses Cassandra under Solr to store information, ensuring this doesn't happen.

✔ Availability and scaling built in. Add a new Cassandra node, and you have a new Solr node. There's no need for a separate search engine cluster with different storage requirements.

Solr provides hit highlighting, faceted search, range queries, and geospatial search support. Part VI covers these features.

Securing Cassandra

DataStax Enterprise offers a range of security features for Cassandra. All data communications are encrypted over SSL, be they internal gossip data or international replication between servers.

Client-to-node encryption is also supported, along with Kerberos authentication communications and internally stored authentication information.

Particularly impressive is the built-in support for encryption of data at rest. This feature has its limitations, though. The commit logs, for example, are not encrypted; operating system-level encryption is required for this.

More seriously, the certificates used for encryption of data within the SSTable structures are stored on the same file system rather than a security device. Practically speaking, this means access to the underlying file system needs to be secured anyway. In extreme scenarios, operating system-level or disk-level management may be a better choice for encryption at rest.

Finding Support for Cassandra

DataStax is the commercial entity providing Cassandra and big data support, services, and extensions. It is a worldwide company with 350 employees (a 100-percent increase from a year ago) spread across 50 countries.

DataStax's leading product is DataStax Enterprise (DSE). DSE combines a Hadoop distribution with Cassandra and additional tools to provide analytics, search, monitoring, and backup.

Managing and monitoring Cassandra

The DataStax OpsCenter is a monitoring tool for Cassandra. It's available in a commercial version and also as a limited free version. This provides a visual dashboard for the health and status of not only Cassandra but also the analytics and search extensions, too.

If you're adding new nodes to a cluster, DataStax OpsCenter gives you the ability to set up automated handling of cluster rebalancing. This capability greatly reduces the burden on database administrators.

Also, configurable alerts and notifications can be sent, based on a range of activities in the cluster. OpsCenter allows alerts to be fired based on, for example, when the CPU usage or data storage size on a particular node breaches a defined performance target. This alerting helps to proactively avoid cluster problems, which can degrade the overall service.

OpsCenter also supports planning for capacity through historical analysis. Historical statistics help predict when new nodes will need to be added. This analysis, too, is configurable visually, with live updates on the state of processing once the cluster is activated.

OpsCenter also has its own API, which allows monitoring information to be plugged into other tools. A good example is a private (internal) cloud-management environment.

Active-active clustering

Most NoSQL databases in this book are either completely commercial or have Enterprise features only in their paid-for, Enterprise version. Cassandra is different. With Cassandra, the base version can do master-master clustering across datacenters.

Actually, it's not so much master-master clustering as it is global data replication, which enables data to be replicated, asynchronously, to datacenters spread throughout the world.

The flip side to a single-cluster, worldwide spread is that a "split brain syndrome" (also called a *network partition*) can develop when networks go down. This situation requires repairing a replica server's data when the network comes back up. Cassandra supports a read-repair mechanism to alleviate this problem, but data can become inconsistent if a split brain syndrome goes on too long.

Part IV
Document Databases

 Visit www.dummies.com/extras/nosql for great Dummies content online.

In this part . . .

- ✔ Creating tree structures.
- ✔ Distributing information.
- ✔ Sharing information with the world.
- ✔ Examining document database products.
- ✔ Visit www.dummies.com/extras/nosql for great Dummies content online.

Chapter 14

Common Features of Document Databases

*W*hen talking about *document databases*, the word *document* refers to a hierarchical structure of data that can contain substructures. This is a more general term than being, for example, like Microsoft Word documents or web pages, although they are certainly two types of documents that can be managed in a document-oriented NoSQL database.

Documents can consist of only binary data or plain text. They can be semi-structured when self-describing data formats like JavaScript Object Notation (JSON) or Extensible Markup Language (XML) are used. They can even be well-structured documents and always conform to a particular data model, such as an XML Schema Definition (XSD).

Document NoSQL databases are flexible and schema agnostic, which means you can load any type of document without the database needing to know the document's structure up front.

Document databases have many uses and share common features, which I explain in the chapter. As you read this chapter, you may be surprised to find out that a document NoSQL database will meet your needs over the other types of NoSQL database mentioned in this book.

Using a Tree-Based Data Model

In Chapter 9, I explain that Bigtable databases require at least some information about the data schema — at a minimum, the table name and column families, although the columns can be variable.

In a document NoSQL database, you can load any type of data without the database having prior knowledge of the data's structure or what the values mean. This flexibility makes these databases great both for prototyping a solution in an "agile" development process and for permitting changes in the stored data after a system goes live. No need for a complex schema redesign within the database for every little change. This isn't the case in traditional relational database management systems (RDBMS).

Bigtable clones allow you to manage sets of data sets; that is, when a Bigtable clone is given a row key, it returns a set of column families. When a Bigtable receives a row key and a column family qualifier, it returns a set of columns, each with a cell value (some with multiple cell values at different timestamps).

Bigtable clones effectively give you three levels of sets: row, family, and column, which can be represented in a tree model. Figure 14-1 shows an example of the online ordering application mentioned in Chapters 7 and 8 structured for a Bigtable clone.

Order Table

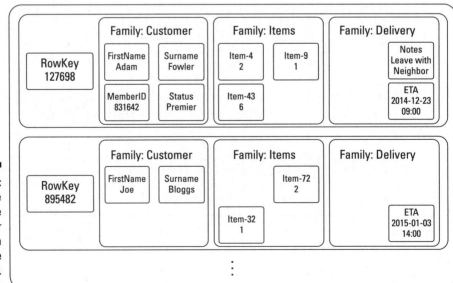

Figure 14-1: Example structure of an order table in a Bigtable clone.

What if you want to go down another level? Or another still? This is where a document database comes in, by providing the flexibility you need. Listing 14-1 is an example of an order document with enhanced information and ample flexibility.

Listing 14-1:   Order XML Document

```xml
<order id="1234">
  <customer id="52">Adam Fowler</customer>
  <items>
    <item qty="2" id="456" unit_price="2.00" price="4.00">Hammer</item>
    <item qty="1" id="111" unit_price="0.79" price="0.79">Hammer Time</item>
  </items>
  <delivery_address lon="-43.24" lat="54.12">
    <street>Some Place</street>
    <town>My City</town>
    …
  </delivery_address>
</order>
```

Of course, you are free to use a less hierarchical, flatter, structure. Listing 14-2 shows a log file management as a tree structure.

Listing 14-2:   A mock Log File in a JSON tree structure

```json
{
  "source": {
    "host": "192.168.1.3", "process": "tomcat", "format": "tomcat-error-log"
  }, "entry": {
    "timestamp": "2014-09-04T10:00:43Z", "level": "error",
    "summary": "Null Pointer Exception at com.package.MyClass:110:2",
    "trace": [
      "com.package.MyClass:110:2",
      "com.package.OtherClass:45:7",
      "com.sun.util.HashtableImpl"
    ]
  }
}
```

In this case, a stack trace error report can be a tree structure. You could, for example, dump information about every live executing process into a file, rather than just the section of code that reported the error. This approach is particularly useful for parallel debugging.

In a Bigtable clone, your application must manage converting the preceding hierarchical document structure to and from a tree structure, whereas a document database can manage it natively.

Storage of document data without "shredding" data across a set of tables is potentially useful if you want to query for a count of error reports to see which applications caused the most errors in a particular code module. Doing so requires a batch analysis job in a Bigtable — but a simple aggregation query in a document database with element indexing enabled.

Handling article documents

Tree structures vary greatly. A semi-structured format like XHTML (the format used by web pages) has, as its name implies, some structure, but you can model the individual paragraphs, headings, and sections in a variety of ways.

A common practice in document databases is to index a property, or an element, no matter where it occurs within a document. For example, you could index all h1 (main headings) and h2 (subheadings) elements regardless of where they occur. Both MarkLogic Server and Microsoft DocumentDB allow this style of indexing.

Document databases are great at providing consistent query over these variable structures. There are many real-life examples of querying over document structures:

- ✔ Stack traces in log files may have a class name field at varying depths in a tree structure.
- ✔ A patient's medical records may mention a drug or condition anywhere in the text notes field.

Managing trades in financial services

One of the most common document formats in the commercial industry is the Financial products Markup Language (FpML). FpML documents are a particular XML schema structure. They're used for trading in long-running financial derivatives.

There are a couple of reasons that FpML need an XML oriented document database rather than a JSON oriented one, or need to be stored in a relational database:

- ✓ JSON doesn't work for storing FpML documents because it doesn't support namespaces, and FpML documents always include elements using the standard FpML namespace and a bank's own internal information in another element namespace — both in the same document.

- ✓ XML Schema Definitions (XSDs) can have parent-child inheritance. A "place," for example, could be a parent class of a "town" or "bridge," with the document mentioning the elements "town" or "bridge," but not "place." This information isn't available for JSON structures, so you can't infer inheritance in a JSON model.

JSON documents are the *lingua franca* of web applications, though. Having a document NoSQL database that supports JSON documents natively, perhaps alongside other formats like XML or plain text, is useful. Don't discount XML given the number of enterprise systems that use it as a native format.

Discovering document structure

Document databases tend to store documents in a compressed on-disk format. In order to do so, the databases need to understand the format of the documents they receive. When you submit JSON or XML documents, for example, a database uses that structure to better manage the data on disk.

Here is an example of a JSON document that represents an online order:

```
{ _id: 1234, customer: 52, customer_name: "Adam Fowler", items: [
  {qty: 2, item: {id: 456, title: "Hammer", unit_price: 2.00}, price: 4.00},
  {qty: 1, item: {id: 111, title: "Hammer Time", unit_price: 0.79}, price: 0.79}
], delivery_address: {street: "some place", town: "My City", … }
}
```

MongoDB stores documents in its own BSON binary representation, which is useful because JSON, like that in the preceding JSON example, has a lot of text in property names. You can save space by compressing or managing these property names as simple numeric identifiers, rather than as long strings.

MarkLogic Server takes a similar approach with XML documents — that is, it stores a compressed representation. All elements and attributes are treated as a term. Each term is assigned a unique ID. This allows MarkLogic to use its own binary tree structure, which saves space when storing XML documents versus storing them as long strings. Listing 14-3 shows an XML representation of the same online order document.

Listing 14-3   An XML Document

```
<order id="1234">
  <customer id="52">Adam Fowler</customer>
  <items>
    <item qty="2" id="456" unit_price="2.00" price="4.00">Hammer</item>
    <item qty="1" id="111" unit_price="0.79" price="0.79">Hammer Time</item>
  </items>
  <delivery_address>
    <street>Some Place</street>
    <town>My City</town>
    ...
  </delivery_address>
</order>
```

Saving space is more important for XML than it is for JSON because XML has closing and starting tags, as you can see in `delivery_address` in the above XML document.

Rather than simply compress data on disk, MarkLogic Server uses these term ids within its search indexes, which are built automatically when a document is written to MarkLogic Server. MarkLogic Server's universal index indexes all structures: elements and attributes, parent and child element relationships, and exact element values.

The universal index indexes everything it finds. This speeds up querying for documents where an element has a particular value, without you having to add specific indexes or instructing the database about the document structure in advance. The universal index also indexes text (words, phrases, and stems). You can find more on MarkLogic's universal index in Part VII.

Microsoft's DocumentDB is a JSON document NoSQL database that also includes a universal index, but only for JSON documents.

Supporting unstructured documents

Fully unstructured information is actually rare. It's more typical to use a container format like JSON or XML and to store large quantities of plain text in particular properties and elements.

There are situations, though, when you receive a lot of text or binary data (think about the average My Documents folder). Here are a couple of ways to manage groups of documents collected from such a hierarchical storage device:

✔ Collections of files may contain a combination of

- Structured files (such as CSV expense information)

- Semi-structured files (such as XML and saved HTML web pages)

- Unstructured files (such as JPEG images, movies, MP3s, word documents, PDFs, and plain text files)

✔ In reality, unstructured formats are actually semi-structured; it's just that you don't normally instruct your database to understand them. However, you may be missing some useful information that you might want to extract and search. For example, JPEG images may contain metadata about

- The camera that took the images

- The prevailing conditions when the image was shot

- The GPS coordinates and elevation where the image was taken

✔ Some databases come with built-in support for extracting this metadata and plain text from binary files. This is great for indexing the plain text for search or to provide for more-structured management of the files' metadata.

✔ MarkLogic Server, for example, includes support for more than 200 binary formats through its use of binary data extraction libraries. These provide an XHTML output, using meta tags for metadata and the body tag for text content. You can integrate other solutions with other document databases to allow automatic extraction of information on ingest.

✔ Many document databases support the concept of a URI path as a primary key, or a unique document ID. Think of this path as being a file system path with an innate hierarchy. Some document databases allow you to list the documents stored under a particular, partial URI. In this way, you can represent a file system in a document database. Some NoSQL databases consider the unique ID as external to the document (MarkLogic), whereas others (MongoDB and Microsoft DocumentDB) use a special id property within the document.

Document Databases as Key-Value Stores

Document databases make great key-value stores. You can use a document URI path to represent a composite key like those in a key-value store. You can use document properties/elements, or metadata fields, to control how the database partitions data.

Document databases also provide a deeper level of data management functionality. This comes at the cost of processing time, which is why key-value stores are used for some JSON document storage use cases — where fast storage and retrieval is more important than advanced management functionality.

Modeling values as documents

Values can be binary information stored as a document. In many uses of a key-value store, though, values are JSON or XML structures. If you want to do advanced processing or indexing of values in a JSON or XML document, then a document database may be a better option.

Document databases provide in-memory read caches, with some (MongoDB) even providing read-only replicas to allow greater parallel reads of the same data. If you have data that's read often, then a document database may provide speedy access to documents that's equivalent to key-value stores' access speed.

Automatic caching of parts of the database is particularly useful if all your data can't fit in the memory of a key-value store, such as Redis.

Using value information

Once the elements/attributes (XML) or properties (JSON) — which I call *elements* from now on to distinguish them from a document's metadata — are indexed, you can perform data queries and aggregation processes over them.

Document databases like MarkLogic Server and Microsoft DocumentDB provide range queries for their typed indexes. This means that, rather than being limited to "element equals X," you can say "element is less than X" or "between X and Y inclusive."

Both MarkLogic Server and Microsoft DocumentDB provide user-defined functions (UDFs). These are server-side functions that take the set of documents matching a query and perform aggregation calculations on them.

These aggregations can be a mean average, a standard deviation, or any other scalar output you devise. These operations are very fast, too, typically operating on the indexes rather than opening each document. This operation contrasts to the Hadoop or internal map/reduce mechanisms of other document databases and key-value stores, which must load the data from disk to perform these calculations.

You can also use these range indexes for fast sorting and filtering operations on result sets. They are immensely useful and allow for more advanced functionality. MarkLogic Server, for example, uses range indexes as the basis for 2D geospatial search.

Patching Documents

In some applications, rather than update and replace a whole document, you may want to change part of it, or a single value. A read, modify, update (RMU) operation on the entire content of a document is quite expensive in terms of processing time, and in many NoSQL databases isn't ACID — meaning another operation could update the document between your application's read and update steps!

Supporting partial updates

A partial update is one where you are updating just one of two values in a document, rather than replacing the whole thing. Perhaps there is a field that holds the number of times a document has been read, or the current product quantity in a warehouse.

Examples of partial updates may be as simple as replacing one element, which is similar to how a RBMS works. Consider the following query:

```
UPDATE Pages SET view_count = view_count + 1 WHERE id = "Page2"
```

If the record is modeled as a document, then a similar patch operation in MarkLogic Server might look like this:

```
<rapi:patch xmlns:rapi="http://marklogic.com/rest-api">
  <rapi:replace select="/view_count" apply="ml.add">1</rapi:replace>
</rapi:patch>
```

Or the equivalent in JSON might look like this:

```
{"patch": [
  {"replace": {
    "select": "$.view_count",
    "apply": "ml.add",
    "content": 1
  } }
] }
```

Document NoSQL databases could be enhanced to implement this functionality in their REST API layer rather than within the database. This implementation would do an internal read, modify, update operation within a transaction, which could lead to a disk I/O penalty similar to an insert of the full document. You want to ensure that these multiple requests per update won't impact your application's performance by performing application load testing at the same level of concurrent requests as the peak period will be in your future production application.

Patching operations can also include appending elements to a parent element within a tree structure. Consider a shopping cart document where a user on a website adds an item to his cart. This could be an append operation at the end of an orderItems element using a document patch.

Streaming changes

The append operation enables you to handle a range of streaming cases efficiently. This operation will identify where in a document new data needs adding, and insert the data. This prevents performance impacts caused by the alternative read-modify-update approach.

For applications that require live information streaming with nearly real-time analysis by an application or human expert, supporting append operations is a potentially game-changing feature.

Consider a video recording that is being analyzed on the fly. Image that you're receiving a video stream from a remotely controlled hexacopter. Along with the video, you're receiving a metadata stream that includes the altitude, position, viewing angle (multiple axes), and the camera's zoom level. You can index this metadata stream by time and append it to a video metadata document's metastream element. For very long videos, to load the whole document and store it temporarily in your system's memory for an update may use up too much RAM — you must load, modify, and then update the whole document's content.

Instead of a very RAM costly read-modify-update cycle, you can stream the changes into the document using an append operation. Moreover, the document is visible to queries in the system while it's being streamed in live, rather than having to wait until the entire stream activity is complete before being made available for query.

Providing alternate structures in real time

NoSQL databases don't use joins to other documents like relational databases do, although some (MarkLogic Server, OrientDB) do allow building of a merged view at the time a document is read.

Instead, an approach called denormalization is used. Denormalization duplicates some information at ingestion time in order to provide access to high-speed reads and queries. Duplication of data is done so that the database doesn't have to process joins at query time.

You may want to quickly produce alternative or merged views as new data arrives in the database. Doings so requires you to use a database trigger to spot the new document and to generate the one or more structures you need.

 Relational database management systems provide a similar concept called *views.* You can construct these on the fly or prebuild them. Prebuilt views are called *materialized views.* These views trade the use of extra disk space for the ability to save memory and processing power at query time. They are, in practical terms, equivalent to adding extra denormalized documents in a NoSQL document database.

Examples of using denormalization include

- ✔ Updating a summary document showing the latest five news items when a new item arrives.

- ✔ Updating multiple searchable program-availability documents on a catchup TV service when a new scheduling document arrives. This merges data from an episode, genre, brand, and scheduling set of documents into multiple program-availability documents.

- ✔ Taking an order document and splitting it into multiple order-item documents in order to allow a relational business intelligence tool to query at a lower granularity.

These use cases require the following database features:

- ✔ If they're easy to update, you can generate these alternative structures in a pre-commit trigger.

  This means the denormalizations are generated as the new document arrives. When the transaction to add documents ends, the denormalizations will become visible at exactly the same time.

- ✔ You can use a post-commit trigger if either of the following occur:

  - Immediate consistency in these views isn't required.

  - Ingest speed is more important than consistency.

- ✔ A post-commit trigger allows the transaction to complete and guarantees that from that point, the denormalizations are generated. This improves the speed of writes at the cost of a few seconds of inconsistency.

Chapter 15

Document Databases in the Enterprise

*I*f a database tells you that data is saved, then you're likely to rely on that assurance. For mission-critical use cases this reliance is vital. Moreover, many industries don't just want changes to their data to be accessible immediately after an update; they also want the indexes used to find the data kept up to date, too — reflecting the current state of the database.

Another issue is the distribution of data around a database cluster. By distributing data, you improve the speed of writes. Distributing data though also means that you may sacrifice the speed of read operations and also of queries. This is because queries need to be handled by many servers. Understanding the tradeoffs for each situation is important.

Document NoSQL databases differ from each other in how they provide the preceding features. They are key for enterprises that want to bet their business on new technology in order to gain competitive advantages.

In this chapter, I discuss the advantages and risks of each approach to consistency and distribution of data in a document oriented NoSQL database.

Remember, there's no right or wrong way to do things; the "right" way simply depends on the situation.

Sharding

If all your new data arrives on the last server in your cluster, write operations will suffer, and as the overloaded server struggles to keep up, read operations will also be affected. This is where sharding comes in.

Sharding is the process of ensuring that data is spread evenly across an entire cluster of servers. Shards can be set up at the time a cluster is implemented (MongoDB), they can be fixed into a number of buckets or partitions that can be moved later (Couchbase, Microsoft DocumentDB), or they can be managed automatically simply by moving a number of documents between servers to keep things balanced (MarkLogic Server).

In this section, I describe different approaches to document record sharding, and how you may apply them.

Key-based sharding

With key-based sharding, the key — the name, URI, or ID — of a document determines which server it's placed on. Like key-value stores and Bigtable clones, some document NoSQL databases assign a range of key values to each server in a cluster. Based on the key of the record and the ranges assigned to each server, a client connector can determine exactly which server to communicate with in order to fetch a particular document. MongoDB and Couchbase database drivers use this approach to sharding.

Some document NoSQL databases, such as MongoDB, allow their replicas to be queried, rather than exist purely as a backup for a primary shard. This allows for greater *read parallelization.* This splits the document access load between both the primary shard and its replicas, increasing overall cluster query performance.

The flip side is that, if asynchronous replication is used, then replicas could "disagree" on the current value of a document. You need to carefully select the client driver and server replication settings to avoid this situation.

Automatic sharding

With automatic sharding, the database randomly assigns a new document to a server, which means the database's developer doesn't have to carefully select a key in order to ensure good write throughput.

Automatic sharding works well for a live cluster, but if you need to scale out or scale back during peak periods, you'll need to rebalance your partitions. For example, a new server with little data will respond quicker than one of the existing servers with lots of data. Using automatic sharding rebalances document among the new (empty) and existing (crowded) servers, increasing average response times.

Rebalancing automatically, rather than based on key range for each server, is an easier operation — you simply move the individual documents you need in order to keep a balance, rather than move them around to maintain fixed range buckets on each server. This means fewer documents to move around, and means you simply move them to a less busy server.

However, no one approach to assigning documents is truly balanced. Some servers will, for reasons unknown to we mortals, perform slightly worse than others, causing partitions to become slightly weighted over time. Rebalancing fixes this problem.

In some databases this rebalancing, or fixed range repartitioning, has to be initiated manually (Couchbase). This then has a batch performance impact across a cluster. Some document databases, like MarkLogic Server, perform this rebalancing live as it needs to. This evens out rebalancing load over time, rather than having to impact cluster performance when manually forced in a short time window.

Preventing Loss of Data

Durability relates to keeping data intact once it's saved. Both ACID-compliant, fully consistent systems and non-ACID, eventually consistent systems are capable of being durable.

Durability is typically achieved either by

- ✔ Always writing the document to disk as it arrives before returning a successful response.

  This impacts the performance of write operations.
- ✔ Writing to memory but writing a journal of the change to disk.

  A journal log entry is a small description of the change. It provides good performance while ensuring durability.

If a server writes to memory only during the transaction, with no journal log, then it's possible for the server to fail before the data is saved on disk. This means the data in memory is lost permanently — it is not durable.

Not all databases guarantee durability by design. Couchbase, for example, only writes to RAM during a write operation. An asynchronous process later on writes the data to disk.

You can use the PersistTo option in Couchbase to ensure that data is forced to disk within the bounds of a write operation.

At the time of this writing, Couchbase 3.0 was in beta and about to be released. This version takes a different approach to durability. It still writes data to RAM, but a new approach — the Couchbase Database Change Protocol (DCP) — is used to stream these changes from RAM to other replicas. This can happen before the originating server saves the data to disk.

By Couchbase's own admission, there is still a small window of time in which data can be lost if a server failure happens. There is no way to predict or fix this problem when it happens because there's no journal — the data is irreversibly lost.

Most databases use a journal log as a good tradeoff between the performance of write operations and durability. MarkLogic Server and MongoDB both use journal files to ensure that data is durable. Microsoft DocumentDB, instead, applies the full change during a transaction, so a journal file isn't needed.

Replicating data locally

Once the data is saved durably to a disk on a single server, what happens if that server fails? The data is safe, but inaccessible. In this situation, data replication within a cluster is useful.

Replication can either occur

- **Within a transaction (called a two-phase commit):** If within a transaction, then all replicas have the same current view of the updated document.
- **After a transaction completes:** In this case, the replica will be updated at some point in the future. Typically, this inconsistency lasts for seconds rather than minutes. This is called *eventually consistent replication.*

Whichever method you use, once it's complete, you're guaranteed that another copy of the data is available elsewhere in the same cluster. If the originating server goes down, the data can still be returned in a query.

Using multiple datacenters

What if you're really having a bad day, and someone digs up a network or power cable to your entire datacenter? This is where database replication comes in.

In database replication, the changes to an entire database across a cluster are streamed as they happen to one or more backup clusters in a remote datacenter(s). Because of the network latency involved, this process generally is done asynchronously as a tradeoff between the speed of write operations and the consistency of remote data.

Because this replication is asynchronous, some data may not be available at the second site if the first site becomes unavailable before the data is replicated. If new writes or updates occur at the backup site when it takes over the service, these changes need to be merged with the saved, but not replicated, data on the original site when you switch back. At times, this process may create a conflict (with two "current" views of the same data) that you must fix manually once inter-cluster communication is restored.

Selectively replicating data

Sometimes though you may have different needs for your other data center clusters. Perhaps you only want a partial set of information replicated to other live clusters, say for reference reasons.

A good example of this is a metadata catalog in which a description of the data each cluster holds is replicated to other sites, but not the data itself. This kind of catalog is useful for very large files that you don't need to replicate to all sites. One non-replicated file store holds the files, while your NoSQL document database holds the metadata catalog.

If you have a small cluster or an individual node (an *austere cluster*) that isn't always connected, database replication isn't a good option, because over time, a backlog of updates could build up and have to be sent all together to the cluster when that *austere cluster* does connect. This situation can cause the secondary cluster to struggle to catch up. An example is a ship, oil rig, or special forces soldier's laptop.

It's also possible that you do want all data replicated, but you must prioritize which data to replicate first. Perhaps a list of all the notes you've made on a device is replicated first, and the notes themselves are replicated later. This is common in certain scenarios:

- **Mobile phone synchronization:** Notes are saved on a phone for offline use and then synced later.

  You can run Couchbase Mobile on a phone to provide for such situations.

- **Austere sites:** These include such places as oil rigs, military bases with intermittent satellite communications, or sneaky people with laptops in remote places. MarkLogic Server supports these types of installations.

This type of replication is sometimes called *mobile synchronization,* or *flexible replication,* or *Query Based Flexible Replication (QBFR)*. The phrase *query based* reflects that a search query is used to bound the data to be replicated, allowing several priority-ordered datasets to be replicated in a push or pull manner.

Managing Consistency

It's perfectly acceptable in some applications to have a slight lag in the time it takes for data to become visible. Facebook posts don't appear instantly to all users. You can also see on Twitter that someone new is following you before the total number of followers is updated. This lag is typically only a few seconds, and for social media that's not a problem. However, the same isn't true in situations such as in the following:

- Primary trading systems for billion dollar transactions
- Emergency medical information in an emergency room
- Target tracking information in a battle group headquarters

It's important to understand the differences in approaches when considering a database for your application. Not all NoSQL databases support full ACID guarantees, unlike their relational database management systems counterparts.

It's not that you're either consistent or inconsistent. Instead, there's a range of consistency levels. Some products support just one level; others allow you to select from a range of levels for each database operation. Here, I cover only the two most extreme consistency models. Refer to specific database products for a complete list of the consistency guarantees they support.

Using eventual consistency

With eventual consistency, a write operation is successful on the server that receives it but all replicas of that data aren't updated at the same time. They are updated later based on system replication settings.

Some databases provide only eventual consistency (Couchbase), whereas others allow tuning of consistency on a per operation basis, depending on the settings of the originating client request (MongoDB, Microsoft DocumentDB).

Most social networks use this consistency model for new posts. This model gives you very fast write operations, because you don't have to wait for all replicas to be updated in order for the write operation to be complete. Inconsistency tends to last only a few seconds while the replicas catch up.

Using ACID consistency

ACID consistency is the gold standard of consistency guarantees. For a full definition of ACID consistency, refer to Chapter 2. An ACID-compliant database ensures that

- ✔ All data is safe in event of failure.
- ✔ Database updates always keep the database in a valid state (no conflicts).
- ✔ One set of operations doesn't interfere with another set of operations.
- ✔ Once the save completes, reading data from any replica will always give the new "current" result.

Some ACID databases go further and allow several changes to be executed within the same transaction. These changes are applied in a single set, ensuring consistency for all documents affected.

Consistency is achieved by shipping all the changes you want applied from the server where a transaction is started, to each replica, then applying the changes, and if all is well the transaction completes. If any one action fails, the entire transaction of changes is rolled back on all replicas. Transaction roll back ensures the data is kept in a consistent state.

MarkLogic Server provides ACID transactions both on the server-side (when applying a set of changes in a single operation) and across several client requests in an application (when applying each change individually, then having a user select 'apply'). Microsoft's DocumentDB provides ACID transactions only on the server-side, when executing a JavaScript stored procedure.

Chapter 16

Document Database Use Cases

. . . .

. . . .

Documents are all around us. From shopping orders to patient notes to books like this one. A world of infinite possibilities exists with documents.

Knowing which use cases can be handled by a document NoSQL database is an increasing challenge. Unlike some other types of NoSQL databases in this book, document database providers are continually adding new features that enable you to turn plain data storage into more functional information.

The use cases I describe in this chapter are industry- and solution-agnostic, which makes sense because there are so many ways to apply document databases. Take each example as a suggested "recipe" and apply it to your particular data-management needs.

Publishing Content

The sale of online books is a big industry. People download whole books to read offline at their leisure or as references in their jobs, for example.

It's a little different with other kinds of digital publications, though. You can access articles in scientific journals, for example, by subscribing to the journal itself, by purchasing a single issue, or by downloading a single article.

Some scientific publishers, with varying degrees of copyright options, allow you to buy access to the images used in their publications. Say that you want to create a slide strictly for 30 students. In that case, the licensing requirements won't be as great as they would be if you were to write and plan to market a book that uses existing published material.

This fine-grained access to content and the associated licensing for its use signifies where digital publishing is today.

Managing content lifecycle

I used to work in the enterprise content management (ECM) and business process management (BPM) software industries. One inescapable realization was that process and content go hand in hand. As content goes through its lifecycle — from creation, to modification, dissemination, and destruction — different business actions generally need to happen.

When you fill in a bank account opening form online, an account opening process starts. This process uses information within that form document, and a sequence of well-known actions, to move the document and business process through a lifecycle.

An account opening document could have the following steps in its lifecycle:

1. *Validation:* Check the form for any semantic or business rule errors. For example, "We don't cover business in a particular part of the UK, such as the Channel Islands."

2. *Identity check:* Check the identity of the user against other systems (for example, check the official ID and credit reports).

3. *Risk assessment:* If the credit report is poor or otherwise not acceptable, a decision is made to manually assess by the appropriate bank employee.

   If the credit check was okay, the process moves to Step 4.

4. *Process for opening account:* This is a holding period during which appropriate systems create the bank account.

5. *Waiting for customer to activate card and account:* Communications are sent out during account opening, and then the account activation pauses until the customer activates their card.

6. *Opening of account is complete:* The process is successful.

The same process applies to publishing:

1. A concept for a book is submitted to a publisher for approval.
2. If the proposal is approved, the author generates a table of contents.
3. The author, if new, goes though initial training.
4. The book is written, produced in a variety of formats, and published to digital and print vendors.

While these processes are happening, it's helpful to use the document lifecycle status as a query field. This means the status metadata either resides in the document itself or is written into the document's metadata by the process. For example, MarkLogic Server allows you to store a separate metadata document alongside the content document, which means that you don't have to store this status information in the document itself.

This approach is useful when the format of the source document isn't designed to hold internal process information. Many publishers use internal XML schema to describe their publications' content, which doesn't allow information about the status of the book and process to be held. So an external metadata association capability is needed in the document database.

Unlike many ECM vendors, very few document NoSQL database vendors support content-centric workflow like those described previously. None have full end-to-end business process management functionality built natively on top of their products.

MarkLogic Server does have a feature called Content Processing Framework (CPF) that provides content-centric workflow. You provide this feature with a definition of the states within the lifecycle (called a *pipeline*) and the list of documents (document collections or URI prefixes) that this pipeline should be applied to.

With this feature, it's possible to build sophisticated workflow-based applications without having to install, integrate, and maintain a separate and complex business process management system.

Distributing content to sales channels

Publishers were among the first to embrace the Extensible Markup Language (XML) as a generic language to describe documents that can be repurposed into different formats as required.

The availability and popular use of XML Stylesheet Language Transformations (XSLT) to convert XML to a variety of other formats, including HTML for web pages and Portable Document Format (PDF) documents, is a key benefit to using XML over other formats like JSON. The use of XML Schema Definitions (XSDs) to describe a common format for exchanging information is also useful.

During the publishing process, you need the ability to repurpose a source document, or documents, into a target format. Publishers may do this at the proofing stage so they can be sure the output looks correct, which generally means these documents are generated and stored alongside the originals in a collection of documents (MarkLogic Server) or attachments (Microsoft DocumentDB).

For other industries, the ability to generate different formats on the fly for occasional use outweighs the need to create and store them just in case they're requested. This concept is called *schema on read* because you morph the data to your target format — the schema — when you request the document.

You can accomplish schema on read in MarkLogic Server by using XSLT for individual documents, or XInclude for merging documents, or a custom XQuery stored procedure to perform any transformation you like. XInclude is a way to merge in other documents at query time. It's a similar, but limited, approach to query joins in the relational database world.

Microsoft provides a similar mechanism for JSON documents via Structured Query Language (SQL) syntax to project, or describe at query time, the structure of the content you want to receive.

This special query syntax is very similar to that used in a relational database management system's (RDBMS) SQL syntax. It allows for repurposing of a number of related document sections, restricting the information returned, and even specifying fixed values and results from aggregation functions (mean average, count, standard deviation, and so on).

Although Microsoft describes pulling together information in a DocumentDB query as a join, it should be pointed out that, unlike a join in a relational database, DocumentDB joins are possible only within sections of the same JSON document. They don't allow joining of multiple documents.

Managing Unstructured Data Feeds

Managing unstructured data is very challenging. Unlike well-designed JSON and XML documents, unstructured data doesn't provide hints to the objects it describes. Structures also vary greatly because human language isn't restricted to a single way of writing.

In this section, I discuss how to manage large quantities of unstructured texts within documents in a document oriented NoSQL database.

Entity extraction and enrichment

Some of these variable structures may be in binary formats. In this situation, you need to extract the text and/or metadata from those formats. When that's done, you can treat this output as a document that can be processed, which could be a text, a JSON, or an XML (including XHTML) document.

Once the data is extracted, it's likely to be a lot of text with no structure. You need to figure out what the "things" mentioned are. These could be, for example, people, places and organizations mentioned by name in the test.

This approach is very common for free text forms such as letters, patient referrals, medical notes, tweets, or news articles.

You'll then probably want to wrap the identified text with a tag — a JSON property or an XML element. So, for example "Adam Fowler" becomes <person>Adam Fowler</person> in XML or "person": "Adam Fowler" in JSON.

Entity extraction is particularly useful if you want to perform a query afterward for all documents that mention Adam Fowler the person. An element lookup is always quicker and more accurate than a full-text search.

How do you get to this point, though? This is where Natural Language Processing (NLP) comes in. You can keep it simple by using a full-text search for a phrase and then a stored procedure to mark up your text. Using MarkLogic Server alerts, for example, enables entity extraction to run fast, asynchronously after adding a document.

For more complex situations or where you want the relationships between entities, not just their mention, you need a more sophisticated solution. Consider the text "Adam Fowler was observed entering Uncommon Ground on Main Street, Medford, WI."

From this text, you get a person's name, a business name, and an address. You also get the fact that Adam Fowler visited the shop Uncommon Ground, which is located on Main Street, Medford, WI.

You can use an open-source tool such as OpenCalais to perform this type of entity and semantic extraction. You can store these results separate from the document or use them to tag the indicated places in the document.

More sophisticated commercial offerings are available, too. The two that I've seen mentioned most frequently by NoSQL-adopting organizations are Smartlogic's Semaphore and TEMIS's Luxid products.

These tools go one step further by providing information about an entity. Returning to the Adam Fowler example, say that the zip code and the longitude and latitude are included with the address.

You can store this enhanced information within the document. Instead of storing

```
<place>Uncommon Ground, Main Street, Medford, WI</place>
```

you store

```
<place lon="-34.567" lat="54.321" zipcode="54451" type="business"
          subtype="coffee">Uncommon Ground, Main Street, Medford,
          WI</place>
```

In this case, if your document database, or the search engine integrated with it, supports geospatial search, you can use the longitude and latitude data. You can also provide a full address summary or link to a Google map using longitude and latitude or the zip code.

The process of adding more information to original content rather than just tagging it is called *entity enrichment*. It's very useful for enhancing ordinary text data, and for allowing the searching of that data.

Managing Changing Data Structures

Each organization has many systems, each with its own data. These individual information silos are typically split by organization area. Examples include HR, customer sales, product quantities available, and complaints. Each of these systems is independent, with their own application managing the data.

Some applications, however, consolidate data from a number of systems within an organization, as well as third party or public data, in order to provide a more flexible application. This provides for a rich array of information with which to mine for useful business answers.

Organizations don't have control over external data-feed formats, and they can be changed at any time without warning. Even worse, many data structures in use today change depending on the application that creates them, rather than the system that stores them.

A good example of this is a tweet. A tweet isn't just a 140-character message — hundreds of fields are behind it, and they vary depending on the application that created the tweet.

In this section, I discuss how this great variety of ever changing data can be handled in a document NoSQL database.

Handling variety

Storing and retrieving variable information is a key benefit of all NoSQL document databases. Indexing and searching their structure, though, is difficult.

Many document databases don't perform these operations natively; instead, they use an external search engine such as Solr (MongoDB) or Elasticsearch (Couchbase) to do so. These search engines typically index either the text in the document or specifically configured elements within the document.

Microsoft's DocumentDB and MarkLogic Server both take a different approach. They have a universal index that examines the documents as they're ingested. They both index the structure as well as the values. This enables you to perform element-value queries (exact match queries) as soon as a document is stored.

Microsoft's implementation even allows you to do range queries (less than, greater than, and so on) over this universal index, whereas with MarkLogic server, range indexes need to be configured individually.

This extra indexing, of course, comes at a cost. It takes extra time at ingest if you want to keep your indexes consistent with your data. It also costs in storage space for the indexes. Either can increase server and storage rental costs.

Both Microsoft's DocumentDB and MarkLogic Server allow you to configure your indexes to a fine-grained level for each database (MarkLogic) or Collection (Microsoft's DocumentDB, which is akin to a "bucket" within a database that manages a set of documents).

Managing change over time

If you change the format of documents, you need to rework your search index configurations. In many search engines, this forces the regeneration of the index of all of your content! A very costly procedure, indeed.

MarkLogic Server gets around redoing a full re-indexing operation by supporting field indexes. In this way, you can query via a single index that is configured to look at element A in one document and element B in another document — the structure is different, but you use a single query to reference the field.

So, for example, as well as having a separate index for "id" within product documents and "prod_id" within order documents, you can have a field index called "product_id" that will include results from both these elements. Doing so would be useful if you were searching for a page on a website, as well as comments about that page, where you could set up an index for "page_name."

Having to manually reconfigure indexes delays the handling of new types of content. You have to perform index changes before making use of the data. This is where a universal index like those in Microsoft's DocumentDB and MarkLogic Server really pays dividends.

Having a universal structural index allows you to search and explore the data you've ingested and then decide to perform different queries over it. You don't have to manually configure the structure before loading content in order to search it immediately.

Where Microsoft's implementation has the advantage is in automatic range index queries because you can perform less than and greater than data operations over numbers and dates.

Where MarkLogic's implementation has the advantage is in providing a full-text search over all content in addition to structure and values. This supports word stemming ("cat" and "cats" both stem to "cat") and word and phrase searches and has configurable diacritic support for languages with interesting dots and dashes over their letters.

MarkLogic Server also includes specialized support for many world languages and is configurable at runtime for specific query needs. An example is a search that is or isn't case-sensitive or diacritic-sensitive or that ignores or includes particular characters as word boundaries.

Consolidating Data

Sometimes an answer isn't available in a single document. Perhaps you need to join multiple streams of information together in order to paint a picture. Maybe instead different systems hold their own data, which needs to be brought together to answer a question.

Handling incoming streams

When building these "answer" documents, your first task is to join the data together. Very few document NoSQL databases (Microsoft DocumentDB, OrientDB, and to a lesser extent, MarkLogic Server) provide support for these joins at query time, which means you have to do this work yourself.

First, though, you need to store the information. Using constructs to store related data is a good start. If you know, for instance, that some tweets and news stories are about the same topic, then tagging them as such in their metadata, or adding them to the same collection, makes sense. In this way, you can quickly look up all data related to the same topic.

Some document databases, for example MarkLogic Server, support adding documents to multiple collections. Others just support one collection for a document. You can work around this issue by using a metadata property, like this JSON document with an internal _topic property:

```
{
  "_id": 1234, "_someInternalProperty":"a value", "_topic": "business",
  "url": "http://bbc.co.uk/some/url" , "title": "A Business Inc. bankrupt",
  "content": "Lorem ipsum dolar sit amet"
}
```

Where metadata properties aren't supported, use an element in the document. A good trick is to use names that start with underscores in order to avoid clashes with fields used by application code, as shown in the preceding example.

In the past, it was normal to receive dumps of information overnight and process them in the wee hours of the morning. Now information is generated 24/7 and needs to be ingested as soon as it arrives. This means your service must operate 24/7 also. No more downtime for system checks, backups, or upgrades.

To handle 24/7 operations, your database cluster needs to support

- ✔ **Online backups:** Back up nodes within the cluster with no loss of service.

- ✔ **Online upgrades:** Take a server offline (another server takes over its data), upgrade the offline server; then bring it back online with no service interruptions.

- ✔ **Data replication:** If a replica server can't take over one server's data, then it can't support online upgrades. You achieve replication through a shared network disk, or disk replication between servers.

These availability constraints are peculiar to 24/7 streamed incoming data. A lot of databases don't need this degree of availability. It's increasingly common to find that service is required 24/7, though, so you need to be aware of these issues.

Amalgamating related data

After you successfully store the data — by the way, well done, because it's no mean feat! — you must join it together.

Say that you use an ID tracing database for banking arrears collection systems. In this case, you want the latest internal information on customers. Perhaps you receive feeds of data from credit reporting agencies, consented email and cell phone records, public twitter messages (including geocoded tweets so you know where they were sent from), and maybe even local phone directory or census information. The consented cell phone and email data typically includes names and addresses, too. (Think of all those web forms you fill in with privacy check boxes.)

You want to integrate this data to provide a picture of a person and where he has lived. Basically, you join the public fragments of his identity. After all, if he moves out of his house and skips the $110,000 he owes the bank on his mortgage, then it's worth trying to find him!

So, you want to create a "Person" document joining information about the particular person at this particular address. Maybe you find his cell phone number, email address, and mortgage records.

You could then mine tweets near his house and see if any cluster at this address. Then look at the profile and tweets to determine whether he is living there, or perhaps his daughter. If it is him, attach this data to the "Person" object.

To ensure that it's the right person, store the provenance information of what you find, and how it was modified or generated. Why did you add the twitter id to the record? What evidence do you have (list of tweets)? How certain are you (percentage match relevance)?

You'll then be able to see whether any of the identifying information in the last couple of months clusters at a new address. Perhaps a rented property in the next town. In this fashion, you can find the debtors new address.

Providing answers as documents

Once you bring all the information together, you need to provide it in a user-friendly way to people who utilize your application.

For catch-up TV services, for example, there's no point in showing episode summaries or a list of all the channels and times for the past two weeks and the next six months that they'll be showing. Instead, it's better to show a set of episodes that the user can watch now, no matter when its start and end dates occurred.

Taking this source information and creating a different amalgamated view at different levels of granularity is called denormalization. This is a very common use case with document-oriented NoSQL databases. Instead of doing joins at query time (as you can do with a relational database), you precompute the joins and store the results as documents, perhaps in a different collection.

Doing so is particularly useful if each of the source documents you need to join together is controlled by a different set of users. The producers of a television show may be responsible for describing the episode, but the network director is responsible for its scheduling.

You need to pull information from the episode and availability documents, perhaps along with series, brand, and platform (for example, Wii, web, set-top box, Apple Store) in order to compose the denormalized *episode-availability* documents.

The best way to think about these denormalized documents is as answer documents. Based on the questions users can ask, what would they expect the answer to look like? Given this information, you can create a set of denormalization operations that make sense for your application.

If you've created denormalizations well, the answer documents will contain all the information that a user needs for a query in order to find them. These documents can then be indexed for query. Alternatively, you can use a search engine to provide a full-text index for *episode-availability* searches.

Although it does take up more space, creating denormalizations reduces query and processing time because only one document is read, and the query doesn't have to process and join together many records in order to provide the single answer the user is looking for.

Producing denormalizations is the document NoSQL database equivalent of a materialized view in the relational database world. Materialized views are pre-computed joins across tables, used to avoid joins at query time. You're trading storage space for query speed and I/O workload. Depending on your application and complexity of the joins, this tradeoff may well be worth making.

Chapter 17

Document Database Products

*I*f you've decided that a document-orientated, schema-free, tree-structured approach is for you, then you have several choices because many great and varied document NoSQL databases are available. But the question, of course, is which one to use?

Perhaps your organization requires the ability to scale out for high-speed writes. Maybe, instead, you have only a few documents with high-value data. Perhaps you're looking for a relational database that your developers are familiar with.

Because the fundamental designs of databases differ, there's no one-size-fits-all approach. These designs are neither wrong nor right; they're just different because each database is designed for a different use. They become "wrong" only if they're applied to the wrong type of problem.

In this chapter, I explain how to make the choice that best suits your needs.

Providing a Memcache Replacement

Memcache is an in memory caching layer that is frequently used to speed up dynamic web applications by lowering database query load.

In some web applications, you must provide an in-memory storage layer — to offload repeated reads from a back-end operational database server or, alternatively, to store transient user session data that lives only while a user is on a website.

Memcached was the original open-source, in-memory key-value store designed for this purpose. It provides either an in-memory store within a single web application's memory space, or a central service to provide memory caching for a number of application servers.

Other similar open-source and commercial options exist. Oracle Coherence is a sophisticated offering, along with Software AG's Terracotta. Hazelcast is a popular open-source in-memory NoSQL option. Redis can also be used for in-memory caching (refer to Part II for more on key-value stores).

Ensuring high-speed reads

The primary purpose of a memcache layer is to attain high-speed reads. With memcache, you don't have to communicate over the network with a database layer that must read data from a disk.

Memcache provides a very lightweight binary protocol that enables applications to issue commands and receive responses to ensure high-speed read and write operations.

This protocol is also supported by other NoSQL databases. Couchbase, for instance, supports this protocol natively, allowing Couchbase to be used as a shared service drop-in replacement for memcache.

Using in-memory document caching

Using Couchbase as a memcache replacement ensures that cached data is replicated quickly around multiple data centers, which is very useful, for example, when a news story is prompting numerous views and tweets. With Couchbase, you can prevent increasing the load on the server by caching this popular story in memory across many servers.

Because Couchbase is a document NoSQL database, it also supports setting up indexes on complex JSON structures. Memcache doesn't provide this type of aggregate storage structure; instead, it concentrates on simpler structures such as sets, maps, and intrinsic types like strings, integers, and so on.

Couchbase is particularly useful when a web application retrieves a cached news item either by a page's URL or by the latest five stories on a particular topic. Because Couchbase provides views and secondary indexes, you can execute exact-match queries against data stored in memory.

Supporting mobile synchronization

Increasingly, services such as Evernote, SugarSync, and Dropbox require that data is stored locally on a disconnected device (like a cell phone) for later synchronization to a central cloud service. These services are particularly critical when devices like cell phones and laptops are disconnected from a network, for example, oil rigs, environmental surveys, or even battlefields.

The creators of such services don't design their own communication and synchronization protocols, probably because doing so is costly, slow, and bug-prone. The good news is that Couchbase has you covered via Couchbase Mobile, which works on mobile devices. Its internal master-master replication protocol allows many different devices to sync with each other and with a central service.

Evaluating Couchbase

Couchbase provides good support for high-speed writes like a key-value store, while also eventually storing data on disk. Its primary use is for an always-on connection for clusters and devices.

Couchbase, however, isn't an ACID-compliant database. There are short windows of time when data is held in memory on one machine but not yet saved to disk or saved on other machines. This situation means data less than a few seconds old can be lost if a server fails.

Couchbase *views* are the basis of its indexing. If you need secondary indexes, then you must create a design document and one or more views. These are updated asynchronously after data is eventually written to disk.

 If data loss windows and inconsistent indexes are big issues in your situation, I suggest waiting for the upcoming version 3.0, which will provide streaming replicas between memory without waiting for disk check-pointing. It also will allow updating query views directly from memory. Combining these capabilities with consistent use of the PersistTo flag on save and the stale=false flag on read will reduce such problems, at the cost of some speed. These settings aren't easy to find on the Couchbase documentation website (http://www.couchbase.com/documentation), so you will have to read the API documentation for the details.

Couchbase is likely hard to beat in terms of speed in the document NoSQL database realm. This speed comes at the cost of consistency and durability and with a lack of automatic indexing and data querying features. Range queries (less than, greater than) aren't supported at all.

Couchbase restricts you to only three replicas of data. In practice, this is probably as many replicas as you want, but all the same, it is a restriction.

If speed is king in your situation — if you're using JSON documents, if you want a memcache replacement, or perhaps you need a persistence layer for your next gazillion-dollar generating mobile app — then Couchbase may be for you.

Providing a Familiar Developer Experience

Developers are picky folks. We get stuck in our ways and want to use only technologies that we're familiar with, and not dirty or weird in some way, although esoteric code may be just the thing for some people, which may be why there are so many different databases out there!

To get developers on board, you need to provide things that work the way developers expect them to. A database needs to be easy to get started with, and it needs to provide powerful tools that don't require lots of legwork — and that they can put to use in, say, about five minutes.

Indexing all your data

Having a schema-free database is one thing, but in order to have query functionality, in most NoSQL databases you must set up indexes on specific fields. So you're really "teaching" the database about the schema of your data.

Microsoft's DocumentDB (for JSON) and MarkLogic Server (for JSON and XML), however, both provide a universal index, which indexes the structure of documents and the content of that document's elements.

DocumentDB provides structural indexing of JSON documents and even provides range queries (less than, greater than operations) alongside the more basic equal/not equal operations. DocumentDB does all this automatically, without you having to "teach" the database about the prior existence of your documents' structure.

Using SQL

Pretty much every computer science graduate over the past 30 years knows how to query and store information held in an RDBMS, which means there are many people fluent in SQL, the language used to query those systems.

Being able to query, join, sort, filter, and project (produce an output in a different structure to the source document) using this familiar language reduces barriers to adoption significantly.

Microsoft provides a RESTful (*R*epresentational *S*tate *T*ransfer) API that accepts SQL as the main query language. This SQL language is ANSI SQL-compliant, allowing complex queries to be processed against DocumentDB using the exact syntax that you would against a relational database, as shown in Listing 17-1.

Listing 17-1:   SQL to Project a JSON Document into a Different Structure

```
SELECT
    family.id AS family,
    child.firstName AS childName,
    pet.givenName AS petName
FROM Families family
JOIN child IN family.children
JOIN pet IN child.pets
```

The SQL query in Listing 17-1, for example, produces the JSON output shown in Listing 17-2.

Listing 17-2:   The Resulting JSON Projection

```
[
  {
    "familyName": "Fowler",
    "childName": "Reginald",
    "petName": "Leo"
  },
  {
    "familyName": "Atkinson",
    "childName": "Reece",
    "petName": "Deefer"
  }
]
```

Programmers familiar with RDBMS should find this query very intuitive.

Linking to your programming language

Of course, high-level programmers won't be attracted to database innards, like the query structure of SQL. They prefer to work with objects, lists, and other higher-level concepts like save, get, and delete. They're a high-brow bunch who sip martinis while reclining on their super-expensive office chairs and coding.

Application objects can be order objects, a list of items in an order, or an address reference. These objects must be mapped to the relevant structures in order to be held in, and queried from, the document database. Listing 17-3 shows an example of a .NET object class used to store family information.

Listing 17-3:   .NET Code for Serialized JSON Objects

```
public class Family
{
    [JsonProperty(PropertyName="id")]
    public string Id;
    public Parent[] parents;
    public Child[] children;
};
public struct Parent
{
    public string familyName;
    public string firstName;
};
public class Child
{
    public string familyName;
    public string firstName;
    public string gender;
    public List<Pet> pets;
};
public class Pet
{
    public string givenName;
};
// create a Family object
Parent mother = new Parent { familyName= "Fowler", firstName="Adam" };
Parent father = new Parent { familyName = "Fowler", firstName = "Wendy" };
Child child = new Child { familyName="Fowler", firstName="Reginald",
                gender="male"};
Pet pet = new Pet { givenName = "Leo" };
Family family = new Family { Id = "Fowler", parents = new Parent [] { mother,
                father}, children = new Child[] { child } };
```

You can use and serialize plain .NET objects directly to and from DocumentDB. These object classes can have optional annotations, which helps migrate an "id" field in the JSON representation to the .NET object's "Id" field (capital I), as you can see in the Family class in Listing 17-3. So, when using DocumentDB, programmers just use the standard coding practices they're used to in .NET.

Evaluating Microsoft DocumentDB

Microsoft's DocumentDB is an impressive new entry in the document NoSQL database space. With tunable consistency, a managed service cloud offering, a universal index for JSON documents with range query support, and JavaScript server-side scripting, DocumentDB is powerful enough for many public cloud NoSQL scenarios.

Currently, DocumentDB is available only on Microsoft Azure, and for a price. It doesn't have an open-source offering, which will limit its adoption by some organizations, though it's likely to be attractive to Windows and .NET programmers who want to take advantage of the benefits of a schema-less NoSQL design with flexible consistency guarantees. These programmers may not want to learn the intricacies of non-Windows environments, like MongoDB on Red Hat Linux, for example.

.NET developers with exposure to SQL or Microsoft SQL Server will find it easy to understand DocumentDB. As a result, DocumentDB will challenge MongoDB in the public cloud — because DocumentDB is more flexible and has better query options when a JSON document model is used.

For private cloud providers and large organizations able to train people on how to maintain free, open-source alternatives, MongoDB will likely maintain its position. If Microsoft ever allows the purchase of DocumentDB for private clouds, this situation could change rapidly.

MarkLogic Server is likely to continue to dominate in cases of advanced queries with geospatial and semantic support; or where binary, text, and XML documents with always-ACID guarantees need to be handled; or in high-security and defense environments.

All the same, Microsoft should be commended for this well-thought-out and feature-rich NoSQL document database. This new entrant along with Oracle's NoSQL key-value store (refer to Part II for more on Oracle NoSQL) and the Cloudant document NoSQL database (which IBM purchased in 2014) proves that NoSQL is making the big boys of the software industry sit up and take notice.

Providing an End-to-End Document Platform

Storing JSON and allowing it to be retrieved and queried with strong consistency guarantees is a great start. However, most enterprise data is stored in XML rather than in JSON. XML is the *lingua franca* (default language) of systems integration. It forms the foundation of web services and acts as a self-describing document format.

- ✔ In addition to XML, plain text documents, delimited files like comma separated values (CSV), and binary documents still need to be managed. If you want to store these formats, extract information from them, and store metadata against the whole result, then you need a more comprehensive end-to-end solution.

- ✔ After managing the data, you may also need to provide very advanced full text and geospatial and semantic search capabilities. Perhaps you also want to return faceted and paginated search results with matching-text snippets, just like a search engine.

- ✔ Perhaps you want to go even further, and take the indexes of all the documents and conduct co-occurrence analysis. This is where you look at two elements in the same document and calculate how often across all documents in a query two values occur together — say, the product and illness fields extracted from some tweets. You may discover that Tylenol and flu often occur together. Perhaps this will lead you to start an advertisement campaign for this combination.

- ✔ This analytic capability is more than summing up or counting existing fields. It requires more mathematical analysis that needs to be done at high speed, preferably over in-memory, ordered range indexes.

Say that you then want to describe how you extracted the information, from which sources, who uploaded it, and what software was used. You can then code this information in Resource Description Framework (RDF) triples, which I discuss in Part V of this book.

You may then want to take all this information, repurpose it, and publish summaries of it. This end-to-end complete lifecycle used to manage documents and the valuable information within them requires many features. To do so in mission-critical systems that require ACID transactional consistency, backups, high availability, and disaster recovery support — potentially over somewhat dodgy networks — makes the task even harder.

MarkLogic Server is designed with built-in support for these really tough problems.

Ensuring consistent fast reads and writes

At the risk of repetition — and boring you to tears — I say once again that providing very fast transaction times while maintaining ACID guarantees on durability and consistency is no easy thing.

Many NoSQL databases that I cover in this part of the book, and indeed entire book, don't provide these guarantees in order to achieve higher throughput times. Many mission-critical systems require these features, though, so it's worth mentioning some approaches to achieving these guarantees while ensuring maximum throughput.

MarkLogic Server writes all data to memory and writes only a small journal log of the changes to disk, which ensures that the data isn't lost. If a server goes down, when it restarts, the journal is replayed, restoring the data. Writing a small journal, rather than all the content, to disk minimizes the disk I/O requirements when writing data, thus increasing overall throughput.

Many databases also lock information for reads and writes while a write operation is updating a particular document. MongoDB currently locks the entire database within a given instance of MongoDB! (Although this will change with upcoming versions of MongoDB.)

To avoid this situation, MarkLogic Server uses the tried-and-true approach called *multi-version concurrency control (MVCC)*. Here's what happens if you have a document at an internal timestamp version of 12:

1. When a transaction starts and modifies the data, rather than change the data, an entirely new document is written.

   Therefore, the database doesn't have to lock people out for reads. All reads that happen after the transaction begins, but before it finishes, see version 12 of the document.

2. Once the document transaction finishes, the new version is given the timestamp version of 13:

   • All reads that happen after this point are guaranteed to see only version 13.

   • Replicas are also updated within the transaction, so even if the primary server fails, all replicas will agree on the current state of the document.

3. All changes are appended as new documents to the end of a database file, both in-memory and on disk.

   In MarkLogic, this is called a *stand*. There are many stands within a *forest,* which is the unit of partitioning in MarkLogic Server. A single server manages multiple forests. They can be merged or migrated as required while the service is live, maintaining a constant and consistent view of the data.

Of course, with new records being added and with old records that are no longer visible being somewhere in the stand files, an occasional cleanup operation is needed to remove old data. This process is generally called *compaction,* but in MarkLogic, it's called a *merge operation*. This is because many stands are typically merged at the same time as old data is removed.

Always appending data means that reads don't have to block other requests, ensuring fast read speeds while still accepting writes. This mechanism is also the basis for providing ACID guarantees for the protection of data and consistency of query and retrieval.

MarkLogic Server also updates all indexes within the transaction boundary. Therefore, it's impossible to get false positives on document updates or deletions, and all documents are discoverable as soon as the transaction creating them completes. No need to wait for a traditional search engine's re-indexing run.

Supporting XML and JSON

MarkLogic Server is built on open standards like XML, XQuery, XPath, and XSLT. XQuery is the language used for stored procedures, reusable code modules, triggers, search alerts, and Content Processing Framework (CPF) actions.

MarkLogic can natively store and index XML and plain text documents, store small binary files within the stands, and manage large binaries transparently directly on disk (but within the managed forest folder).

You handle JSON documents by transposing them to and from an XML representation with a special XML namespace, which in practice, is handled transparently by the REST API. You pass in JSON and retrieve JSON just as you do with MongoDB or Microsoft's DocumentDB, as shown here:

```
<person id="1234">Adam Fowler</person>
```

The XML representation on disk is highly compressed. Each XML element name is very text-heavy, and there's a start tag and an end tag, as shown in the preceding example. Rather than store this long string, MarkLogic Server uses its own proprietary binary format.

MarkLogic Server replaces the tag with a term id and inherently handles the parent-child relationships within XML documents, which saves a lot of disk space — enough so that, on an average installation, the search indexes plus the compressed document's content equal the size of the original XML document.

This trick can be applied to JSON, too, and MarkLogic is adding native JSON support in MarkLogic Server version 8. In addition, MarkLogic is also adding full server-side JavaScript support. You will be able to write triggers, user-defined functions, search alert actions, and CPF workflow actions in JavaScript.

In addition, the exact functions and parameters currently available in XQuery will be available to JavaScript developers. JavaScript modules will also be capable of being referenced and called from XQuery, without special handling. This will provide the best of both worlds — the most powerful, expressive, and efficient language for working with XML in XQuery; and the most natural language for working with JSON in JavaScript. Except you'll be able to mix and match depending on your skills as a developer.

Using advanced content search

There are document NoSQL databases, and then there are enterprise search engines. Often integrating the two means having search indexes inconsistent with your database documents, or duplicated information — some indexes in the database with the same information or additional indexes in the search engine.

MarkLogic Server was built to apply the lessons from search engines to schema-less document management. This means the same functionality you expect from Microsoft FAST, HP Autonomy, IBM OmniFind, or the Google Search Appliance can be found within MarkLogic Server.

In addition to a universal document structure and value (exact-match) index, MarkLogic Server allows range index (less than, greater than) operations. This range query support has been extended to include bounding box, circle radius, and polygon geospatial search, with server-side heat map calculations and "distance from center of search" analytics returned with search results.

MarkLogic Server's search features don't include a couple of features provided by dedicated search vendors (you can find more on search engines in Part VI):

- ✔ An out-of-the-box user interface application that you can configure without using code.

- ✔ Connectors to other systems. This is because MarkLogic Server aims to have data streamed into it, rather than going out at timed intervals via connectors to pull in content.

Range index distance calculations allows for complex relevancy scoring. A good example is for searching for a hotel in London. Say that you want a hotel near the city center but also want a highly rated hotel. These two metrics can both contribute to the relevancy calculation of the hotel document in question, providing a balanced recommendation score for hotels.

This is just one example of the myriad search capabilities built into MarkLogic Server. Many of these capabilities, such as alerting, aren't as feature-rich in pure-play enterprise search engines, let alone in NoSQL databases.

Securing documents

Many of MarkLogic's customers are public sector organizations in the United States Department of Defense. In these areas, securing access to information is key. MarkLogic Server has advanced security features built in. These features are available for commercial companies, too.

MarkLogic Server's compartment security feature isn't available for commercial customers based in the United States because of government licensing agreements. Outside the United States though, this feature is available for commercial use.

MarkLogic supports authentication of users via encrypted passwords held in the database itself, or in external systems. These external systems include generic LDAP (Lightweight Directory Access Protocol) authentication support and Kerberos Active Directory token support, which allows single sign-on functionality when accessing MarkLogic from a Windows or Internet Explorer client. Digital certificates are also supported for securing access.

Authorization happens through roles and permissions. Users are assigned roles in the system. These roles may come from internal settings or, again, from an external directory through LDAP. Permissions are then set against documents for particular roles. This is called *role based access control (RBAC)*.

If you add two roles to a system, both with read access to the same document, then a user with either one of those roles can access the document.

In some situations, though, you want to ensure that only users with all of a set of roles can access a document. This is called *compartment security* and is used by defense organizations worldwide.

Consider the following compartments:

- ✔ **Nationality:** British, American, Russian
- ✔ **Organization:** CIA, NSA, DoD, UK SIS, UK NCA, FSB
- ✔ **Classification:** Unclassified, Official, Secret, Top Secret
- ✔ **Compartment:** Operation Squirrel, Operation Chastise, ULTRA

If a document has read permissions set for the roles American, Secret, and Operation Chastise, then only users with all three roles have access to that document.

Compartment security effectively enforces AND logic on roles instead of the normal OR logic. Roles must be in named compartments for compartment security to be enabled, though.

These permissions are indexed by MarkLogic in a hidden index. Any search or document retrieval operation, therefore, is always masked by these permissions, which makes securing documents very fast as the indexes are cached in memory.

Users performing a search never see documents they don't have permission for, including things like paginated search summaries and total matching records counts.

These security guarantees are in contrast to many other systems where a mismatch between the document database, application, and search engine security permissions can lead to "ghost" false positive results. You see that a result is there, and maybe it's a unique ID, but you don't see data from the database describing the result, which indicates that content exists that you should never see.

Security permissions in MarkLogic are also applied to every function in the system. A set of execute permissions is available to lock down functionality. Custom permissions can be added and checked for by code in these functions. Execute permissions can even be temporarily bypassed for specific application reasons using *amps* — amps are configuration settings of a

MarkLogic application server to allow privileged code to be executed only in very specific circumstances.

Wire protocols in MarkLogic, such as XML Database Connectivity (XDBC, the XML equivalent of Windows' ODBC), HTTP REST, and administrative web applications are all secured using SSL/TLS.

MarkLogic Server also holds a U.S. Department of Defense Common Criteria certification at an EAL2 (Evaluation Assurance Level 2) standard. It is the only NoSQL database to hold accreditation under Common Criteria. This means its security has been tested and verified such that its development and testing procedures comply with industry best practice for security.

All these features combined provide what MarkLogic calls *government-grade security*.

Evaluating MarkLogic Server

MarkLogic Server has a great many functions, including NoSQL database, search engine, and application services (REST API). Its list of enterprise features, including full ACID compliance, backup and restore functions, cross-datacenter replication, and security, are unsurpassed in the NoSQL space. This makes MarkLogic Server attractive for mission-critical applications.

MarkLogic Server is currently hard to come to grips with because of its use of XQuery. Although XQuery is a very capable language and the best language for processing XML, not everyone is familiar with it. MarkLogic Server version 8, with its server-side JavaScript support, will alleviate this issue.

MarkLogic Server, like Microsoft's DocumentDB, is a commercial-only offering. The download license provides six months of free use for developmental purposes, after which you have to talk with a MarkLogic sales representative in order to extend or purchase a license. This is alleviated somewhat by a lower-end Essential Enterprise license. Unlike many open-source NoSQL databases where an expensive commercial version is always required for cross-datacenter replication, backup and restore functions, integrated analytics, and other enterprise features, this less-advanced edition of MarkLogic provides these features as standard. This new licensing scheme was introduced in late 2013 to counter the common perception that MarkLogic Server was too expensive.

MarkLogic Server is also available on U.S. and UK government purchasing lists, as GSA and GCloud, respectively.

MarkLogic Server also has limited official programming language driver support. Currently, an XDBC Java and .NET API, and REST based the Java API are available as official drivers. A basic JavaScript Node.js driver will also be available with the release of version 8. These REST API-based drivers are being open-sourced now, though, which should improve development releases.

Unofficial drivers are also available as open-source projects for JavaScript (MLJS — for use in both Node.js and browser applications), Ruby (ActiveDocument), C# .NET (MLDotNet), and C++ (mlcplusplus).

MLJS, MLDotNet, and mlcplusplus are all projects I manage on my GitHub account at `https://github.com/adamfowleruk`.

The lack of an out-of-the-box configurable search web interface is also a problem when comparing MarkLogic Server's search capabilities to other search vendors. This problem is limited, though, with many customers choosing to use wrap search functionality as one of many functions within their NoSQL-based applications.

For end-to-end document-orientated applications with unstructured search, perhaps a mix of document formats (XML, JSON, binary, text), and complex information management requirements, MarkLogic Server is a good choice.

Providing a Web Application Back End

It's a very exciting time, with web startups and new networked mobile apps springing up all over the place. If this describes your situation, then you need a NoSQL database that is flexible enough to handle changes in document schema so that old and new versions of your app can coexist with the same data back end.

You also need a simple data model. If you support multiple platforms, you need this model to work seamlessly across platforms without any complex document parsers, which probably means JSON rather than XML documents.

If you're building a web app that communicates either directly to the database or via a data services API that you create, then you want this functionality to be simple, too. In this case, a JSON data structure that can be passed by any device through any tier to your database will make developing an application easier.

Many web startups and application developers who don't want to spend money on software initially but want their database to expand along with the popularity of their application use MongoDB. MongoDB, especially running as a managed cloud service, provides an inexpensive and easy-to-start API required for these types of applications. The software doesn't provide all the advanced query and analytics capabilities of Microsoft's DocumentDB or MarkLogic Server, but that isn't a problem because its primary audience consists of web application developers in startup companies.

Trading consistency for speed

In many mobile and social applications, the latest data doesn't return with every query; however, that's no great loss if, for example, you get a new follower on Twitter and the count of followers doesn't update for, say, six seconds. Allowing this inconsistency means that the database doesn't have to update the master node and the replicas (typically two) during a write operation.

Trading this consistency in a document database like MongoDB means that the database doesn't have to update the master node and the replicas during a write operation. MongoDB also supports writing to RAM and journaling to disk, so if you want durability of data with eventual consistency to replicas then MongoDB can be used for this. This allows MongoDB to provide high write speeds.

MongoDB currently locks its database file on each MongoDB instance when performing a write. This means only one write can happen at a time (although this issue will be addressed in version 2.8). Even worse, all reads are locked out until a write completes. To work around this problem, run multiple instances per server (perhaps one per two CPU cores). This approach is called *micro-sharding*.

Normally you operate one instance of a NoSQL database per server and manage multiple shards on that server (as discussed in Chapter 15) — with MongoDB micro-sharding you have to run multiple copies of MongoDB on each server, each with a single shard. This is of course a higher CPU and I/O load on the server.

Consistency levels aren't enforced by the MongoDB server; they are selected by the client API driver, which allows clients to selectively choose the consistency for their writes and reads.

To ensure that all replicas are updated and that the data is completely flushed to disk before an operation completes, you can select the ALL replicas option for the write operation.

Similarly, you can set read consistency options. For example, you can ask for a majority of replicas, or all replicas, to agree on the "current" state of a record for the read operation before a copy of the record is returned to the client.

Sticking with JavaScript and JSON

If you're writing a web application, then you probably employ several web developers, and they're probably familiar with clever JavaScript tricks and know how to model data effectively in JSON.

Ideally, you want those developers to use their existing set of skills when it comes to operating your database. You want to save and retrieve JSON. When you query, you want a query definition that's in JSON. You might not be a relational database expert with years of Structured Query Language (SQL) experience; however, you want to same functionality exposed in a way familiar to your JavaScript and JSON fluent web developers.

MongoDB's query mechanism uses a JSON structure. The response you get is a JSON result set, with a list of JSON documents; it's all very easy to understand and use from a web developer's perspective, which is why MongoDB is so popular.

Finding a web community

MongoDB's simplicity and JavaScript-centric characteristics make it a natural starting place for developers. This is reflected by the strength of the MongoDB online community

Partly it's because MongoDB, Inc. (formerly 10gen) has an excellent developer-centric, local meet-up strategy and strong marketing behind it. Every week in MongoDB offices worldwide, people show up and work on apps with their sales and consulting staff.

MongoDB is also prevalent on web forums. If you hit upon a problem, chances are you can find a solution on StackOverflow.com. This is a double-edged sword, though — because it may be that people are having a lot of problems!

Evaluating MongoDB

MongoDB is a solid database when used as a back end for web applications. Its JavaScript and JSON centricity make it easy to understand and use straightaway.

Being able to choose what level of consistency and durability you have is also useful. It's up to you, as a developer, to understand this trade off, though, and the benefits and costs each gives you.

Currently, the main thing limiting MongoDB's use in mission-critical enterprise installations — as opposed to large enterprises that are using MongoDB as a cache or for noncritical operations — is its lack of enterprise features.

The recent 2.6 version did introduce rolling backups, data durability settings, and basic index intersection. Basic RBAC (role based access control, mentioned earlier in this chapter) was also added, but not at the document level. You can secure access only by using roles to collections and databases, not individual documents.

Also, fundamental changes need to be made to MongoDB's architecture to allow better scaling. Support for multi-core processors that doesn't require you to start multiple instances is one such change.

Another is the need to define a *compound index.* Say that you have a query with three query terms and a sort order. In order to facilitate this query, rather than add an index for each term and define the sort order in the query, you must define a compound index for every combination of query terms you use and their sort order. This approach requires a lot of indexing and index space. MongoDB has begun to address this issue, but it hasn't entirely removed the need for compound indexes.

The database-wide write lock is also a problem in systems that require large parallel write operations. This fundamental design exists because MongoDB uses memory-mapped files. An entirely new persistence mechanism will be required to resolve this, and this will take time to test, debug, and prove.

MongoDB's funding rounds in 2013 were aimed at helping it solve these fundamental design challenges in the coming years, and MongoDB is on its way to achieving this goal with the new features in the 2.6 and 2.8 releases.

The bottom line is that MongoDB is easy to grasp and is already used by many companies to build very useful applications. If you have a web application or need a JSON data model in a NoSQL database with built-in querying, consider adopting MongoDB, especially if you need a free database or a private installation. Currently, neither of these scenarios are supported by Microsoft's DocumentDB.

Chapter 18

MongoDB

. . . .

In This Chapter

▶ Working with open-source software

▶ Supporting MongoDB

. . . .

MongoDB is the poster child for the NoSQL database movement. If asked to name a NoSQL database, most people will say MongoDB, and many people start with MongoDB when looking at NoSQL technology. This popularity is both a blessing and a curse. It's obviously good for MongoDB, Inc. (formerly 10gen). On the flip side, though, people try to use MongoDB for purposes it was not designed for, or try to apply relational database approaches to this fundamentally different database model.

MongoDB is a good NoSQL document database with a range of features that, in the open-source NoSQL world, are hard to beat. Starting your NoSQL career with MongoDB is a good approach to take.

In this chapter, I describe how MongoDB can be used, and where support can be found for your own implementation.

Using an Open-Source Document Database

Some companies can't afford to purchase commercial software, support, or consulting, at least at the outset. If this describes your company, you may want to start with the free open-source version of MongoDB, which you can find at `https://www.mongodb.org/downloads`.

MongoDB's use of the GNU Affero General Public License (AGPL) v3.0 means that anyone can download the software source code, compile it, and use it to provide a database service, either for her own applications or as a shared public cloud computing service.

Doing so reduces the costs and complexities of adopting MongoDB. Several cloud providers on Amazon and Azure offer hosted MongoDB database services.

MongoDB's core database code is available under the GNU AGPL v3.0 license. MongoDB is unique in using this particular license. This differs from the standard GNU GPL in ensuring that, if a modified version of MongoDB is created and run on a public service (for example, in the Amazon or Azure clouds), then the source code for that modification must be released back to the community under the same GNU AGPL v3.0 license. Some commercial companies may find this requirement problematic, because it may prevent them from producing their own enhanced MongoDB and making it available as a unique commercial service on the public cloud.

Handling JSON documents

MongoDB natively handles JSON documents. Like XML, JSON documents' property names can be quite verbose text. MongoDB uses its own BSON (short for Binary JSON) storage format to reduce the amount of space and processing required to store JSON documents. This binary representation provides efficient serialization that is useful for storage and network transmission.

This internal operation is handled transparently by the client drivers and MongoDB. Developers never need to worry about this implementation detail.

Finding a language binding

One of the main strengths of MongoDB is the range of official programming language drivers it supports. In fact, it officially supports ten drivers. These drivers are released under Apache License v2.0, allowing you to extend the drivers, or fix them as needed, and to redistribute the code.

Also, more than 32 unofficial drivers (the code is not reviewed by MongoDB) under a variety of licenses are available, which is by far the most language drivers I've come across for any NoSQL database.

Whether you want a modern-day or older esoteric programming language, MongoDB probably has a language binding for you, as shown here:

> ✔ **Official:** C, C++, C#, Java, Node.js, Perl, PHP, Python, Ruby, Scala
>
> ✔ **Unofficial:** ActionScript 3, Clojure, ColdFusion, D, Dart, Delphi, Entity, Erlang, Factor, Fantom, F#, Go, Groovy, JavaScript, Lisp, Lua, MATLAB, Node.js, Objective C, OCaml, Opa, Perl, PHP, PowerShell, Prolog, Python, R, REST, Ruby, Scala, Racket, Smalltalk

If your language binding isn't mentioned in the preceding list, then you really are using something rare and wonderful for your applications!

Effective indexing

Storing data is one thing, finding it again is quite another! Retrieving a document using a document ID, or (primary) key, is supported by every NoSQL document database.

In many situations, though, you may want a list of all comments on a web page or all recipes for puddings (my personal favorite!). This requires retrieving a list of documents based not on their key but on other information within the document — for example, a page_id JSON property. These indexed fields are commonly referred to as *secondary indexes.* Adding an index to these fields allows you to use them in queries against the MongoDB database.

In some situations, you may want to search by several of these fields at a time, such as for all pudding recipes that contain chocolate but are gluten free. MongoDB solves this issue by allowing you to create a *compound index,* which is basically an index for all three fields (recipe type, ingredients, is gluten free), perhaps ordered according to the name of the recipe.

You can create a compound index for each combination of query fields and sort orders you need. The flip side is that you need an index for every single combination. If you want to add a query term for only five-star recipes, then you need yet another compound index, maybe several for different sorting orders, too.

Other document NoSQL databases (MarkLogic Server and Microsoft DocumentDB) and search engines solve this matter by allowing an intersection of the results of each individual index. In this way, there's no need for compound indexes, just a single index per field and a piece of math to perform an intersection on each index lookup's document id list. This approach reduces the amount of administration required for the database and the space needed for the index on disk and in memory.

You also need to think about how to structure your documents so that you can create effective indexes for querying. MongoDB, in true NoSQL style, doesn't support cross-document joins, which means that your document structure must contain all the information needed to resolve a query. Essentially, you construct your documents to look like the "answers" you're looking for. The process of merging information to provide effective answers is called denormalization and is a key skill required for working with NoSQL databases.

MongoDB doesn't support a universal index — you need to manually configure every index. In its 2.6 version, MongoDB introduced basic geospatial support through the adoption of the GeoJSON standard.

Likewise, advanced full-text searches aren't supported in MongoDB. A common pattern is to integrate the Solr search engine with MongoDB (see Part VI of this book for details on Solr). This provides eventually consistent full-text searches of your documents. However, in this case, you must write part of your application according to MongoDB's programming API and part in accordance with Solr's. If, however, you need full-text indexing in MongoDB, this is the approach to take.

Finding Support for MongoDB

MongoDB, Inc., is the commercial company behind most of the development and innovation of the MongoDB NoSQL database, and it is one of the largest NoSQL companies in terms of investments, raising $150 million through October 2013.

This funding round was purely to improve MongoDB and help it become an enterprise-class product ready for high-end mission-critical workloads. So far, MongoDB has added geospatial search and started improving support for index intersection and security. MongoDB has also added a database write journal to ensure data durability in the event of a system failure.

Over the next two to three years, we should begin seeing better database locking, fully composable search indexes, and security permissions at the document level. At the moment these are lacking in MongoDB.

MongoDB in the cloud

MongoDB, Inc., provides advice on running MongoDB on a wide variety of cloud platforms, which isn't surprising because MongoDB emerged from the 10gen company's cloud application requirement.

MongoDB supports the following public cloud platforms:

- ✔ Amazon EC2
- ✔ dotCloud
- ✔ Google Compute Engine
- ✔ Joyent Cloud
- ✔ Rackspace Cloud
- ✔ Red Hat OpenShift
- ✔ VMWare Cloud Foundry
- ✔ Windows Azure

There is, of course, nothing stopping you from downloading MongoDB and installing it on your private cloud. This, too, is supported.

Licensing advanced features

Not all functionality is available on the free download version of MongoDB. If you want any of the following functionality, you must buy MongoDB Enterprise from MongoDB, Inc.

- ✔ **MongoDB Management Service (MMS):** Enables disaster recovery replication to a second cluster and is a systems monitoring tool.
- ✔ **Security integrations:** Includes Kerberos, LDAP authentication, and auditing.
- ✔ **Enterprise software integration:** Integrates MongoDB with your organization's monitoring tools through SNMP (Simple Network Management Protocol).
- ✔ **Certified operating system support:** Includes full testing and bug fixes for operating systems.
- ✔ **On-demand training:** Provides access to online training portal.
- ✔ **24/7 support:** Includes software support and bug fixes.
- ✔ **Commercial license:** Enables you to use MongoDB as an embedded database in a commercial product or service you sell.

In practice, disaster recovery replication to a second or subsequent site is required for enterprise application software. If you're a large enterprise thinking about betting part of your business on a NoSQL document database, you need disaster recovery replication, which means forking out the money for an Enterprise License Agreement.

Ensuring a sustainable partner

MongoDB, Inc., now has the funding required to improve its product and market it to organizations worldwide. With offices all over the globe, you can find official support locally, specific to your needs when using MongoDB, including regular health checks, presales architecture and deployment advice, and expert consulting services, all for a significant price, of course. If you're working on your first major project, this advice can be invaluable. For example, it can help you spot ways to apply best practices and avoid common pitfalls.

As a principal sales engineer, I know how valuable early-stage consulting advice is. You may need only 20 days of consultancy over a year's time, but it helps ensure a successful project. It's also generally a good idea to have a health check a few months after you go live because estimates on the size requirements of systems never exactly match their scale of actual predicted use, or growth of use. So, it's best to do an early-stage tweak of a few post-deployment settings in order to tune your database appropriately. For this, expert advice is best — so buy a few of those consultancy days.

The document NoSQL database landscape is now in prime time. With IBM buying Cloudant and Microsoft building DocumentDB — from scratch — it's clear that these types of databases are the most valuable applications of NoSQL technology.

With the entry of the big boys of IBM and Microsoft, and Oracle with its NoSQL key-value store, competition will begin to get tight. The market is no longer immature and full of startups competing for cutting-edge customers.

Enterprise capabilities and rich functionality that help reduce development and administration costs will become increasingly important, as will security, data durability, consistency, and systems monitoring.

MongoDB must meet the expectations of investment groups providing it with funding. It will be interesting to see how MongoDB reacts to competition from IBM Cloudant and especially Microsoft's DocumentDB. DocumentDB seems aimed squarely at providing just a little more than MongoDB does, but of course at a commercial software price.

For now, though, MongoDB's status as a leading document NoSQL database vendor, along with the others I discuss in this part of the book, is assured. With a large installation base, the ability to be installed in private clouds, and many experienced developers on the market, MongoDB will be hard pressed to be surpassed by Microsoft for a while yet.

Part V
Graph and Triple Stores

 Visit www.dummies.com/extras/nosql for great Dummies content online.

In this part . . .

✔ Applying standards.

✔ Managing metadata.

✔ Accessing unstructured information.

✔ Examining triple store and graph products.

✔ Visit www.dummies.com/extras/nosql for great Dummies content online.

Chapter 19

Common Features of Triple and Graph Stores

In This Chapter

▶ Architecting triples and quads

▶ Applying standards

▶ Managing ontologies

I want to begin this chapter by asking, "Why do you need a triple store or graph store?" Do you really need a web of interconnected data, or can you simply tag your data and infer relationships according to the records that share the same tags?

If you do have a complex set of interconnected data, then you need to decide what query functionality you need to support your application. Are you querying for data, or trying to mathematically analyze the graph itself?

In order to get the facts, or assertions, that you require, are you manually adding them, importing them from another system, or determining them through logical rules, called *inferencing*? By inferencing, I mean that if Luke is the son of Anakin, and Anakin's mother is called Shmi, then you can infer that Luke's grandmother is Shmi.

The tool you select for the job — whether it's a simple document store with metadata support, a triple store, or a graph store — will flow from your answers to the preceding questions.

In this chapter, I discuss the basic model of graph stores and triple stores, how they differ, and why you might consider using them.

Deciding on Graph or Triple Stores

I deliberately separated the terms graph store and triple store in this book. The reason is pretty simple. Although the underlying structures are the same, the analysis done on them is drastically different.

This difference means that graph and triple stores, by necessity, are architected differently. In the future, they may share a common underpinning, but not all the architectural issues of distributing graphs across multiple machines have been addressed at this point in time.

Triple queries

A triple store managed individual assertions. For most use cases you can simply think of an assertion as a "fact." These assertions describe subjects' properties and the relationships between subjects. The data model consists of many simple *subject – predicate – object* triples, as shown in Figure 19-1.

Figure 19-1:
Simple
subject –
predicate –
object triple.

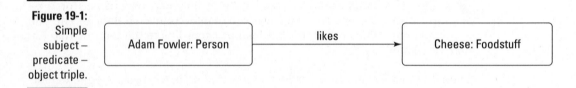

This subject – predicate – object triple allows complex webs of assertions, called graphs, to be built up. One triple could describe the type of the subject, another an integer property belonging to it, and another a relationship to another subject.

Figure 19-2 shows a simple graph of subjects and their relationships, but no properties for each subject. You can see that each relationship and type is described using a particular vocabulary. Each vocabulary is called an *ontology*.

Each ontology describes a set of types, perhaps with inheritance and "same as" relationships to other types in other ontologies. These ontologies are described using the same triple data model in documents composed of Resource Description Framework (RDF) statements.

In graph theory these subjects are called *vertices,* and each relationship is called an *edge*. In a graph, both vertices and edges can have properties describing them.

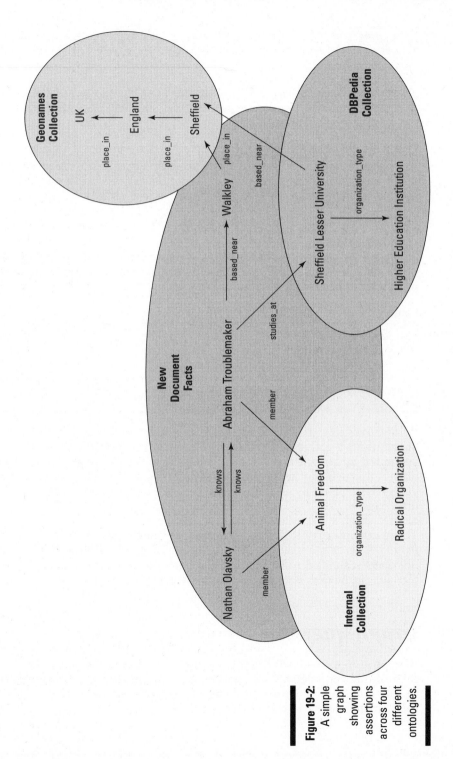

Figure 19-2:
A simple graph showing assertions across four different ontologies.

Every graph store is a triple store because both share the same concepts. However, not every triple store is a graph store because of the queries that each can process.

A triple store typically answers queries for facts. Listing 19-1 shows a simple query (based on the graph in Figure 19-2) to return all facts about the first ten subjects of type `person`.

Listing 19-1:   Simple SPARQL Query

```
SELECT ?s ?p ?o WHERE {
  ?s rdf:type :person .
  ?s ?p ?o .
} LIMIT 10
```

In a more complex example, you may look for subjects who are related to other subjects through several relationships across the graph, as illustrated in Listing 19-2.

Listing 19-2:   Complex SPARQL Query

```
SELECT ?s WHERE {
  ?s rdf:type :person .
  ?s :knows ?s2 .
  ?s2 rdf:type :person .
  ?s2 :likes :cheese .
} LIMIT 10
```

In Listing 19-2, you aren't looking for a directly related subject but for one separated by a single *hop* (that is, a query on an object related to another object) through another vertex, or relationship, in the graph. In Listing 19-2, you're asking for a list of the first ten people who know someone who likes cheese.

These examples SPARQL queries share one thing in common: They return a list of triples as the result of the operation. They are queries for data itself, not queries about the state of the relationships between subjects, the size of a graph, or the degree of separation between subjects in a graph.

Graph queries

A graph store provides the ability to discover information about the relationships or a network of relationships. Graph stores can respond to queries for data, too, and are also concerned with the mathematical relationships between vertices.

Generally, you don't find these graph operations in triple stores:

- ✔ **Shortest path:** Finds the minimum number of hops between two vertices and the route taken.
- ✔ **All paths:** Finds all routes between two vertices.
- ✔ **Closeness:** Given a set of vertices, returns how closely they match within a graph.
- ✔ **Betweenness:** Given a set of vertices, returns how far apart they are within a graph.
- ✔ **Subgraph:** Either finds a part of the graph that satisfies the given constraints or returns whether a named graph contains a specified partial graph.

These algorithms are mathematically much harder queries to satisfy than simply returning a set of facts. This is because these algorithms could traverse the graph to an unpredictable depth of search from the first object in the database.

Triple queries, on the other hand, are always bounded by a depth within their queries and operate on a known set of vertices as specified in the queries themselves.

Describing relationships

Graph stores also allow their relationships, or edges, to be described using properties. This convention isn't supported in RDF in triple stores. Instead, you create a special subject to represent the relationships itself, add the properties to this intermediate subject.

This process does lead to more complex queries, but they can be handled using the query style shown in Listing 19-2.

Making a decision

The differences between the graph and triple store data models lead to great differences in architecture. Because of the number of hops possible in graph queries, a graph store typically requires all its data to be held on a single server in order to make queries fast.

A triple store, on the other hand, can distribute its data in the same manner as other NoSQL databases, with a specialized triple index to allow distributed queries to be spread among servers in a cluster.

In the future, it may be possible to distribute a graph store while maintaining speed — by detecting wholly independent graphs stored alongside others and separating them between servers. Alternatively, you can use graph analysis to find the nearest related vertices and store them near each other on the same server, which minimizes the number of cross-server relationships, and thus the queries required.

Whether you choose a triple or graph store isn't a question of which architecture you prefer; instead, the question is which type of queries you prefer.

The majority of data models use triples to provide the same flexibility in modeling relationships as you get in schema-less NoSQL's document models. They are basically schema-less relationships: You are free to add, remove, and edit them without informing the database beforehand of the particular types of relationship you're going to add.

Triple stores are concerned with storing and retrieving data, not returning complex metrics or statistics about the interconnectedness of the subjects themselves.

Triple stores are also built on the open RDF set of standards and the SPARQL query language. Graph stores each have their own terminology, slightly different data models, and query operations.

If you need to query information about the graph structure, then choose a graph store. If you only need to query information about subjects within that graph, then choose a triple store.

From this point on, I use the term *triple store* to refer to both triple and graph stores, unless stated otherwise.

Deciding on Triples or Quads

The subject – predicate – object data model is a very flexible one. It allows you to describe individual assertions.

There are situations though when the subject – predicate – object model is too simple, typically because your assertion makes sense only in a particular context. For example, when describing a particular patient in one medical trial versus another trial, or maybe you're describing the status of one person within two different social groups.

Thankfully, you can easily model context within a triple store. Triple stores have the concept of a *named graph*. Rather than simply add all your assertions globally, you add them to a named part of the graph.

You can use this graph name to restrict queries to a particular subset of the information. In this way, you don't need to change the underlying ontology or the data model used in order to support the concept of context.

In the preceding example, you could have a different named graph for each medical trial or each social group. If you specify the named graph in your query, you restrict the context queried. If you don't specify the named graph, you get a query across all your data.

Note that each triple can be stored in only a single named graph. This means you must to carefully select what you use as your context and graph name. If you don't, then you may find yourself in a situation where you need to use two contexts for a single set of triples.

The way the graph name is implemented on some NoSQL databases means the triples are stored within a document, and the document can be linked to multiple collections. The collection name in these systems is synonymous with the graph name. This allows a little more flexibility, even if it's a little "naughty" when compared to the W3C specifications. MarkLogic Server provides this capability if you need it.

By creating a database for all triples in a particular application, when querying across them, you're automatically saying they all have value. In most situations, therefore, you don't need a context. In this situation, you can ignore the context of the data and just keep thinking in terms of triples, rather than quads.

If you need the context concept and you can add a property to a subject without making your queries complex, or altering an ontology, then do so, because this approach is more flexible.

If you absolutely need to use context without adding your own properties outside of an ontology, then using the graph name for context will give you the quads you need.

Storing RDF

The first standard you need to become familiar with when dealing with triples is the Resource Description Framework (RDF). This standard describes the components of the RDF data model, which includes subjects, predicates, objects, and how they are described.

This standard is vast and too complex to detail in this book. The best reference I've found is *Semantic Web for the Working Ontologist*, Second Edition by Dean Allemang and James Hendler, published by Morgan Kaufmann. This book discusses practical ways to apply and model RDF solutions.

Applying Standards

Sir Tim Berners-Lee has a lot of talented people working with him at the World Wide Web Consortium (W3C). These people like to create standards based on feedback from scholars and industry.

Applying open standards allows organizations like your own to find a wider range of talented people with transferable skills they can apply to their projects. This is much easier to find then expertise on proprietary methods.

There is a difference between proprietary and open software and proprietary and open standards:

- A proprietary (commercial) piece of software can support open standards.

- Open-source software can invent its own data models and query languages, and not support open standards.

Be sure you don't confuse the two when deciding on the total cost of ownership of software.

Here are a few key RDF concepts that are explained in detail in the *working ontologist* book:

- **URI:** The unique identifier of a subject or a predicate.

- **Namespace:** A namespace allows packaging up of objects in an ontology. Namespaces allow you to mix internal RDF constructs and third-party ontologies.

- **RDF type:** Used to assert that a subject is an instantiation of a particular type. Not equivalent to a class. RDF supports inheritance between RDF types, including across ontologies.

- **Subject:** The entity you're describing — for example, physical (person, place) or conceptual (meeting, event). Takes the form of a URI.

- **Predicate:** The edge, or relationship, between the subject and the object. Takes the form of a URI.

- **Object:** Either another subject URI when describing relationships between subjects, or an intrinsic property value like an integer age or string name.

A key difference between RDF and other specifications is that there are multiple expression formats for RDF data, not just a single language. Common languages are N-Triples, Turtle, and RDF/XML.

Which format you choose depends on the tools you're using. A person who understands RDF in one format should be able to pick up another format easily enough without formal retraining.

In addition to RDF, there are other related standards in the ecosystem. Here are the standards you need to become familiar with:

- ✔ **SPARQL:** Semantic querying language. Triple store equivalent of SQL. Able also to construct new triples and return as a result set. (An example of *projection*.)
- ✔ **RDF Schema (known as RDFS):** RDFS helps define the valid statements allowed for a particular schema.
- ✔ **OWL (the Web Ontology Language):** Sometimes referred to as RDFS+. A subset of OWL is commonly used to supplement RDF Schema definitions.
- ✔ **SKOS (Simple Knowledge Organization System):** W3C standard recommendation that describes using RDF to manage controlled vocabularies, thesauri, taxonomies, and folksonomies.

These specifications allow you to define not only the data in your database but also the structure within that data and how it's organized.

You can use a triple store by utilizing a single RDF serialization like N-Triples, and SPARQL to query the information the database contains. It's good to know about these other specifications, however, when you're designing ontologies that you share with the outside world.

Querying with SPARQL

SPARQL is a recursive acronym that stands for SPARQL Protocol and RDF Query Language. SPARQL uses a variant of the Turtle language to provide a query mechanism on databases that store RDF information.

SPARQL provides several modes of operation:

- ✔ **Select:** Returns a set of matching triples from the triple store
- ✔ **Ask:** Returns whether a query matches a set of triples
- ✔ **Construct:** Creates new triples based on data in the triple store (similar to projection)

These operations can be restricted to portions of the database using a Where clause.

As shown in Listing 19-1, select statements can be very simple. The sample in listing 19-1 returns all triples in the database that match the given expression.

You can construct more complex queries to find particular subjects that match a query across relationships in the graph, as shown in Listing 19-2.

Using SPARQL 1.1

An update to the SPARQL standard is now very common and often people looking to implement a triple store request the 1.1 version of the SPARQL standard.

Version 1.1 provides a "group by" structuring mechanism and allows aggregation functions to be performed over triples.

Listing 19-3 shows both an aggregation function (AVG for mean average) and a GROUP BY clause. This query returns the average age of purchasers for each product ordered from a website.

Listing 19-3:   Product Average Purchaser Age Query and Result

```
SELECT (AVG(?age) AS ?averageage) WHERE {
    ?product :id ?id .
    ?product :title ?title .
    ?order rdf:type :order .
    ?order :has_item ?product .
    ?order :owner ?owner .
    ?owner :age ?age .
} GROUP BY ?title
```

SPARQL 1.1 also provides a HAVING keyword that acts like a filter clause, except it operates over the result of an aggregation specified in the SELECT clause, rather than a bound variable within the WHERE clause.

Modifying a named graph

An often overlooked specification is the W3C SPARQL 1.1 graph store protocol. This is a single web address (called a HTTP endpoint — HTTP being Hypertext Transfer Protocol, the protocol that powers the web) that allows clients to create, modify, get, and delete named graphs within a triple store.

This is a simple specification that can be easier to work with than the more complex SPARQL 1.1 Update mechanism. The graph store protocol is easy to use because you can take any Turtle RDF file and use a simple web request to create a graph, or add new data to an existing graph.

SPARQL 1.1 Update is a variation of SPARQL that allows the insertion and deletion of triples within a named graph. It also provides graph deletion via the DROP operation and copy, load, move, and add operations.

Managing Triple Store Structures

Triple stores provide great flexibility by allowing different systems to use the same data model to describe things. That comes at the cost of allowing people to describe things in a very open and flexible way!

RDF Schema (RDFS), OWL, and SKOS allow developers to use the familiar RDF mechanism to describe how these structures interrelate to each other and the existing relations and values.

Describing your ontology

An ontology is a semantic model in place within an RDF store. A single store can contain information across many ontologies. Indeed, you can use two ontologies to describe different aspects of the same subject.

The main tool used to describe the structures in an RDF ontology is the RDF Schema Language (RDFS). Listing 19-4 illustrates a simple example of an RDF Schema.

Listing 19-4:   Some Assertions

```
:title rdfs:domain :product .
:service rdfs:subClassOf :product .
:period rdfs:domain :service .
:foodstuff rdfs:subClassOf :product .
:expiry rdfs:domain :foodstuff .
```

Listing 19-5 shows how RDF Schema are used in practice.

Listing 19-5:   Triples Within This RDF Schema

```
:SoftwareSupport rdf:type :service .
:SoftwareSupport :period "12 months" .
:SoftwareSupport :title "Software Support" .
:Camenbert rdf:type :foodstuff .
:Camembert :title "Camembert Cheese" .
:Camembert :expiry "2014-12-24"^^xs:date .
```

The preceding schema implies the following:

- ✔ Software support is a type of product.
- ✔ Camembert is a type of product.
- ✔ Both have a title in the product domain, rather than the service or food-stuff domains.

Relationships within triples are directional, thus the semantic web industry's frequent references to *directed graphs*. The relationship is from one subject to one object. In many situations, there is an opposite case, for example:

- ✔ fatherOf (or motherOf) and sonOf
- ✔ purchased and owns
- ✔ ordered and customer

The Web Ontology Language, OWL, provides extensions to RDF Schema that help model more complex scenarios, including that in Listing 19-6.

Listing 19-6:   Simple Use of the OWL inverseOf Property

```
:person rdf:type owl:Class .
:fatherOf rdf:type owl:ObjectProperty;
    rdfs:domain :person;
    rdfs:range :person;
    owl:inverseOf :sonOf .
:sonOf rdf:type owl:ObjectProperty;
    rdfs:domain :person;
    rdfs:range :person;
    owl:inverseOf :fatherOf .
```

As you can see in Listing 19-6, the `inverseOf` predicate can be used to specify that relationships are the opposite of each other. This enables the presence of one relationship to infer that the other relationship also exists in the opposite direction.

Of course, many more sophisticated examples are available. You can probably think immediately of other ways to apply this concept.

My personal favorite use of inferencing is to shorten paths within queries. You know from the preceding triples that Adam has an order, the order contains several items, and items have genres. So, you can infer a single fact: Adam is interested in databases. Being able to infer this fact can greatly simplify future queries. It allows a preference engine to use data without knowing how the ordering system is structured in the database.

Enhancing your vocabulary with SKOS

A common requirement in using a triple store is to define concepts and how objects fit within those concepts. Examples include

- ✔ Book categories in a library
- ✔ Equivalent terms in the English language
- ✔ Broadening and narrowing the focus of a concept using related terms

SKOS is used to define vocabularies to describe the preceding scenarios' data modeling needs.

A *concept* is the core SKOS type. Concepts can have preferred labels and alternative labels. Labels provide human readable descriptions. A concept can have a variety of other properties, too, including a note on the scope of the concept. This provides clarification to a user of the ontology as to how a concept should be used.

A concept can also have relationships to narrower or broader concepts. A concept can also describe relationships as close matches or exact matches.

Listing 19-7 is an example SKOS ontology used to describe customers and what class of customer they are with a company.

Listing 19-7:   SKOS Vocabulary to Describe Customer Relationships

```
amazon:primecustomer a skos:concept ;
  skos:prefLabel "Amazon Prime Customer"@en ;
  skos:broader amazon:customer .
amazon:customer a skos:concept ;
  skos:prefLabel "Amazon Customer"@en ;
  skos:broader :customer ;
  skos:narrower amazon:primecustomer .
```

SKOS provides a web linkable mechanism for describing thesauri, taxonomies, folksonomies, and controlled vocabularies. This can provide a very valuable data modeling technique.

In particular, SKOS provides a great way to power drop-down lists and hierarchical navigation user-interface components. So, consider SKOS for times when you need a general-purpose, cross-platform way to define a shared vocabulary, especially if the resulting data ends up in a triple store.

Describing data provenance

In the day-to-day use of databases you likely create, update, and delete data with abandon. In this book, you find out how to gather information from disparate sources and store all of it together, using document or semantic mechanisms to create new content or infer facts.

In larger systems, or systems used over time, you can end up with very complicated interconnected pieces of information. You may receive an innocuous tweet that shows a person may be of interest to the police. Then decide six months later, after examining lots of other data, that this person's house should be raided.

How do you prove that the chain of information and events you received, assessments you made, and decisions taken were reasonable and justified for this action to take place?

Similarly, records, especially documents held in document-orientated NoSQL databases, are changed by people who are often in the same organization. This is even more the case when you're dealing with distributed systems like a Wiki. How do you describe the changes that content goes through over time, who changed it, and why? This kind of documentation is known as *data provenance.*

You can invent a number of ways to describe these activities. However, a wonderful standard based on RDF has emerged to describe such changes of data over time.

The W3C (yes, those people again!) PROV Ontology (PROV-O) provides a way to describe documents, versions of those documents, changes, the people responsible, and even the software or mechanism used to make the change!

PROV-O describes some core classes:

- prov:Entity: The subject being created, changed, or used as input
- prov:Activity: The process by which an entity is modified
- prov:Agent: The person or process carrying out the activity on an entity

These three core classes can be used to describe a range of actions and changes to content. They can form the basis for systems to help prove governance is being followed within a data update or action chain.

PROV-O comprises many properties and relationships. There's not room in this book to describe all of them, nor could my tired ole hands type them! But here is a selection I like to briefly mention:

- wasGenertedBy: Indicates which agent generated a particular entity

- wasDerivedFrom: Shows versioning chains or where data was amalgamated

- startedAtTime, endedAtTime: Provide information on how the activity was performed

- actedOnBehalfOf: Allows a process agent to indicate, for example, which human agent it was running for; also, used to determine when one person performs an operation at the request of another

Regardless of your requirements for tracking modifications of records or for describing actions, you can use PROV-O as a standards-compliant basis for managing the records of changes to data in your organization.

PROV-O is a group of standards that includes validator services that can be created and run against a triple store using PROV-O data. It's a standard well worth being familiar with if you need to store data on changes information held in your NoSQL database.

Chapter 20

Triple Stores in the Enterprise

● ●

In This Chapter

▶ Taking care of your data

▶ Managing facts about data alongside source data itself

● ●

*A*s with any other type of database system, there are best practices for organizing and setting up triple stores to ensure consistent and reliable service. There is a difference, though, between triple stores and graph stores. That is, two different architectural approaches are taken in the design of triple stores and graph stores. These two approaches are due to different types of queries — graph wide analysis functions and listing records (subjects), and their properties that match some criteria. These differences lead to tradeoffs related to ensuring data durability, supporting high availability of associated services, and providing for disaster recovery.

In this chapter, I discuss the issues around maintaining a consistent view of data across both triple stores and graph stores. I also talk about a common enterprise use case of using a triple store to store facts about and relationships between data that is managed in other systems.

Ensuring Data Integrity

Most enterprises expect a database to preserve their data and to protect it from corruption during normal operations. This can be achieved through server side features, or settings in a client driver. Whatever the approach, the ultimate aim is to store multiple copies of the latest data, ensuring that even if one copy is lost the data stays safe and accessible.

Enabling ACID compliance

Many of the triple and graph databases featured in this book are ACID-compliant. I talk about this in Chapter 2. As a reminder, ACID compliance means that a database must guarantee the following:

- ✔ **Atomicity:** Each change, or set of changes, happens as a single unit. In a transaction, either all the changes are applied or all are abandoned (that is, a *rollback* occurs in which the database is restored to its previous state).

- ✔ **Consistency:** The database moves from one consistent state to another. Once data is added, a following request will receive view of the data.

- ✔ **Isolation:** Each transaction is independent of other transactions running at the same time so that, ideally, each transaction can be played one after the other with the same results. This arrangement is called being *fully serializable*.

- ✔ **Durability:** Once data is confirmed as being saved, you're guaranteed it won't be lost.

These properties are important features for mission-critical systems where you need absolute guarantees for data safety and consistency. In some situations, relaxing these rules is absolutely fine. A good example is a tweet appearing for some people immediately, but for others with a few seconds delay.

For highly interconnected systems where data is dependent on other data, or where complex relationships are formed, ACID compliance is a necessity. This is because of the unpredictable interdependency of all the subjects held in a triple store.

Graph stores tend to guarantee ACID properties only on their primary master server. Because of the complex math involved, graph stores tend not to be *sharded* — that is, they don't have part of their data residing on different servers. I discuss sharding's advantages for other NoSQL databases in Chapter 15, but in the following I talk about sharding in terms of consistency and cross-record query throughput.

It's much quicker for the math involved to have all the data on one server. Practically, this means that you have two or more big servers, as described here:

- ✔ All clients talk only to the first server, which I'll call the *master*. Therefore, that database can easily provide ACID guarantees.

> ✔ For the server's replica(s) though, replication may ship data changes asynchronously, rather than within the same transaction boundary. This is normal on other NoSQL databases and relational databases, but usually only between two separate clusters in different data centers rather than two servers in the same cluster.

Graph stores ship changes asynchronously for the master and the replica(s) within the same data center. So, although graph stores like Neo4j and AllegroGraph are technically ACID-compliant, they don't guarantee the same-site consistency that other NoSQL databases covered in this book do. This is because of the two approaches to building a triple or graph store.

A better option is to select either a graph store or triple store approach, based on the query functionality you need.

✔ **Single server for a whole database:** High server costs. Other servers act as disaster recovery or delayed read replicas. You get very fast graph analysis algorithms, though.

✔ **Multiserver, sharded database:** Lower server costs. Other servers are masters for portions of the data, and highly available replicas for other servers in the cluster. This option produces slower, complex graph analysis functions, but you can still do fast SPARQL-style triple queries for individual records held just one a single server.

In an asynchronous, eventually consistent replica, it's possible that, after a failure, some of the saved data will not be available on the replica.

Sharding and replication for high availability

The simplest way to provide high availability is to replicate the data saved on one server to another server. Doing so within the transaction boundary means that, if the master dies on the next CPU cycle after saving data, the data is guaranteed to be available on its replica(s), too.

This is the approach ACID-compliant NoSQL databases generally take. Rather than have these replica servers sit idle, each one is also a master for different parts of the entire triple store.

So, if one server goes down, another server can take over the first server's shards (partitions), and the service can continue uninterrupted. This is called *a highly available* service and is the approach that MarkLogic Server and OrientDB take.

An alternative and easier implementation is to make each replica eventually consistent with respect to its view of the data from the master. If a master goes down, you may lose access to a small frame of data, but the service as a whole remains highly available.

If you can handle this level of inconsistency, then ArangoDB (from Franz, Inc.) may be a good open-source alternative to MarkLogic Server and OrientDB. ArangoDB is busy working on providing fully consistent replicas, but they're not quite there yet.

Replication for disaster recovery

The replication approach that graph stores provide in the same data center, and the replication approach three triple stores mentioned previously provide between data centers, is an eventually consistent full copy of data.

Secondary clusters of MarkLogic Server, OrientDB, and ArangoDB are eventually consistent with their primary clusters. This tradeoff is common across all types of databases that are distributed globally.

Primary clusters of Neo4j and AllegroGraph also employ this method between servers in the same site. Their master servers hold the entire database, and replica servers on the same site are updated with changes regularly, but asynchronously.

In addition to replicating the master to local replicas, consider replicating the data to a remote replica, too, in case the primary data center is taken offline by a network or power interruption.

Storing Documents with Triples

An emerging pattern is for document NoSQL databases to integrate triple store functionality. This makes sense. Document NoSQL databases typically provide

✔ The ability to store many elements/properties within a single document

✔ Concept of a collection for a group of documents

✔ Ability to create specialized indexes over structures within their content

✔ Ability to join different query terms together to satisfy a request to match a document

You can map these properties onto their equivalent triple store functionality. Specialized indexes are used to ensure that the triple store-specific query functionality is fast. These databases then simply adopt the open standards of RDF and SPARQL to act as a triple store to the outside world.

Also document NoSQL databases don't support relationships among documents. By applying triple store technology to these databases, you can represent a document as a subject, either explicitly or implicitly, and use triples to describe them, their metadata, relationships, and origin.

Some of these databases, such as OrientDB, are also capable of using triples to describe containment relationships within documents. As a result, you can request a merged document (say a book) that is created at query time from many related documents (chapters, images, and so on).

This functionality is provided in two ways, depending on the approach you take with the triple store:

- ✔ Use a document as a representation of a subject/vertex and a relationship/edge (ArangoDB).
- ✔ Use a document as a container for many triples (OrientDB, MarkLogic Server).

Neo4j and AllegroGraph don't provide this functionality, as it focuses solely on providing a graph store.

You can find more information on this hybrid approach, including additional functionality, in Part VII of this book.

Describing documents

Some of the databases mentioned in this part (Part V), such as OrientDB and ArangoDB, don't support storage of metadata about documents outside of the documents themselves.

By creating a subject type for a document, you can graft document metadata functionality into these databases. This subject type can hold the ID field of the document and have a predicate and object for every piece of metadata required.

You can construct this extra metadata automatically by using a custom API entry point in the database's own APIs, or perhaps by constructing specialized database triggers that execute when the document is saved and extracted. Alternatively, you can add this metadata accordingly with additional API calls from your application.

Combining queries

Once you start implementing this joined approach between the document and semantic worlds, you may get to a point where you need to perform a combined query.

With a *combined query,* you query both the document and the triple store in order to answer a question related to all the information in your database.

A combined query could be a document provenance query where you want to return all documents in a particular collection that have, for example, a "genre" field of a particular value and that also were added by a semantically described organization called "Big Data Recordings, Inc."

Another likely possibility is that the document you're storing is text that was semantically extracted and enriched. (Refer to Part IV for more on this process.) This means that the text in the document was analyzed, and from the text you extracted, for example, names of people, places, and organizations and how they relate to one another.

If this document changes, the semantic data will change also. In this case, you want to be able to replace the set of information extracted from the document and stored in the triple store. There are two mechanisms for doing so:

- ✔ **Use a named graph.** Use the document ID, or a variation of it, for the name of a graph and store all extracted triples in that graph, which makes it easy to update the extracted metadata as a whole. This process works for all triple stores.

    The advantage of a named graph is that it works across triple store implementations. The downside is that you have to manually create server-side code to execute one query against the triple store and another against the document store in order to resolve your complex document provenance query.

- ✔ **Store the triples in the document they were extracted from.** If your document structure supports embedding different namespaces of information, like MarkLogic Server, you can store an XML representation of the triples in an element inside the document.

    This approach offers the advantage of linking all the required indexes in the same document ID (MarkLogic Server calls this a URI). MarkLogic Server has a built-in search engine that includes support for full text, range (less than, greater than) queries, as well as semantic (SPARQL) queries.

This means you can construct a MarkLogic Server Search API query that, in a single hit of the indexes (called a *search index resolution*), can answer the entire query. This works regardless of the ontology or document search query needed. It's just a different type of index inside the same document.

The AllegroGraph graph store product takes a different approach to joining a document NoSQL database to a graph store. It provides an API to integrate to a MongoDB document store. This allows you to use SPARQL to find subjects that match a SPARQL query and that relate to documents that match a MongoDB query, which is achieved using standard SPARQL queries and AllegroGraph's own custom MongoDB-linked functions.

Chapter 21

Triple Store Use Cases

In This Chapter

▶ Handling unstructured information

▶ Reconstructing processes

▶ Applying inductive logic

▶ Establishing social relationships

● ●

Semantics, triples, and graphs offer a whole new world that's unfamiliar to many people with a database background. This makes it very exciting!

You first need to get hold of the data needed to build your graph, which you can find at from websites that publish Linked Open Data (LOD), or you can extract them from your own content. Two examples of LOD websites are dbpedia (`http://dbpedia.org`), which provides a semantically modeled extra of Wikipedia data, and geonames (`http://geonames.org`), which provides a catalogue of places, countries, and geospatial coordinates.

You may then need to track where you found this information, how you acquired it, and the changes made to the information over time. This *provenance* information can be key in legal and defense industries.

Perhaps you need to merge all the new triples you have added from your own organizations' data with reference information from other systems and sources. Several techniques are available that can help you accomplish this task. For example, you can add extra properties to a Place from imported Geonames data, or you can create your own subclass of Place, such as a Theme Park, and describe that location.

You then need to support providing answers to potentially difficult questions by using the information you store. Because the social graph is the most wide-ranging example of a complex graph model, in this chapter, I spend some time talking about the links between people and other subjects in a triple store, and the types of queries a triple store holding this type of data can address.

In this chapter, I also extract facts from existing data, use additional facts from third-party sources, and use semantic data to store an audit trail of changes to records over time.

Extracting Semantic Facts

Semantic facts are properly called *assertions*. For most use cases, using the term *facts* is an easier mental model to picture, so I use the term facts throughout. An assertion is a single triple of subject – predicate – and object. This could be "Adam is a Person" or "Adam is aged 33."

All database software can easily handle structured information like these facts. This data is effectively a list of fields and their values, as I discussed in Chapter 19. Unstructured text, though, is very difficult for computers, and indeed humans, to deal with.

Free text indexing and proximity searches can help you to some extent. For example, a proximity search displays documents in which matching terms occur, and you can infer a relationship between text within a document by using proximity-search limits such as NEAR queries (for example, "Adam NEAR/3 age" which means searching for where "Adam" is mentioned within three words of "Age"). To do anything useful, though, you need a more comprehensive approach.

In this section, I describe how to analyze the text in unstructured content in order to extract semantic facts, so you can provide a rich query using semantic technology over information extracted from text documents.

Extracting context with subjects

Natural Language Processing (NLP) is the process of looking at words, phrases, and sentences and identifying not only things (people, places, organizations, and so on) but also their relationships.

You can store this information as subjects, properties, and relationships — as you do in triple stores. Several pieces of software are available to help you do so. Here are the most popular ones:

- ✔ **OpenCalais:** An open-source semantic extraction tool
- ✔ **Smartlogic Semaphore Server:** A commercial entity extraction and enrichment tool that can also generate triples
- ✔ **TEMIS Luxid:** Another common commercial entity extraction and enrichment tool

All of these tools provide entity extraction (identify things) with entity enrichment (add extra information about those things). They also have the ability to generate an output report. This report can be in a list of semantic assertions (OpenCalais) in RDF or XML format. You can also place these facts in a separate RDF document, or you can tag text inline in the original document. All these tools generate XML and/or RDF output.

You can then store this output in a document database or a triple store, or you can utilize a hybrid of the two. Doing so facilitates an accurate semantic search. It also allows the information within unstructured text to be combined with other semantic facts ingested from elsewhere (for example, DBpedia, Wikipedia's RDF version; or GeoNames, a public geospatial database in RDF).

Forward inferencing

Inferencing is the ability to take a set of assertions and extrapolate them to other assertions. You can perform *backward inferencing* and forward *inferencing.*

Here's an example of backward inferencing: If Leo is the son of Adam, and Adam is the son of Cliff, then you can reason that Leo is the grandson of Cliff. You can "prove" a new fact by referencing others in the database. That is, in order to infer the new triple, you use information available earlier in the text.

Forward inferencing, on the other hand, is the process of inferring what may happen in the future (or be true in the future), when after analysing all existing information, all facts that can be inferred are inferred.

Forward inferencing is typically done at ingestion time, which does lead to slower performance, but it also means that you don't have to do this work at query time. In this respect, forward inferencing is similar in effect to the denormalization approach of other NoSQL databases.

Forward inferencing does allow you to build quite sophisticated webs of stored and inferred facts, which users can employ as helpful shortcuts. A good example is a product recommendations — for instance, "You may like product *x* because you liked product *y,* and others who liked product *y* also liked product *x.*"

If you don't create your inferencing rules carefully, you can end up in a situation where inferencing gets out of hand by creating billions of triples that may not, in fact, be accurate! This can lead to aborted triple ingestion, poor performance, or a significant waste of storage.

This proliferation can happen by the inferencing rules clashing. An example is if you infer that all objects with names are people, but in fact find that many cars and pets have names. You will have a lot of incorrect triples generated stating that all these cars and pets are people!

Tracking Provenance

Being able to prove that a decision was made or that a process was followed because of a certain set of facts is a difficult business. It generally takes weeks or months to trawl through content to discover who knew what and when and why things happened as they did.

However, triple stores store assertions so that they can be queried later. Graph stores go one step further by allowing you to take a subgraph and ask for other matching graphs that are stored.

One example of a provenance query is to find collusion in financial markets. If you see a pattern of traders at two investment banks communicating with each other prior to companies' marketplace events, then you may see a pattern of fraud.

These patterns can be modeled as graphs of interconnected people, organizations, activities, and other semantic relationships such as "Adam called Freddie the Fraudster."

Auditing data changes over time

The World Wide Web Consortium (W3C) has created a set of standards under the PROV Ontology (PROV-O) banner to track changes to data.

This ontology includes support for a variety of subject types, including people, organizations, computer programs, activities, and entities (typically content used as input or output).

For example, as a police force receives reports over time, an analysis can be updated. Each change is described, and the list of sources for the report increases to reflect the data the report is based on.

This information can, in turn, be used to create an action plan. A police risk assessment and threat analysis as well as an arrest plan can be based on this information prior to a raid.

By using the output of the police report analysis and a semantic query over provenance information, you can prove that the appropriate process was followed to support a raid on the premises of the "guilty" entity.

Building a Web of Facts

You can create a triple store that answers questions by using other peoples' data instead of just your own. The Resource Description Framework (RDF) standard was created to allow this web of interconnected data to be built. This approach is generally referred to as the *Semantic Web*.

There's also a growing movement of open-data publishing. This movement has led governments, public sector organizations, research institutions, and some commercial organizations to open up their information and license it to be reused.

Combining the concepts of open-data publishing and RDF and SPARQL allows you to create Linked Open Data (LOD), which is published data under an open license that refers to other sources of linked open data on other websites.

A news article from the BBC might mention a place that's linked to the GeoNames geographical RDF dataset. It could also mention a person with a profile on DBpedia — the RDF version of Wikipedia.

Over time, these links develop and are changed to produce a global Semantic Web of information. This is the culmination of Sir Tim Berners-Lee's vision for a web of interconnected data that can be navigated by computers, just as the World Wide Web is navigated by humans using web browsers.

Taking advantage of open data

You can find many great datasets, ranging from the U.S. Geological Survey (USGS) data about places within the United States to information about Medicare spending per patient, or even to names of newborns since 2007 in the United States.

Not all open data is published according to RDF specifications; therefore, it isn't ready to be stored immediately in a triple store. For example:

- ✔ Of the 108,606 datasets on the U.S. government's open-data website (https://www.data.gov), only 143 are available in RDF, whereas 13,087 are available in XML, 6,149 are available in JSON, and 6,606 are available in CSV.

- ✔ At http://data.gov.uk (the UK's equivalent to data.gov), of the 15,287 published datasets, 167 are available in RDF, 265 are available in XML, 3,186 are available in CSV, and 22 are available in JSON.

Many of these datasets are easy to convert to an RDF format, but the problem is you have to manually figure out how to do this conversion yourself, for every dataset encountered.

Currently, these publishing mechanisms are published only as static data files rather than as a SPARQL endpoint that can be queried and composed in other RDF data stores. You can search for a dataset, but not for the dataset itself. Hopefully, this will change in the future as open-data publishing develops.

Incorporating data from GeoNames

GeoNames is a database of geographic information that covers a vast range of information, including

- ✔ Continents, countries, counties, towns, and administrative boundaries
- ✔ Mountains, forests, and streams
- ✔ Parks
- ✔ Roads
- ✔ Farms
- ✔ Zip Codes
- ✔ Undersea locations

All this information is licensed under the Creative Commons Attribution version 3.0 license. This means you're free to use the information so long as you clearly state who created it.

All the information in GeoNames is linked to a longitude and latitude point on the Earth, allowing for geospatial search and indexing.

Consider a text document that mentions a town. You can link this document to the town within GeoNames, which enables you to search for all documents in a country even if that document doesn't explicitly contain the country's name!

Places in GeoNames are also linked to their DBpedia entries, if one exists. This is a practical example of Linked Open Data in action.

Incorporating data from DBpedia

DBpedia contains a semantic extraction of information available within Wikipedia. It's a crowd-sourced effort created by volunteers and made available under both the Creative Commons Attribution-ShareAlike 3.0 license and the Free Documentation License.

As of this writing, DBpedia provides data on 4.58 million entities, with 583 million facts in 125 languages! It's a huge resource, and it enables you to provide contextual information to help end users navigate through information.

This information is available for download in the N-Triples and N-Quad formats. A description of the DBpedia ontology is available in the Web Ontology Language (OWL) on its website (www.w3.org/2004/OWL).

Linked open-data publishing

Once you have your own data linked to other linked open-data sources, you may want to publish your own information. You can use a triple store to do so. If you have protected internal information, you may want to extract, or replicate, particular named graphs from your internal servers to a publically accessible server hosting "published" information.

You can use this publishing server to host flat file N-Triples for static downloads. You can also use it to provide a live SPARQL query endpoint to the web for others to interactively query and to download subsets of your data as they need it.

SPARQL, as a query language, allows you to join, at query time, remotely stored information from other SPARQL endpoints. This is a great way to perform ad hoc queries across multiple datasets. The following example is a SPARQL 1.1 Federated query to two different endpoints:

```
PREFIX foaf: <http://xmlns.com/foaf/0.1/>
SELECT ?person ?interest ?known
WHERE
{
  SERVICE <http://people.example.org/sparql> {
    ?person foaf:name ?name .
    OPTIONAL {
      ?person foaf:interest ?interest .
      SERVICE <http://people2.example.org/sparql> {
        ?person foaf:knows ?known . } }
  }
}
```

You can find the entire example at `www.w3.org/TR/sparql11-federated-query/#optionalTwoServices`. The SPARQL 1.1 Federated Query document is a product of the whole of the `W3C SPARQL Working Group`.

Migrating RDBMS data

When performing entity enrichment on NoSQL databases, it's common to pull reference information from relational database management systems.

Again, those clever people who contribute to W3C working groups have you covered, by way of a language called R2RML, which stands for RDB to RDF Mapping Language. This enables you to define transforms to convert a relational schema to a target RDF ontology. R2RML and related standards are available here: `www.w3.org/2001/sw/rdb2rdf`

In some situations, though, you want to quickly ingest information before performing data refactoring or inferencing. For example, you may want to store the original information so that you can assert PROV-O provenance information on the data before reworking it.

In this situation, you can use the Direct Mapping of relational data to RDF. You can find details on this standard here: `www.w3.org/TR/rdb-direct-mapping`

In the past, I've used direct mapping to perform a tongue-in-cheek demo to illustrate ingesting relational data into a triple store for inferencing and querying. You can find this video on YouTube at `https://www.youtube.com/watch?v=4cUqMzsu0F4`

Managing the Social Graph

Social relationships between people provide a classic example of how a relationship graph is used. It's been said that all people on the planet are separated by only six degrees — that is, we're all within six steps of knowing someone who knows someone, who knows someone . . .

Social graphs are important in several instances, including the following:

✔ **Social networks:** Include the likes of Facebook, Twitter, and LinkedIn.

✔ **Professional organizations:** To identify individuals or groups in large organizations with required expertise. Also can be used for organizational charts.

✔ **Organized crime detection:** Police and security organizations perform multi-year million-dollar investigations of organized crime networks with many points of contact and relationships.

✔ **Family tree:** Includes many parent, grandparent, uncle, and other relationships. Some assertions from such research may or may not be accurate. One source may list a George Fowler who may or may not be the same George Fowler in another source.

Managing this information has its challenges. Different approaches can be taken, depending on whether you're describing relationships between people or whether you're describing individuals and their activities.

Storing social information

You can find ontologies to model social data. One of the oldest, but still useful, models is Friend of a Friend (FOAF).

The FOAF RDF model gives individuals the ability to describe themselves, their interests, their contact details, as well as a list of people they know. This model includes Linked Open Data links to their contacts' FOAF descriptions, when it's known.

This data can be discovered and mined to produce spheres of influence around particular subject areas. The downside is that typically only Semantic Web computer scientists use FOAF to describe themselves on their websites!

When describing family trees, most people use the Genealogical Data Communication (GEDCOM) file format. This file format is designed specifically for this information rather than combining with other data. Using a common RDF-based expression would instead have allowed this data to be easily integrated into a triple store.

However, the Defense Advanced Research Projects Agency (DARPA) funded the DARPA Agent Markup Language (DAML) to model family relationships. Despite its spooky name, this project created an RDF expression of GEDCOM. You can find this standard documented at www.daml.org/2001/01/gedcom/gedcom.

Performing social graph queries

Triple and graph stores can be used to perform queries on a social graph in several ways. For example, to

✔ Suggest a product to users based on similar items purchased by other people.

✔ Suggest that users add new friends based on their being friends of your existing friends.

✔ Suggest groups that users can be a member of based on existing group memberships, friends with similar group memberships, or others with similar likes and dislikes who aren't in their network.

You can do the preceding by constructing SPARQL to enable users to do the following:

1. Find all customers who share the same or who have similar product purchases.

2. Order customers by descending value of the number of matches.

3. Find all products those people have ordered that the user hasn't.

4. Order the list of products by descending value according to the total number of orders for each item across all similar customers.

Here's an example of using SPARQL to find potential new friends in a social network (listing friends of my friends who are not me):

```
SELECT ?newfriend WHERE {
  ?me ex:username "adamfowler" .
  ?me ex:friend ?friend .
  ?friend ex:friend ?newfriend .
  FILTER NOT EXISTS (?me ex:friend ?newfriend) .
  FILTER NOT EXISTS (?me = ?newfriend ) .
} limit 10
```

Selecting friends based on second-level matches is pretty straightforward. To enable users to find the first ten people who are potential friends, you can use SPARQL as you did in the preceding example.

The preceding example shows traversal of a graph of relationships using SPARQL. Group membership suggestions use a similar query, except instead of traversing friends of friends, you traverse memberships of groups.

Chapter 22

Triple Store Products

* *

In This Chapter

▶ Documenting relationships

▶ Creating scripts

▶ Running fast graph traversal operations

* *

*W*ith two key approaches to managing semantic facts — triple stores with RDF and graph stores — you have a wide variety of functionality to consider. This abundance makes choosing which database to use difficult.

My advice is to follow the queries. Both graph and triple stores are capable in their data models of describing things — subjects or vertices — and their properties and relationships. So, the deciding factor isn't a list of features; it's what you want to do with the queries.

Perhaps you want to store a set of facts on related concepts, maybe to drive a product-suggestion engine, or to link disparate data sources or reports, or just to provide a very flexible data model for querying that, unlike other NoSQL databases, includes relationships. In this case, a triple store may well work for you.

In other situations, you may need a graph store. You may need to identify the similarities (or not) between different networks. Perhaps you're looking for parts of your data that match a known pattern of fraud. Maybe you're powering a navigation application and need the shortest path between two points.

Once you decide which route to take — triple store or graph store — you need to choose which product to use. Is the key difference its open source or commercial license? Maybe you also need to incorporate hybrid features such as a document NoSQL database. Or perhaps you need a rich and expressive graph query language.

But don't be overwhelmed. Use this chapter to get a flavor of which system is most likely to have the functionality you need. Given the variability in this section, I heartily recommend carefully reading your chosen vendor's website, too, in order to discover whether all the features you need are supported.

Managing Documents and Triples

Document NoSQL databases offer a rich way to store and manage variably structured data. Although document NoSQL databases enable grouping of data through collections or secondary indexes, what they don't provide is the concept of relationships between records held within them.

Document NoSQL databases also don't allow you to detail complex relationships about the entities mentioned within documents — for example, people, places, organizations, or anything about which you've found information.

ArangoDB, MarkLogic Server, and OrientDB all allow you to manage documents alongside triples in the same database. They are all examples of distributed triple stores — not graph stores. Their features vary significantly, though, in what you can do with documents and triples.

Storing documents and relationships

An obvious place to start in unpicking your requirements is by mapping the relationships between documents. This can be achieved through the following methods:

- ✔ **Provenance of data storage:** This includes changes applied over time and links to previous versions or source documents, perhaps by using the World Wide Web Consortium's (W3C) PROV Ontology (PROV-O).

- ✔ **Entity extraction:** This involves storing facts extracted from free text about things like people, places, and organizations, along with the fact that they're mentioned in particular documents.

- ✔ **Management of compound documents:** This includes complex documents that contain other documents that exist in their own right — for example, modular documentation that can be merged together in workbooks, online help, or textbooks.

Each of these situations requires management of data relationships between records (documents). Each one also requires linking the subject described to one or more source documents in your database. For example, a police report might mention a gang name and a meeting of three people on October 23. These facts can be extracted into person, organization, and event RDF types.

A separate document could contain the fact that this organization will be purchasing guns from a particular arms dealer. This linkage provides another person instance and another event (which may or may not be the same as the previously mentioned event).

These documents aren't directly related. Instead, they're related by way of the extracted entities mentioned in the text they contain. You need to maintain the links between the extracted subjects and the source documents, though, because you may need to prove where you found the facts for a later court case or investigation.

For instance, say that a police department creates a document requesting an operation to intercept expected criminal activity, and it bases that request on the preceding kind of research. In that case, the police need to store the provenance of their data. The resulting document may undergo multiple versions, but it's based on material in the police report's source documents.

Once the operation is completed, each officer needs to write a statement. A final file is created as evidence to submit to the prosecutor's office. This file comprises summary information, all source intelligence, and the officers' statements.

In checking evidence, the prosecutors need to know who changed what, when, and how; with what software, and why? What was the reasoning behind an arrest (was it the content of other documents, for example)?

Each individual document exists as a record in its own right, but the final submission exists only because these other documents are combined. This is an example of a *compound document pattern*. A prosecution file could contain an overview describing the contents of the file, multiple statements made by witnesses, transcripts of an interview of the accused, and photographs of a crime scene.

All three databases discussed in this book allow you to store triples that relate to documents. After all, all you need to do is create an RDF class to represent a document, with a property that links to the ID of the document you're making statements about. Use of these facts is left up to your application.

OrientDB also enables you to create triples that relate documents based on their data. Say that you have a JSON order document that has a list of order items. These order items could have a "product-id" field related to the "_id" field within a product document. You can configure OrientDB to automatically use this information to infer facts about their relationship. Even better, if you want to present a single order document containing all related data, you can request OrientDB to do so at document fetch time.

MarkLogic Server provides different document and triple functionality. You can embed semantic facts within XML documents themselves. These facts are still available in any standard semantic (SPARQL) query. Then, if the document is updated, the facts are updated. No need for a separate and RDF-only way to update facts. This approach is particularly useful when you're using an entity enrichment process with products like TEMIS, SmartLogic, and OpenCalais. You can take the output from these processes and store them as a document. Here your semantic work is done — all the facts and the original source text is indexed.

MarkLogic Server's internal XML representation of facts doesn't use RDF/XML. This means you must store these in-document facts as sem:triple XML elements. This implementation detail is hidden when you're using standard interfaces like the W3C Graph Store and SPARQL protocols.

ArangoDB allows you to store documents and triples. It uses a document to store triples, much like MarkLogic Server does. These are specific classes of documents in ArangoDB, though. ArangoDB doesn't support embedding triples within documents like MarkLogic Server or automatically inferring document relationships like OrientDB.

Combining documents in real time

OrientDB's capability to hold the relationships of documents to one another based on property values in their data is very useful. It allows you to update individual documents but request a full compound document as required.

OrientDB provides a lazy loading method for fetching these complex documents and populating Java objects with their data. This makes processing the main object fast while providing the entire graph of object relationships to the programmer.

OrientDB also allows the specification of a *fetch plan*. This allows you to customize how data is loaded when following these document relationships. If you know, for example, that a list of related content needs only the first ten linked documents, then you can specify that. You can also restrict the data returned to the field level for each object.

Combined search

MarkLogic Server is unique in this book in that it provides a very feature-rich search engine and triple store built in to the same database engine as a single product.

This enables you to do some interesting content searches in MarkLogic. Consider a situation like the preceding example where a document has triples embedded within it.

You can perform a query like "Find me all police reports that mention members of Dodgy Company, Inc., that contain the word 'fraud,' that were reported at locations in New England, and that were reported between March and July 2014." New England isn't a defined region, so it is provided as a geospatial polygon (an ordered list of points — like connect the dot drawings).

This search contains several types of queries:

- ✔ **Geospatial:** Denotes longitude and latitude places in the document within the specified polygon for New England.
- ✔ **Range:** A date range must be matched.
- ✔ **Word/Phrase:** The word "fraud" must be mentioned. This requires full text indexing and stemming support. (So "frauds" would also match.)
- ✔ **Collection:** I want only documents in the police reports collection.
- ✔ **Semantic:** You're looking for documents that mention people who are members of Dodgy Company, Inc.

MarkLogic uses term indexes to provide the types of queries listed above. Each individual query returns a set of document IDs. These are then intersected so that only documents that match all of the terms are returned.

I've assumed AND logic between terms, but there's nothing stopping you from defining very complex tree-like criteria, with queries within queries, as well as NOT and OR logic.

This checking of term lists is very quick because they're cached in memory and store a list of matching document IDs for each indexed value. Supporting a variety of composable index queries allows semantic (SPARQL) queries to also be combined with all the preceding query types.

Evaluating ArangoDB

ArangoDB is the most popular NoSQL database available that has an open-source license and that provides both document store and triple store capabilities. These two features aren't yet deeply linked, but they can be used together, if required.

ArangoDB claims to be an ACID-compliant database. This is true only for the master. ArangoDB writes to the master, but replicas receive changes on an asynchronous basis. As a result, client code gets an eventually consistent, non-ACID view of the database, unless it always accesses the master.

ArangoDB, like many NoSQL databases in this book, also supports sharding of the triple store. This allows very large databases to be split across (relatively!) cheap commodity servers.

Unlike other triple stores, ArangoDB does support graph query functions such as shortest path and distance calculation. Careful management of sharding is required to ensure efficient performance of distributed graph queries and to avoid many (relatively slow) network trips to other servers to complete a single graph query.

ArangoDB also supplies its own Annotation Query Language (AQL), eschewing support for RDF and W3C standards like SPARQL.

ArangoDB is an appropriate choice if you want a single eventually consistent database cluster that provides JSON document storage and triple store features in the same product, and if you need an open-source license.

Evaluating OrientDB

OrientDB is a very interesting NoSQL database. It's fully ACID-compliant and can run in fully serializable or read committed modes. It's high availability replicas are also updated with ACID consistency, ensuring that all data is saved and all replicas have the same current view of data.

Even more interestingly, OrientDB uses the open-source Hazelcast in-memory NoSQL database to provide high availability replication. I didn't include Hazelcast in this book because it's in-memory only — it doesn't store data to disk, and thus isn't fully durable. However, it's a very promising ACID-compliant NoSQL technology, as evidenced by its use in OrientDB.

OrientDB has an impressive array of features. JSON, binary, and RDF storage are all supported. It also allows (optionally) you to enforce schema constraints on documents within it.

OrientDB also has a range of connectors for both ingestion and query. Several Extract, Transform, and Load (ETL) connectors are available to import data from elsewhere (JDBC, row, and JSON). In addition, a Java Database Connectivity (JDBC) driver is available for querying; it allows OrientDB to be queried like any relational database or via the Java Persistence API (JPA) in the Java programming language.

You must manage sharding by manually configuring several partitions (called *clusters,* confusingly in OrientDB) and explicitly specifying which partition you want each record update saved to. This forces a manual check on the application developer to ensure consistent performance cluster-wide.

OrientDB has great support for compound JSON documents through its interleaved semantics and document capabilities.

A community license is available under Apache 2 terms, although most functionality is available only in the commercial edition. Favorable commercial licensing terms are also available for startups or small organizations.

OrientDB also doesn't support open standards integration such as RDF data import/export or SPARQL query language support. Instead, it provides its own customized HTTP and JSON-based API for these functions.

If you need a JSON database with triple support and compound documents, then OrientDB could well be the database for you.

Evaluating MarkLogic Server

MarkLogic Server is a long-established database vendor; it emerged in 2001 as a provider of an XML database with enterprise search technology built in. MarkLogic Server predates the modern usage of the term "NoSQL," although its architecture is definitely similar to that of newer NoSQL databases.

MarkLogic Server's triple store support is built upon a document NoSQL database foundation. Triples are stored as XML in documents. A special triple index (actually several indexes) ensures that queries across facts held in these documents, or embedded within XML documents, are available at speed in semantic (SPARQL) queries.

This functionality was introduced in version 7 in 2013 and is part of a multi-release cycle of improvements to semantics support in MarkLogic Server. Version 8 will include support for a wider range of SPARQL features, including SPARQL 1.1 update and SPARQL 1.1 aggregations (sum, count, and so on). Version 9 will complete the roadmap for delivering full semantics capability.

At the moment, MarkLogic Server's SPARQL 1.1 support isn't as extensive as some competitors' products, although many triple and graph stores haven't implemented SPARQL at all.

The commercial-only model will not appeal to some people who have their own dedicated development teams and prefer to learn and enhance open source software instead. There's a free, full-featured Enterprise Developer version, with a fixed time limit of six months, after which you must approach MarkLogic to purchase a license.

A change to the licensing terms in version 7 in late 2013 led to a new "Essential Enterprise" edition that's available for purchase at a much lower price point than previous versions. This entry level edition is limited to nine production server instances, but is otherwise fully featured, including support for security, high availability, disaster recovery, and backup/restore as standard.

Although MarkLogic Server provides both a document database and a triple store and compound search within documents across both content and semantic querying, integration of these two types of query is weaker than it is in OrientDB. There's no support for compound documents using the semantics capability, although by using XInclude, you have some support on the document database side.

If you need a secure Common Criteria-certified NoSQL database with document management, triple store, and advanced search capabilities, then MarkLogic Server is a good option.

Scripting Graphs

Storing and retrieving triples is great, but you can achieve more by applying open standards in new and interesting ways.

AllegroGraph from Franz is a triple store that supports open standards and allows you to use them to script the database. This provides for advanced triple and quad functionality across indexing, inferencing, defining reusable functions, and integrating with third-party products.

Automatic indexing

AllegroGraph stores seven indexes for every triple in the database. These indexes are composed of the subject, predicate, object, graph, and identifier — a unique ID for every triple stored. The seven indexes are

- ✔ **S P O G I:** Used when the subject is known to find a list of triples.

- ✔ **P O S G I:** Used to find unknown subjects that contain known predicates and objects.

- ✔ **O S P G I:** Used when only the object is known.

- ✔ **G S P O I, G P O S I, G O S P I:** Used when a subgraph is specified, one for each of the preceding three scenarios.

- ✔ **I:** A full index of all triples by identifier. Useful for fast multi-triple actions, such as deletions.

All triples in AllegroGraph have the these seven indexes, which helps to quicken both triple (fact returning) queries and subgraph queries that require graph traversal.

Using the SPIN API

The SPARQL Inferencing Notation (SPIN) API provides behavior for objects held within a triple store.

SPIN allows you to define a named piece of SPARQL that can be referenced as a function in future SPARQL queries. An example is a SPARQL CONSTRUCT query that returns an ?area bound variable to calculate the area of an instance of a rectangle subject.

You create a function by associating a class with a SPIN rule, which in turn is an RDF representation of a SPARQL query. The SPIN API was submitted by semantic web researchers from Rensselaer Polytechnic Institute in New York, TopQuadrant, and OpenLinkSW. Franz has implemented the SPIN API in its AllegroGraph triple store product.

SPIN is used in AllegroGraph to

- ✔ Encode SPARQL queries as RDF triples.
- ✔ Define rules and constraints.

✔ Define new SPARQL functions that can be used in filters or to return extra bound variables (called *magic properties* in AllegroGraph).

✔ Store SPARQL functions as templates.

These stored SPARQL queries have their own URI, which makes referencing them easy.

AllegroGraph uses SPIN to provide free text, temporal and geospatial search, and a Social Networking Analysis (SNA) library. You can use SNA to define reusable functions, thus easing the work for query developers.

JavaScript scripting

AllegroGraph also allows you to pass in Lisp (or LISP) and JavaScript functions via a HTTP service, which enables you to execute arbitrary server-side JavaScript code in the triple store.

The JavaScript API provided allows developers to add triples, query triples, execute SPARQL, and loop through result sets using a cursor mechanism. This allows you to step through results one page at a time.

Using this mechanism, you can even define a new HTTP endpoint service. You provide the API with the service name, HTTP method (GET, PUT, POST, DELETE), and a callback function. This function is executed each time a request is received. The same API is available to implement your service to do whatever functionality you require.

Triple-level security

AllegroGraph provides security at the triple level. As a result, administrators can set allow/deny rules for particular subjects, predicates, objects, or graph URIs for roles.

Multiple filters are composed together so that they always produce the same result regardless of the order in which they're defined. There are two types of filter:

✔ **Allow:** Only allows triples matching the pattern; removes all other triples.

✔ **Deny:** Allows triples, except the ones specified by the filter.

In complex situations where you want to deny a subgraph, you may want to apply filters to named graphs rather than to the triples.

Security filters apply only to remote HTTP clients. Local Lisp clients have full access to all triples in the database, regardless of what filters are in place.

Integrating with Solr and MongoDB

AllegroGraph provides its own free-text search API. If you need to go beyond this basic functionality, you can integrate the Solr search engine, too. Using Solr for free-text searches returns a set of matching AllegroGraph triples.

Solr provides support for multiple languages; has customizable tokenizers and stemmers to handle language rules; and allows ranking, word boosting, faceted search, text clustering, and hit highlighting.

Unlike the native free-text indexer, the Solr search indexes are updated asynchronously at some point after the triples are added to AllegroGraph. You must manage this indexing to ensure that you don't return out-of-date views of triples or miss triple results entirely.

You can also use AllegroGraph to store semantic triples that are linked to MongoDB documents. You create links to MongoDB documents by using triples of the following form:

```
ex:someSubject <http://www.franz.com/hasMongoId> 1234
```

A *magic predicate* is used to provide functions that allow querying of MongoDB data using SPARQL. This enables you to submit JSON property queries within a string to the mongo:find function. This JSON is used as a query by example. This means the JSON will restrict matches to just those documents with the exact same properties and values.

Here's an example SPARQL query:

```
prefix mongo: <http://franz.com/ns/allegrograph/4.7/mongo/>
prefix f: <http://www.franz.com/>
select ?good ?bad {
  ?good mongo:find '{ Alignment: "Good" }' .
  ?bad mongo:find '{ Alignment: Bad" }' .
  ?good f:likes ?bad .
}
```

In the preceding code, note that, rather than returning a document, the mongo:find function returns the list of subject URIs with associated documents that match the query. This functionality is particularly useful if you have extracted semantic data that you need to store in a triple store, but store complex data documents inside MongoDB.

Providing links means you avoid the classic "shredding a document in to many subjects and properties" problem common to trying to store a document within a triple store. (The shredding problem also applies to relational databases, as mentioned in Chapter 2 of this book.)

Evaluating AllegroGraph

AllegroGraph is a commercial graph store product that provides very rich functionality. Franz, the company behind AllegroGraph, follows the accepted and emerging standards while providing its own APIs where gaps exist. This provides customers with a best-of-both-worlds approach to open standards support. You can use the standards while Franz provides added SPARQL functions and other scripting mechanisms to allow you to go beyond out of the box functionality in your application.

AllegroGraph doesn't support sharding or highly available operations. If a server fails, you must manually switch the service to another server using network routing rules or similar techniques.

AllegroGraph is commercial software. A free version, limited to 5 million triples, is available. A developer version, limited to 50 million triples, is also available. The enterprise version has no limits.

AllegroGraph does support online backups with point-in-time recovery. It also provides a useful triple-level security implementation. Its extensive support for open standards such as SPARQL 1.0 and 1.1, the SPIN API, CLIF++ and RDFS++ reasoning, and stored procedures in Lisp with JavaScript scripting will make it popular to many developers.

Using a Distributed Graph Store

For some difficult network math problems, you want a dedicated graph-store approach. Although a graph store means holding all data on a single node, or a copy on every node in a highly available cluster, having all the data locally allows for fast graph traversal operations.

Neo4j provides support for nodes and relationships. Nodes can have one or more labels. Labels are similar to RDF types. Property indexes can be added for specific labels. Any node with a given label will have that labels defined properties indexed.

Adding metadata to relationships

Unlike the RDF data model and SPARQL query standard, Neo4j enables you to add properties to relationships, rather than just nodes. This is especially important when you need to hold information about the relationship itself. A good example is in-car route planning where you store each town as a node. The towns nearest it are stored as nodes, too, with a "next to" relationship between them. The distance between each town is stored as a property of the relationship.

If you model car route planning in an RDF triple store, you can store the "journey segment" between towns as a node (subject), with a normal subject property of distance. Each town can have a "touches journey" relationship to the journey segment. In this way, the queries are more verbose, and although they involve more node traversals, the use case can be solved using the RDF data and SPARQL query models.

Optimizing for query speed

Although you can perform property queries in Neo4j without adding dedicated property indexes, significantly higher query speed is possible by adding indexes.

Indexes can be configured for any property. These are scoped by the label and property name. If a property is used for lookup by a number of different node labels, you need to configure multiple indexes.

Indexes can enforce uniqueness constraints, which allows for a useful guarantee when you need to generate, store, and enforce unique ID properties.

You need to index only the properties you use in queries. If you don't use properties in queries, then adding indexes for these properties won't help your query performance; they'll just take up disk space.

Using custom graph languages

Neo4j provides a rich custom query language called *Cypher* that enables you to configure complex graph queries, including properties and labels attached to nodes and relationships.

If you're experienced with the Structured Query Language (SQL) of Relational Database Management Systems (RDBMS), the Cypher query language will be familiar. An example of a cypher query is shown in Listing 22-1, in which all actors who performed in any movie with the title *Top Gun* are found.

Listing 22-1   Example Cypher Query

```
MATCH (a:Movie { title: 'Top Gun' })
OPTIONAL MATCH (a)-;[r:ACTS_IN]-()
RETURN r
```

This query shows an optional match query. The query returns the *Top Gun* movie node and all actors in the movie.

Cypher enables very sophisticated programming, including the programming of each loop, create, merge, and delete operation.

Neo4j has an interesting web page on modeling (shredding) different data structures in a graph store. You can find it here: `http://neo4j.com/docs/2.1.5/tutorial-comparing-models.html`

Evaluating Neo4j

Neo4j is the leading open-source graph store. It provides ACID-compliant transactions on the primary master node. Writes can be arranged at any node in a highly available cluster, with a two-phase commit ensuring that the master always has the latest copy of the data in the cluster.

The default isolation level is read committed. This means that long-running transactions will see information committed in other transactions that occur within the same time period as the long-running transaction. For a long-running transaction that performs the same query twice — once at the start of a transaction and once at the end — both queries in the same transaction could see different views of the data for the same query.

Not all replicas are kept in sync with the master in all situations, though. Replica updates provide "optimistic transactional consistency." That is, if the replica can't be updated, the transaction still commits on the master. The replica will be updated later on. Thus replicas are eventually consistent.

Neo4j provides a range of graph operations including shortest path, Dijkstra, and A* algorithms. Neo4j also provides a graph traversal API for managing sophisticated graph operations.

Many of the enterprise features are available only in the paid-for Neo4j Enterprise Edition from Neo Technology, Inc. The enterprise edition is also provided under the AGPL license. However, this license requires you to either pay for the enterprise edition or license your Neo4j-based application `built on it` under an open-source license.

Neo4j does have a startup license that is discounted, too. A community edition is freely available for commercial applications, but it's severely limited. No support is provided in the community edition for backups, highly available clustering, or systems management.

It's also worth noting that because Neo4j is designed for heavy graph traversal problems, all the data of the graph must be storable in each and every node in the cluster. This means you must invest in significant hardware for large graphs. Neo4j's documentation recommends good-quality, fast SSDs for production.

Neo4j 2.1 included a fix, available only in the enterprise edition, for good performance on systems with six or more processor cores. Any server you buy now will have more than six cores, so this is worth noting. It's also worth doing significant performance testing at a realistic scale before going in to production with your application.

Neo4j doesn't support the open standards of RDF or SPARQL, because it is designed for graph problems rather than triple storage and querying, although it can also be used for those tasks, too.

If you have a sophisticated set of hard graph traversal problems or need to embed a graph store in a Java-based application, then Neo4j may well be a very good choice, given its concentration on solving hard graph problems.

Chapter 23

Neo4j and Neo Technologies

In This Chapter

▶ Capitalizing on Neo4j

▶ Getting support for Neo4j

Neo4j is the most popular open-source graph store available today. Neo4j allows the storage of nodes and relationships and uses properties to annotate these types of objects. A typing system is provided by tagging nodes with labels.

Sophisticated queries are supported with the feature-rich Cypher Query Language. The syntax of Cypher is easy to pick up if you're familiar with the Structured Query Language (SQL) of relational database management systems. Also, using the correct color coding in a Cypher syntax-highlighting text editor makes the queries rather pretty in their own right! Lots of nice brackets, parentheses, and arrows.

Neo4j's commercial offering — Neo4j Enterprise from Neo Technologies — provides functionality for mission-critical applications, including high availability, full and incremental backups, and systems monitoring. Neo4j specializes in providing an embeddable and feature-rich graph store designed for the most complex graph problems and for storing billions of nodes and relationships.

In this chapter, I discuss the open source software, its commercial counterpart, and the company with the same name that provides support for both.

Exploiting Neo4j

Neo4j goes beyond the simpler triple store data and query model to provide support for advanced path-oriented algorithms. A path is any route between nodes or a set of traversals that match a particular query.

In this section, I talk about Neo4j's key benefits and why you may wish to adopt it for your graph store needs.

Advanced path-finding algorithms

Queries can be performed that return a set of paths. These paths can be traversed by specialist algorithms in order to answer complex graph questions.

A common use for a graph store is to find the shortest path between two nodes, for example:

- ✔ For route planning applications for car navigation systems
- ✔ For social distance or influence calculations weighted by interactions between people on the network
- ✔ For determining the most efficient path to route traffic through a data network

The algorithm that's most often used for this analysis is Dijkstra's algorithm, named after Edsger Dijkstra. The Dijkstra algorithm works by analyzing each individual link from the source to the destination, remembering the shortest route found and discarding longer paths, until the shortest possible route is found.

At a high-level, the algorithm works by traversing the graph starting with all nodes related to node A, each with a particular starting distance. The distance from this node to its relations is added to the initial distance. As the links to non-visited nodes expands, nodes with too great a distance are eliminated until eventually the shortest path is discovered.

The complexity of this graph traversal can sometimes be simplified by applying known tests during traversal. Perhaps it's possible to determine the estimated cost before traversing a whole graph — for example, assuming that highways are quicker than minor roads for long journeys. This combination of assumptions to choose the next path to analyze is formalized in the A* algorithm.

Specifically, the A* algorithm used weighted comparisons based on some property of each connection in the graph.

Both the A* algorithm and Dijkstra's algorithm are supported by Neo4j. Neo4j also allows you to plug in your own traversal algorithms using its Traversal Framework Java API.

Scaling up versus scaling out

It's hard to perform well on a distributed cluster when you're traversing a large number of paths between nodes, rather than pulling back properties on nodes with a limited number of relations in a query. This is why Neo4j stores all data on a single server. Setting up replicas is possible, but each replica contains a full copy of the data, rather than subsets of the data of the whole graph. This approach differs from triple stores, which share the data between each server in a cluster, using a sharding approach instead.

Although using a single node for all data provides good query speed for complex graph operations, this does come at a cost — because for very large graphs, you may need to use high-specification server hardware instead of multiple small and inexpensive commodity servers.

The Neo4j documentation recommends, for instance, that each server use fast Solid State Disks (SSDs) as the primary storage mechanism. Given that SSDs provide less capacity than traditional magnetic spinning disks, you will need more space in your server for SSDs. You'll also probably want to create a virtual disk array (a RAID array) so that you can spread the write load across all disks.

The I/O subsystem of the servers must also be capable of fully utilizing the number of SSDs attached to it. This typically requires a dedicated I/O controller card in the server.

Requiring high-specification hardware in order to provide greater data storage and query speed is an example of *vertical scaling*. You basically buy an ever-bigger (taller) server to handle more load.

Buying double the specification of a machine may cost three times as much, whereas buying two servers of the same specification costs only twice as much. For this reason, vertical scaling is more costly than the horizontal scaling of other NoSQL databases.

If you absolutely need high-performance graph operations and are happy to pay for the privilege, then the tradeoff between cost and speed may be worth it.

Complying with open standards

The dominant standards in the triple store and linked (open) data world are

- Resource Description Framework (RDF) for the data model
- Web Ontology Language (OWL) for defining an ontology
- SPARQL Protocol and RDF Query Language (SPARQL) for query

Neo4j doesn't, out of the box, support any of these standards; however, you can find a variety of third-party plug-ins and approaches that enable you to use Neo4j as a standards-compliant triple store.

These plug-ins may not directly map RDF concepts onto those in Neo4j, so be sure to read about each one in depth before adopting it. Because the plug-ins aren't officially supported by Neo4j, they aren't full-featured, nor do they perform as well as the open standards-based support that's built into other triple stores. You need to test these plugins before implementing them. They are useful as an add-on to an existing Neo4j graph store, though.

Using Neo4j for Linked Data applications is documented on the Neo4j documentation website at `www.neo4j.org/develop/linked_data`.

Finding Support for Neo4j

Neo Technologies is the primary commercial company behind the development of Neo4j. As well as offering services and support, it offers an Enterprise Edition.

The Enterprise Edition of Neo4j provides the following enhanced features:

- ✔ Certification on Windows and Linux
- ✔ Emergency patches
- ✔ Enterprise lock manager to prevent deadlocks
- ✔ High-performance cache for heap sizes greater than 8GB
- ✔ Highly available clustering
- ✔ Hot backups, both full and incremental
- ✔ Advanced system monitoring
- ✔ Commercial email and 24/7 phone support
- ✔ Ability to embed the Enterprise Edition in commercial, closed source, applications

If you're using Neo4j for production in mission-critical systems, these features are probably vital, so evaluating the Enterprise Edition is worth the effort.

Clustering

Neo4j's Enterprise Edition provides support for highly available clustering. A Neo4j master server manages the primary data store for all write operations.

You can add other servers to the cluster to provide for failover in case the master fails and to spread out the query load. These replicas are updated during a write transaction using an optimistic commit. An optimistic commit is one where you assume that the write operation has succeeded without specifically checking for it. This usually happens on secondary replicas.

If one of the replicas is unavailable, it will be updated at a later date. Therefore, Neo4j doesn't guarantee ACID consistency across an entire cluster. The inconsistency may last for a very short window of time, but timing is important in situations where the master fails before a replica is updated.

High-performance caching

When operating as a cluster, a client API operation can land on any Neo4j instance, which is okay in many cases. If you receive many queries for the same data, you want to cache them in memory — doing so is faster than always fetching data from disk.

Neo4j provides two types of cache:

- **File buffer cache:** Caches the data on disk in the same, efficiently compressed format.

- This also acts as a write-through cache when you're entering new data into Neo4j and journaling it to disk.

- **Object cache:** Stores nodes, relationships and their properties in a format for efficient in-memory graph traversal.

- This supports multiple techniques, defaulting to the high-performance cache (hpc).

By providing these caches, Neo4j helps to increase the speed of both high ingest rates and common read queries.

Cache-based sharding

If your dataset is very large, you need to carefully manage what data is loaded into Neo4j's memory to be sure you're not constantly adding and removing data from the caches.

A good way of doing so is to send particular API calls to the same server. You may, for instance, know that user A performs a lot of operations on the same set of nodes. By always directing this user to the same server, you ensure that the user's data is on only a single server's cache. This approach in Neo4j is called *cache-based sharding*. Remember, it's the cache that is sharded, not the Neo4j database itself.

Finding local support

Neo Technologies has offices in the United States, Europe, and the Far East. In the United States it's based in San Mateo, California. The company has European offices in Malmö in Sweden; in London in the UK; in Munich and Dresden in Germany; and in France. It also has an office in Malaysia.

Neo Technologies provides 24/7 premium support for enterprise customers. Services are also available for education and for help in the design, implementation, rollout, and production phases of a deployment project.

Finding skills

As I indicated earlier, Neo4j is the dominant graph store in the NoSQL database world. It's used extensively in both the open-source community edition as well as in production in large enterprises.

Many computer scientists with an interest in graph theory are familiar with Neo4j, both in theory and practice. Therefore, you can find a broad range of developers.

For existing organizations, the requirement to learn Cypher will be a barrier, although its similarity to the SQL of relational databases will help with this requirement. Third-party extensions are available to link Neo4j with more common open standards such as RDF, SPARQL, and OWL.

Part VI
Search Engines

 Visit www.dummies.com/extras/nosql for great Dummies content online.

In this part . . .

- ✔ Organizing data stores.
- ✔ Building user interfaces.
- ✔ Delivering to external customers.
- ✔ Examining search engine products.
- ✔ Visit www.dummies.com/extras/nosql for great Dummies content online.

Chapter 24

Common Features of Search Engines

*T*he most visible part of a search engine is the search box. Google popularized the simple text box as the standard for allowing people to search vast arrays of digital content.

Words are imprecise, though. Do you mean John Smith the person or John Smith the beer? Do you mean guinea pig sex or determining the gender of a guinea pig? A mistake can cost time, but it can also bring a nasty surprise!

Really understanding how a search engine works allows you to create a shopping list of functionality that you actually need, rather than just conduct a "beauty pageant" of the search engines with the most features.

You probably need to fully implement only a few features rather than implement basic support for many features, and identifying the right features can save a lot of time.

In this chapter, I discuss all the features you'll commonly find in search engines, and how they can be applied for fun and profit.

Dissecting a Search Engine

Although the most visible part of a search engine is the little text box on a web page, there are many behind-the-scene features that make the text box work.

In this section, I discuss how a search engine goes beyond the normal database concept of querying, and why you should consider search when selecting a NoSQL database.

Search versus query

A search is different from a query. A *query* retrieves information, based on whether it exactly matches the query. Querying for orders that include a specific item or for items in a specific price range are good examples.

A *search*, on the other hand, is inexact and doesn't require strict adherence to a common data model. Terms may be required or optional, with potentially complex Boolean logic. A relevancy score is typically calculated rather than simply stating "match" or "not a match" in a query. These relevancy calculations are tunable and greatly improve a typical user's search experience.

Search engines also provide hints for narrowing searches. In addition to providing a page of results and relevancy scores for each result, you may also be presented with information about the whole result set, which are called *facets*. Facets allow, for example, narrowing a product search by a product category, by price range, or by the date that the product was added.

Facets enhance the users' experiences by allowing them to discover ways to improve their original search criteria without prior knowledge of data structures.

Web crawlers

Web crawlers are automated programs that check for updates to known websites and follow links to new websites and pages, indexing all content they find on the way. They may also take a copy of the state of a web page at the time of indexing.

When you're trying out search, the first order of business is finding some content! That content can be highly structured relational database records, such as the content on e-commerce websites. Or it may be entirely free text, or something in between, such as a Microsoft Word document or a web page with some structure.

You begin by crawling the authoritative source system(s). Some databases have built-in indexing that allows real-time indexing. The vast majority of search engines, though, index remote content and update their indexes periodically. These indexes out of date, but a lot of content stays the same, so you don't need to find it within minutes after it's published.

Web search engines start with a list of URLs (Uniform Resource Locators). When crawling these URLs, they read the text on the web pages and index it; they also add newly discovered links to the queue of indexed pages. This single type of crawler can discover all linked web pages on the web.

Your organization may need to crawl a variety of systems. If so, note that many search engines, such as IBM OmniFind, HP Autonomy, and Microsoft FAST, have connectors to a variety of different sources.

These crawlers are typically provided by stand-alone search engines. Some search engines are embedded within databases, like MarkLogic's NoSQL document database. These embedded search engines index their own content, so they don't include crawlers for other systems, which means that you must move or copy content into the NoSQL database in order to have it indexed.

Although this requires more storage, the advantage of a real-time index for content stored in a NoSQL database may outweigh the disadvantages of a separate search engine. The primary disadvantage of a separate search engine is that crawling occurs on a periodic schedule, leading to inconsistent data results and false positives — where the document no longer exists or doesn't match the search query.

Indexing

After you find content, you need to decide what you want to index. You can simply store the document title, the link, and the date the content was last updated. Alternatively, you can extract the text from the content so you can list the words mentioned in the document.

You can go further and store a copy of the page as it was when indexed. This is a particularly popular feature in Google search results — especially if a page was recently deleted by its author, and you still want to access the page as it was when indexed.

A standard index stores a document ID followed by a list of the words mentioned within it. When you're performing a query, though, this approach isn't particularly useful. It's much better to store document IDs as a list under each unique word mentioned. Doing so enables a search engine to quickly determine the set of documents that match a query.

This is called an *inverted index* and is the key to having good search performance. The more content you index, the more important it is that inverted indexes are stored so that query times are fast. Be sure to ask your vendor about its product's index structure and about the scale at which it performs well.

Of course, you may want to index more than words. You can index date fields (updated, created, indexed at), numbers (page count, version), phrases, or even things like geospatial coordinates of places mentioned in content. These are collectively called *terms*, and their lists of matching documents are called *term lists*.

If a query you want to perform requires that all words, dates, and numeric terms match, the search engine will perform an intersection of the matching term lists, which means that the search engine returns results only on documents that include all three *term lists*. This is known as AND Boolean logic.

More useful perhaps is OR Boolean logic, which means that documents with more of the matching terms are given a higher relevancy score. The calculation of relevancy varies depending on the given situation.

For example, you may think results on recent news are more relevant than older news stories. In addition to this, you may also want to attach more relevancy to those in which the terms you entered are matched more frequently in the same document. The problem here, though, is that a document of 20 words (say a tweet) that mentions your word once may be more relevant than a 20-page document that also mentions the same word once. One word in 20 is a high frequency within the document.

A common way to offset relevancy problems is to calculate TF-IDF (Term Frequency-Inverse Document Frequency):

- *Term frequency* is how often a term appears in a given document.
- *Inverse document frequency* is the total number of documents divided by the number of documents mentioning that term.

There are various ways to calculate term frequency and inverse document frequency. I mention it to make the point that indexing and relevancy scoring are useful features, and ones that simple query in most databases cannot handle on their own.

Searching

Once you have all the lovely indexes, you need a way to query them that doesn't baffle your application's users. Google is so popular because a simple text box can be used for both simple word searches and for searches for very complex criteria, such as restricting the country of matched web pages, or the age of web pages returned.

Using a search grammar

The key to making searching easy is to use an easy-to-understand text format, which relates to what's called a *search grammar*. Most search engines provide a free-text Google-like grammar.

Here you see an example of a search grammar in use:

```
"grazing land" AND rent site:uk -arable -scotland 2013..2014
```

This example of Google search text includes several terms:

- ✔ **Phrase:** A phrase of words that must be next to each other, like `"grazing land"`.
- ✔ **Boolean AND:** `AND` joins the phrase and following word search and requires that both match.
- ✔ **Word:** Typically, the word includes stems, so in this case, `rent` also includes renting, rents, and rented.
- ✔ **Domain:** Here, the domain is the UK website domain name (`site:uk`).
- ✔ **Negation:** Here, pages with the words `arable` (for crop land) and `scotland` are excluded.
- ✔ **Range:** Here the date ranges for the years `2013` to `2014` are included.

This type of grammar is very easy to grasp and remember for future searches. These rules combined with parentheses enable you to perform very sophisticated searches.

Specialist publishers often provide enhanced search services that enable users to query across hundreds of terms in a single search. This capability is especially useful for niche datasets, such as financial services news reports and filings data.

Many search engines provide a default grammar, with some allowing you to customize the grammars and how they're parsed, which is a plus if you're considering moving from one search engine to another one that's more scalable, but in doing so, you don't want to burden the users of your application with having to learn how to use a new search grammar.

Pagination

The earlier Google search query yields over 54,000 results. There's no point in showing a user such a big list! Sorting by relevancy and showing the ten most-relevant matches is generally enough. All search engines provide this capability.

You may want the user interface you create to provide quick "skip" navigation to next and previous pages, and perhaps to the first page.

Sorting

Sorting by relevancy is often the best bet, but in some circumstances, a user may want to override the order of results. This is most common in publishing scenarios where a user orders by "most recent" first or on an e-commerce website where the user chooses to show the least expensive product first.

Most search engine interfaces provide a drop-down menu that has helpful options for sorting.

Faceting

A *facet* is an aspect of the search results that users may decide to use to further narrow their searches. Facets provide user-friendly ways of traversing search results to find exactly what's needed. A facet has a name and shows many values, each with the number of records returned that match the value (for example, searching for Harry Potter on Amazon shows a product type facet with values book (55) and DVD (8)).

Advanced faceting can include hierarchical facet values, calculated buckets such as "Jun 2013" and "Jul 2013" (rather than individual dates) and even heat map regions for display as an overlay on a web map.

Snippeting

For text queries, you may often want to show one or more sections of text that match the given text terms, rather than simply state that a large document matches the query. This process is called *snippeting*.

It's quite common for search engines to include three snippets per result, although you can configure this along with the number of characters or words to return in each snippet.

On Google, these snippets are shown with the continuation characters (. . .) separating them. Matching words are shown in bold within the snippets.

Using dictionaries and thesauri

As an extension to word stemming, you may want to support dictionaries and thesauri. These are particularly useful for finding synonyms.

Law enforcement agencies, in particular, are awash with synonyms. Drug dealers may call narcotics "products," with each product referred to by a slang term as well as by its chemical or scientific name. Using a third-party thesaurus (for example, in OpenOffice format) or your own internally managed one can add breadth to a search term.

Indexing Data Stores

Corporate systems house a large amount of valuable organizational data. These systems vary from department to department and between different classes of business.

If you need to keep such systems in place but provide a single search capability over all of them, you need a search engine that can connect to these corporate systems.

Alternatively, you can consolidate a variety of IT applications on a common data platform. This platform may have search capabilities built into the database. Doing so enables you to instantly update indexes, which results in proactive alerts as new content arrives.

Using common connectors

You may want to index a variety of enterprise systems, with each containing useful information for your organization's staff.

These systems include

- **Relational databases:** Used for indexing products sold on a website.
- **Network file shares:** Shared network drives, covering commonly formatted file documents such as Microsoft Word and Excel. These store content very similar to that found on any office computer.
- **Microsoft SharePoint:** This and other enterprise content management (ECM) systems like IBM FileNet and EMC Documentum control access to managed and versioned documents.

- ✔ **Email:** For email discovery and records management, storing and searching the text of emails and their attachments, as well as social relationships is useful (who emails whom, and how often).

- ✔ **Forms and images:** Paper forms sent in by customers are scanned as images; then, using optical character recognition (OCR) technology, words are extracted from the pages.

- ✔ **Metadata:** Data about data. Usually properties of a document or file. Includes date created, by whom, when last accessed or updated, title, keywords, and so on. May also include information extracted from the file itself, like the camera used to take a photo.

If you need to index these external content sources, then a stand-alone search engine may be useful.

Periodic indexing

These connectors are typically pull-based. That is, they run on a timed interval for each data source. Therefore, they're always outdated. This isn't an issue for a lot of content, such as products that are rarely updated, other than regarding their availability. For organization's internal processes data, though, and certainly for financial services or feeds of live defense data, outdated content can lead to financial losses or, in the latter case, the risk of harm to personnel.

In such situations, you may want to push data onto a common data platform. A NoSQL database is ideal for this purpose, especially where a great variety of data is being stored.

If a NoSQL database has a built-in search engine, you can update its indexes at the same time the data is updated.

Many NoSQL databases embed a third-party search engine like Solr but don't provide live updated indexes. If you need an absolutely live set of indexes, you need a NoSQL database that has a built-in search engine.

Alerting

One advantage of live indexes is that they bring alerting within reach. *Alerting* is where a query is saved, and a user receives an alert box when new documents arrive that match the saved query.

This is particularly useful in the following situations:

- ✔ A user completes a manual search and wants to be notified when new matching content arrives.

- ✔ It's particularly useful for human expert information analysis use cases, be it commercial or otherwise. Or imagine that a business deal is on hold waiting for the arrival of certain matching content that will allow the process to continue (for example, proof of address documentation for a new client).

- ✔ Content needs to be processed if it matches a query. This is common in entity extraction and enrichment.

- ✔ A good example is matching an address in order to embed geospatial coordinates within a record. This enables geospatial search, rather than just text search.

In most search engines, only a subset of the search features are available when you're saving searches for alerts. Be sure that your search engine supports all the common query types that you want your users to be able to use for alerting.

Using reverse queries

A *reverse query* is where you say, "Give me all saved searches that match this document" rather than "Give me all documents that match this search." Search engines that support thousands rather than only a handful of search alerts incorporate a special reverse query index to ensure scalability. A reverse index is where a search is saved as a document and its search plan is indexed. This approach results in fast candidate matching when a new record arrives in the system.

Matchmaking queries

You can also combine reverse queries with normal forward queries. Doing so is useful where a record contains search criteria as well as data. This behavior is customary in matchmaking queries.

Here are some examples of matchmaking queries:

- ✔ People searching for jobs have criteria for the jobs they're seeking; equally, employers have criteria for the positions being sought.

- ✔ A dating website comprises information about individuals as well as the criteria those individuals have in making a match.

These queries can't be satisfied by manual queries or alerts alone; rather, they require a combination of forward and reverse query matching.

Here's an example of how a search engine might process this kind of matching:

1. Notice of a new job is added to a website.

2. An alert is sent to a user because the notice matches her job-search criteria.

3. Before sending the alert, the alert-processing code checks to make sure that the person matches the criteria of the employer, too.

4. If there is a match, an alert is sent to the user.

   A separate alert process may also send information about relevant new job seekers to the employer.

Matchmaking queries can be done with overnight batch processing, but this results in long lead-times on matches, which isn't desirable in some cases (such as short-lived auction listings on the web).

Chapter 25

Search Engines in the Enterprise

In This Chapter

▶ Finding unstructured data

▶ Providing a user-friendly search experience

*P*roviding search engine functionality for your local computer files is easy, and the same is true for adding basic text search to a web shop front end.

Where things start to get really complex is when you try and provide a single search application over multiple sources of information. Not only are the data formats different but also the individual systems are different.

Some data must have text snippets in search results; others need image previews. Each data source displays its own set of facets about its data. Some of these facets (or search fields) may be similar across different systems. The security access rules are also different within each system, requiring a central concept of identity and permissions to map effectively in a search application.

This is why *enterprise search* — that is, searching across a large enterprise's information stores — is a difficult problem to solve. However, you can mitigate this complexity in a number of ways.

In this chapter I discuss the unique issues of applying search across a large Enterprise, and making such a complex system accessible to end users.

Searching the Enterprise

Web search engines have long had to index web pages, images, PDF files, word documents, and other formats. As a result, the main issue in enterprise search solutions stems from the differences between source systems' architectures (the systems where the content resides) and the variety of available data. For example, there is a great variance in the functionality needed to easily collate different data from a range of sources and in how to provide a consistent way to manage the indexes of that data.

In this section, I talk about the variety of systems that typically contain useful data that needs searching, and how to recognize challenges that arise because of the differences in implementation between these systems.

Connecting to systems

As I discuss in detail in Chapter 24, many *enterprise search* engines provide out-of-the-box connectors for source systems; IBM OmniFind, HP Autonomy, and Microsoft FAST all have connectors for common systems and databases.

These connectors provide an easy way to pull data from many sources into a single repository — there's no need to code your own integrations. The downside is that these connectors invariably are run on a timed basis; they don't show the exact live state of all your enterprise's data, which is very similar to how web search engines work.

In some cases, you may be better off consolidating all your unstructured data in a common database platform. NoSQL document databases are ideal for this situation, because they provide a schema-free way to store data sourced from a variety of systems.

This data consolidation also means you reduce costs by replacing multiple data sources used to power your custom applications with a single *enterprise data platform*. Another side benefit is that you're not duplicating the storage of data, unlike traditional search engines where the primary data store's own indexes are separate from the search engines.

Finally, because a database with search capabilities knows when new data arrives, there's the possibility of real time, or at least improved latency, between the data and the search indexes.

Ensuring data security

An often overlooked problem is that of mapping different stores' security models onto a common model used to lock down information in the search application.

A relational database has a very different security model from an enterprise content management system, which in turn differs from a network file share.

Being able to reconcile roles and users in one system with roles and users in other systems is vital to ensuring the security of data. If this is not done correctly, then the best case scenario is that only the existence of a document (for example, its title or source system ID) is revealed in the search results. This is called a *false positive* because, when users try to access the source document, they're told they don't have permission to do so. For high-security systems, you don't even want users to know the document exists!

Now for the worst case scenario. If someone uses "the right" search words in a query, entire paragraphs of the should-be secured document are revealed in the snippets of the search results! A "snippet" showing text that matches a query may contain 30 words. A user could keep typing the last three words in each snippet to reveal the next 30 words — until the whole document is read!

In an *enterprise search* application, it's vital that a standard security model and auditing checks be created and enforced in order to prevent data leakage. To a certain extent, a consolidated single database is easier to secure (if security of records is provided by the database itself) than multiple systems linked to a single search engine through role mappings.

Creating a Search Application

Search has become the default way we all find information on websites. You no longer click through departments and categories on websites to find what you want; instead, you simply type a description of what you're looking for in a search bar.

Providing a user-friendly search experience, therefore, is vital in ensuring that customers find your products quickly and that the product is right for them, and it helps you in terms of sales.

In this section, I discuss how users access a system, both from an interface usability standpoint and in common search engine features used to aid users in locating the most relevant results.

Configuring user interfaces

Many *enterprise search* engines provide their own web application for searching through their catalogs. You can configure your application so that it's branded, and you can design its navigation system according to your website's user-interface styles and layout.

Some search engines provide *widgets* — small pieces of JavaScript web application code — that you can embed into your website. This is a good approach if you want fine control over how the site looks, but don't want to write a search web application entirely from scratch.

Other search engines, especially those embedded within databases, provide an API, which gives you an easy way to access advanced search functionality, without having to create the entire user interface yourself.

However, for complex custom applications, you may have to live with the API approach and writing your own application; otherwise, your website might wind up looking like a competitor's.

What a good search API gives you

Users don't just want an empty text field in which to type search text. They need guidance on what terms or phrases to use, and how to drill down into search results. A good search API provides some or all of the following features:

- ✔ **Suggestions:** Phrases or criteria that appear as the user types. The suggestions could be phrases from search indexes or could be based on previous or commonly used search terms.

- ✔ **Facets:** Facets are a listing of fields and the most common values for them from the matching search results. They show values for particular fields in the whole search result (not just the ten results shown in the first page) and how common that value is. Facets are great for narrowing result sets.

- ✔ **Grammar:** A rich default or configurable search grammar that is easy to use and expressive in the ease of control over the search experience that the users have when using it. Here are some examples:

  - • Double quotes to specify phrases

  - • AND and OR keywords with parentheses to indicate complex Boolean logic

  - • The negation character (-) to exclude a search term

- ✔ **Snippets:** For text searches. Snippets are one or more short sections of the matching text with the matching search terms highlighted.

✔ **Similar results:** For each search result shown, also listing the three most similar records to this search result.

Similar result matching is useful for identifying common sets of documents in the results that are closely related by content.

✔ **Preview:** For images or documents. These are previews of the matching image, or document cover, or PDF front page, shown as a thumbnail in the search results.

Going beyond basic search with analytics

Rather than just providing the ten most-relevant search results, it's sometimes more appropriate to display statistics about the results to the user. The use of facets is the most typical example of returning information about the set of search results. Figure 25-1 shows how Amazon uses snippets to assist in navigation.

As you can see in Figure 25-1, the Children's Books category facet has many values (ten shown, more available), and each value has a count of the number of results matching. For example, the Children's Books Science Fiction and Fantasy value with a count of 419 matching search results. These clickable facet values allow users to drill into the datasets.

However, in some search engines, you can configure the preceding mechanism to provide other aggregated statistics for document values. Here are some statistics that you can calculate from facet or other range index calculations:

✔ Count of the number of results matching a particular facet value.

✔ Age buckets for children's reading age groups (refer to Children's Books Age Range in Figure 25-1).

✔ Average age of people diagnosed with conditions, grouped by condition name, across a search of medical records.

✔ Geographic dispersal of search results across a country, typically shown as either a heat map or color-coded counties/states/countries.

✔ Co-occurrence of different fields in the search results. How often a particular actor is shown in each genre of the search results, for example. This is an example of *two-way co-occurrence.*

amazon.co.uk
Prime

Shop by
Department ▾   **Search**   Advanced Search   Browse Genres   Best Sellers   New & Future Releases

Adam's Amazon   Today's Deals   Gift Cards   Sell   Help

harry potter   **Go**

Hello, Adam
Your Account ▾   Your
Prime ▾   🛒 **Basket** ▾   Wish
List ▾

Christmas Store
First Thoughts of Christmas › Shop now

Books   Children's Books ▾   Browse Genres   Best Sellers   New & Future Releases   Paperbacks   Top Offers   Textbooks   Audiobooks   Sell Your Books

1-16 of 1,274 results for **Books** : Children's Books : **Children's Books** : '"harry potter"'

Related Searches: harry potter and the philosopher's stone, harry potter, harry potter box set, harry potter set.

Sort by   Relevance

Show results for

‹ Any Category
‹ Books
Children's Books
Children's Science Fiction & Fantasy (419)
Children's School Fiction (36)
Action & Adventure (102)
Fiction (911)
Novelty & Activity Books (84)
Film & TV (49)
Family, Friends & Social Issues (35)
Legends, Myths & Fables (19)
Fairy & Folk Tales (14)
Children's Humour (28)
+ See more

Children's Books Age Range

| Ages 0-2 | Ages 3-4 | Ages 5-8 | Ages 9-11 | Ages 12-16 |

LOOK INSIDE!

Harry Potter and the Philosopher's Stone: 1/7 (Harry Potter 1) by J.K. Rowling (1 Sep 2014)
★★★★★ ▾ (1,717)

£3.85 Paperback *Prime*
Get it by Monday, Oct 27
£0.00 kindleunlimited
Subscribers read for £0.00. Learn more.
£4.99 Kindle Purchase

More buying choices - Paperback
£2.10 new (39 offers)
£2.05 used (4 offers)

FREE Delivery on orders over £10
Trade-in eligible for an Amazon gift card
Other Formats: Hardcover, Audio CD

Figure 25-1:
Amazon
search
results
showing
facets.

Some search engines support N-way co-occurrences, which is particularly useful for discovering patterns you didn't know existed. Examples include products mentioned with other products or with medical conditions on Twitter.

All of these calculations are performed at high speeds by accessing just the search indexes. These can be calculated as one of the following:

- ✔ Part of the search results (such as for facets or heat maps)
- ✔ A separate statistical operation over the same indexes (such as co-occurrence)

A typical way to provide analytics over a dataset is to delegate the responsibility to a business intelligence tool such as Cognos, Business Objects, or Tableau. The problem with these tools is that they typically pull information from the data store and perform analytics over a stored copy of the data. This is called a *data warehouse*. The problem is that the information isn't in real time; often it's updated only once in 24 hours.

If BI tools don't pull a copy of the data, then performing a wide ranging analysis affects the performance of the underlying database or search engine, which has obvious implications for the cost of hardware and software licenses to provide analytical functionality. Business intelligence (BI) tools typically charge per user, making the cost prohibitive for end-user applications.

Using the built-in analytical capabilities of the database or search engine may be a better solution. Rather than shift vast amounts of data to a BI tool, you perform fast calculations over an in-memory copy of the search indexes.

Doing so enables the support of many users for both search and analytical workloads. Many organizations in financial services and government are looking at NoSQL databases with search functionality to provide near-real-time analytics for their data, without a complex, separate BI or data warehouse infrastructure.

Chapter 26

Search Engine Use Cases

In This Chapter

▶ Enabling customers to find your products online

▶ Making best use of all your enterprise's data

▶ Supporting proactive user working processes

Search applications vary widely both in the kind of information that's cataloged and in how users interact with search engines. For example, a hotel-booking website differs greatly from eBay's site, which is different from Amazon's site. Each use case has its particular features and approaches.

In this chapter, I discuss some aspects involved in providing user-friendly search capabilities in your application and in providing the behavior that you want your application to have.

Searching E-Commerce Products

There is an old adage in sales — *"A customer not only needs your product, they need to know that they need your product."* However, the trick is to lead customers not only to the product most relevant to their search terms, but to what they really need.

The simplest form of search is a search of a single-product catalog; for example, searching for printer toner on Amazon.

In this chapter, I discuss how to use a search engine to provide e-commerce website product search capabilities.

Amazon-type cataloguing

Many people, myself included, see `Amazon.com` as the default place to go when shopping online. Some key features make it the go-to place, and those features have nothing to do with the variety of products available or to Amazon's size.

Instead, the features are more personal in nature. For example, when I search for a book on a particular topic, Amazon lets me know what other people think about the book and how it compares to similar titles. I also appreciate Amazon's relevant suggestions based other shoppers' purchases. (I find this aspect of Amazon's search technology to be weirdly accurate!)

A list of recommendations isn't typically what people expect from a search engine interface, but, at its core, recommendations are absolutely powered by search indexes. This search isn't over the products themselves; rather, the search is of purchases, order history, and products I've viewed but not yet bought.

Geospatial distance scoring

Every hotel website of note provides a search-based interface that shows summary information about the hotel and often a map view of the results as well. Positional search functionality is called *geospatial search*, which I introduce in Chapter 25.

Figure 26-1 shows the trivago website, which is my default site for finding hotel deals. It provides *search federation* rather than just its own indexes. With search federation, trivago performs a search over a wide range of hotel websites and displays the consolidated result — it does not store the hotel availability information itself, instead asking individual hotel providers' websites.

The interesting thing about the view in Figure 26-1 is that the order of the results is determined not by a field within the hotel's description, but rather by a value calculated from a difference of the field's information and my search criteria.

I didn't ask for just all hotels with positions within a particular area; I asked for the distance from them to a central point to be calculated and used for sorting.

Some search engines go further, allowing you to take this geospatial distance and use it to affect relevancy scoring. I may prefer closer hotels but want this factor weighed against hotels with good ratings. Therefore, the website's search engine recommends hotels that are further away at a higher relevance if they have substantially better reviews.

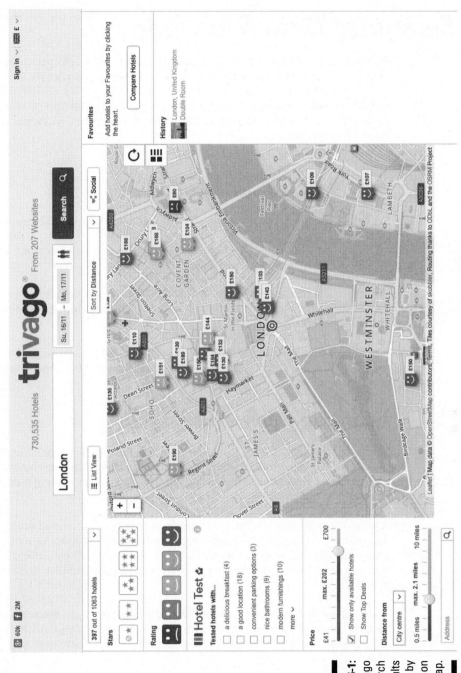

Figure 26-1:
Trivago
hotel search
results
ordered by
distance on
a map.

Enterprise Data Searching

Being able to bring together disparate types of data while providing a single search interface is the main challenge in *enterprise searches*.

In this section, I discuss challenges around discovering and providing a consistent search interface over the variety of information stores present in a modern enterprise.

Storing web data

Web data includes the text on web pages, images shown on those pages, and files linked for downloads on those pages. Being able to extract text from web-page markup while preserving paragraphs and concepts of a summary or title are basic features of web search indexers.

Web data also requires that metadata and text be extracted from binary files. Where an image was taken, on what camera, and at what resolution are now common search criteria.

Similarly, being able to extract text from PDFs and Word documents and metadata such as author and publisher is also useful for search applications.

Searching corporate data

Most corporate data is still held on people's laptops, network file shares, or increasingly in email or instant messages. Understanding the similarities and differences between these types of data is key to creating a user-friendly search experience.

A good example is searching by people. Perhaps it's an email address within an email, or a person's full name in the author field of a document, or an employee id in an instant message. Being able to identify all these different sources as the same person is a useful piece of functionality in an *enterprise search* engine.

As I mention in Chapter 25, reconciling the different data source's security models into a single search security model and enforcing auditing are essential to preventing unauthorized access to corporate data in a search engine.

Searching application data

Many applications include their own search functionality. You can provide a single search interface for this information in one of two ways. You can

- ✔ Consolidate the information, or an extract, in a central search engine.
- ✔ Federate the query, effectively performing one query on each of a set of sources and consolidating and interpreting the results, showing one search result set to the user.

Because application versions and functionality change over time, setting up and maintaining a federated search engine is complex. For example, each application provides its own subset of search functionality that may or may not map well onto a central search grammar. You often end up with the lowest common denominator of functionality when implementing search federation.

A consolidated index does cost more in storage, but it allows fine control over what is indexed and which search functionality is exposed to end users. Also, you can consolidate multiple databases into a single data and search platform, which reduces cost when compared to the search federation approach.

Alerting

Users don't want to waste their time staring at a search interface and pressing the refresh button. Similarly, lengthy, complex business processes that pause while waiting for new content to arrive can be hard to manage.

With search alerts, a search can be saved and actions can be configured to perform useful functionality when new content that matches the search criteria arrives.

In this section, I discuss the various interesting ways that alerting can be used in order to support more proactive and responsive working practices.

Enabling proactive working

Imagine a senior police investigator whose job requires surveillance of all drug-related activity in one area of a city. This investigator can't be effective if he has to scan through reports and arrests every day. A better route for him is to include specific, related terms in search query over all this content, including, for example, names of organizations and individuals of interest, a geospatial area he works in, crime terms such as drug names, or people's nicknames.

By saving his exact information query requirements as an alert, the investigator is notified about new, relevant information as it arrives, which shortens the time it takes to react to new information.

Finding bad guys

Using the preceding intelligence-gathering scenario, a long-term investigative officer might be made aware of crucial and actionable intelligence that could prevent a crime. The same mechanism can be used across public data sources. This gathering of information from public sources is called *open-source intelligence*. Here "open" refers to the fact information is published to the web and requires no special description devices or legal warrants to obtain, and includes mining such sources as Twitter, Facebook, data.gov and other publicly available sources for data of interest.

When new data arrives, the NoSQL database can perform some of the analysis and enrichment functions before adding the data to the search engine's index and making it available to intelligence officers. This way, the officer doesn't have to do the enrichment manually, trawling through paragraphs of text and highlighting and tagging key terms and phrases, and he winds up with a rich set of search fields to save for search alerts with minimal human work.

Another example is in a military context. Suppose that, by using alerting, an agent discovers that a person of interest isn't in the current operation's targeted area as expected, but in an entirely different location. This information could prevent a failed mission and perhaps even civilian casualties. Moreover, the data could lead to a better use of resources.

In defense and intelligence search use cases, it's important to combine a range of functions, but especially geospatial search. Knowing where and when things occur is key to planning operations. Also very important are links (relationships) between physical objects, such as people and places, and also intangible objects, such as meetings, organizational hierarchies, and social networks of influence. This emerging approach is called *object-based intelligence* and includes aspects of full text, geospatial, and semantic (web of facts and relationships) search.

Chapter 27

Types of Search Engines

*S*earch engines are as diverse as the kinds of content they index. Large software companies acquired enterprise-level search engines aimed at corporate data five to ten years ago. These search engines are largely outdated or are embedded within applications used by their purchasers.

During the same period, Google has become the dominant player in web crawling and search. Through Google's Search Appliance (GSA), its patented algorithms and simple search interface provide ample service on the public web and on corporate websites.

Open-source projects were developed, incorporating lessons learned in web search technology, and closed the gap left by stagnant enterprise search engines. These open source products are undergoing rapid development at the moment and, to achieve scale, are integrating many of the architectural design features of NoSQL databases. Indeed, many search engines are often integrated into NoSQL databases to provide unstructured search.

In this chapter, I discuss the uses of these search engines, and how they can be used both alongside and instead of a NoSQL database.

Using Common Open-Source Text Indexing

Apache's Lucene, the most popular open-source indexing and search engine technology, has been around since 1999. It's written in Java and is a lightweight library aimed purely at indexing text within fields and providing search functionality over those indexes.

In this section, I discuss the challenges around text indexing, and software typically used to solve those challenges.

Using Lucene

Lucene performs text indexing and search; it's not an end-to-end search engine. This means its developers concentrated on building a very flexible indexing mechanism that supports multiple fields in an indexed document.

Lucene doesn't include web crawlers, binary text extractors, or advanced search functionality such as faceting. It's purely for full-text indexing and search, which it does very well.

Lucene's key innovation is that it is an embeddable library that allows you to index a wide range of source data for full-text searches. It powers many search engines and websites in its own right, being embedded into these products.

Distributing Lucene

Lucene isn't a distributed search server environment. Instead, you present Lucene with text to be indexed in fields of a document, and it allows searches to run against the indexes. This flexibility makes it appropriate for a wide range of uses.

To provide indexing for terabytes of data, you need to select an open-source search engine that uses a library like Lucene for its full-text indexing, and fortunately, there are several to choose from. The most popular ones are Apache Solr and Elasticsearch.

These search engines approach clustering and distributed querying the same way NoSQL databases I talk about elsewhere in this book do. Instead of being databases, though, products like Solr and Elasticsearch hold document extracts and indexes and distribute those pieces of data.

Evaluating Lucene/SolrCloud

SolrCloud provides Lucene with a highly available, failure-tolerant, distributed indexing and search layer. You can use SolrCloud to enable a Solr cluster to do the following:

✔ Create multiple replica shard searches that can be distributed across different servers holding the same information, providing faster query response times.

✔ Create multiple master shards so that data can be split across multiple machines, which reduces the indexes per machine and optimizes write operations. It also increases the amount of an index that can fit into memory, which improves query times.

SolrCloud (Solr version 4 and above) operates a master-slave replication mechanism. This means a write happens locally and is eventually pushed to all replicas. Therefore, a Lucene/Solr cluster is eventually consistent — clients may not see a new or updated document for a while, although usually only for milliseconds. This delay could be an issue if you absolutely need an up to date view of your data. A good example of this is when looking for the latest billion dollar trade you just made.

Solr also acts as a NoSQL database, allowing documents to be written and committed. They can also be patched without a full replacement, much as they are in document NoSQL databases.

A manual commit is required to ensure that the documents are written to the transaction log and, thus, preserved if a server failure occurs.

SolrCloud uses Apache ZooKeeper to track the state of the cluster and to elect new master shards in the event of server failure. This prevents a "split brain" of two parts of the same cluster operating independently.

Apache also recommends that you set up ZooKeeper in a highly available manner, spread over a set of servers. This is called a *ZooKeeper ensemble*. Apache also recommends doing so on dedicated hardware, because if you don't, you will have to restart ZooKeeper to modify and do updates. If it is also located on a Solr machine, a forced failover will occur.

ZooKeeper is required for all new database client applications to connect to in order to determine the state of the cluster and perform a query. To ensure that your SolrCloud instance is highly available, you must set up a ZooKeeper ensemble across multiple machines. Otherwise, you'll have a very stable SolrCloud cluster that no one can query!

Solr doesn't handle disaster recovery clusters. The current recommendation is to set up two SolrCloud clusters that know nothing about each other. When adding documents (updating indexes), you must commit changes to both clusters. As a result, application developers bear the burden of establishing consistency.

SolrCloud is a solid, distributed search platform, though. It goes beyond what is provided by Lucene — it isn't merely a distributed set of indexes. These features make Solr a leading open-source search engine that will appeal to many developers of enterprise Java applications. SolrCloud offers:

- ✔ Faceted navigation and filtering
- ✔ Geospatial search, including points and polygons
- ✔ Structured search format as well as a free text search grammar
- ✔ Text analytics
- ✔ Dynamic fields, allowing new fields to be incorporated into existing indexes without reconfiguration of an entire system
- ✔ Multiple search index configurations for the same field
- ✔ Configurable caching
- ✔ Storage of XML, JSON, CSV, and binary documents
- ✔ Text extraction from binary documents using Apache Tika and metadata extraction using Apache UIMA

Solr is accessible via an HTTP-based API, allowing any programming language to use the search platform's services.

Combining Document Stores and Search Engines

The way to guarantee the highest write performance of a database with a real-time, advanced search engine is to use a database that is a search engine. MarkLogic server is unique in the NoSQL database landscape by being built using search engine indexing techniques from the start, rather than just for storing and retrieving data and having search indexing and query execution added on later.

MarkLogic Server is built with data integrity and consistency foremost in its design, while also providing for clusters of hundreds of servers in a highly available cluster.

In this section, I discuss MarkLogic Server's approach to search indexing and query.

Universal indexing

A useful feature to enable search to be used instantly in MarkLogic Server is the universal index. When a document is added to MarkLogic, certain information is automatically indexed without special configuration being required. This indexed information is

✔ All elements and properties within the document

✔ Parent-child relationships of elements within elements

✔ Exact values of each element and attribute

✔ Words, word stems, and phrases

✔ Security permissions on the document

✔ All associated properties, including collections and creation and update times, which are stored in an XML document

The universal index allows any (XML or JSON) content to be added to the database and made immediately available for search. This is particularly useful in situations where you're loading an unknown set of content and need to browse it before adding specialized indexes.

MarkLogic Server also includes support for text and metadata extraction for more than 200 binary file types, including common office document formats, email, and image and video metadata.

Using range indexes

After you load your data and browse it via the universal index, you can start adding data-aware indexes, which are often referred to as *secondary indexes* in NoSQL.

Typically, range indexes are set up on numeric and data types to provide support for range queries. A range query includes one or more less than and greater than operations.

You set up range indexes by storing an ordered set of values and a list of the documents they relate to — for example, ascertaining all news articles in September by taking a block of document ids between two date values.

Operating on in-memory data

Indexes in MarkLogic Server are cached in a server's memory, using whatever spare memory capacity is available. This makes operations on that data very fast. In addition to range queries, you can use range indexes for sorting and faceted navigation.

You can also use range indexes to perform mathematical functions over field values across a set of results. The most common calculation is a count of the documents mentioning a particular value, which is used to calculate facets.

Other operations are also supported, including summation, average (mean, mode, and median), standard deviation, and variance. You can also write user-defined functions in C++ and plug them into MarkLogic Server at runtime to provide custom, complex range mathematical calculations. This approach is like Hadoop's in-database MapReduce operation, except it's much faster and without the baggage of a large Hadoop installation.

Other operations on range indexes include calculating heat map density of search results, which can be overlaid on a map. You can also perform co-occurrence calculations, which allows you to take two or more fields in each search result and see how often their values occur simultaneously. This is useful for discovering patterns, such as the link between medical conditions and products mentioned on Twitter.

Retrieving fine-grained results

Most search engines provide search queries over the entire document. MarkLogic Server, however, allows you to specify a subset of the document and perform a search for it. This is particularly useful when you want to restrict the search to a specific section, rather than search a whole document or one field. Examples include book summaries, comments on an article, or just the text of a tweet (tweets actually have dozens of fields; they're not just a short string of text).

Evaluating MarkLogic

MarkLogic Server is an enterprise NoSQL database, providing functionality demanded by enterprise-grade mission-critical applications. MarkLogic Server favors consistency and durability of data and the operation of rich functionality on that data more than it does throughput speed for adding new data, and querying that data.

If you have sophisticated search requirements including full text, free schema, binary content, XML and JSON, real-time alerting, and support for text, semantic and geospatial search across hundreds of terabytes of mission-critical data, then I recommend that you check out MarkLogic Server.

The downside to a database that also does search is that the front-end user interface is lacking in functionality when compared to legacy enterprise search platforms such as HP Autonomy, IBM OmniFind, and Microsoft FAST.

MarkLogic does provide an HTTP-based API supporting document operation and structure and free text grammar search, but you must develop the user interface yourself.

MarkLogic includes an application builder web application that you can use to configure a basic search web application. In a convenient wizard driven interface, The application generated by this wizard is very simple though, always requiring customization via code to create a final production-ready application.

MarkLogic provides a range of open-source language bindings, including Java, JavaScript, C# .NET, Ruby on Rails, C++, and PHP. This means you can plug MarkLogic Server into your application stack of choice.

MarkLogic Server does lag behind other enterprise search platforms in that it doesn't provide natural language processing (NLP) functionality — for example, splitting "Hotels in London" into a product type query of "hotel" and a geospatial query matching hotels near to the center of London.

Although it's a closed-source project, MarkLogic provides detailed documentation and free online training courses. Meetups are also available for MarkLogic in the United States, Europe, and Japan.

MarkLogic Server is the only NoSQL database product mentioned in a variety of analyst reports, including those covering both data management and search, from a range of analyst firms.

Evaluating Enterprise Search

There are many legacy search engines deployed in enterprises today. Understanding those available is useful when deciding to adopt them, or replace them with a modern alternative for use with NoSQL databases.

Here are the most commonly used legacy enterprise search engines:

- HP Autonomy, which incorporates the Verity K2 search engine business
- IBM OmniFind
- Oracle Endeca
- Microsoft FAST

These search engines haven't undergone significant development as stand-alone products in recent years, but they have been embedded in their sponsor companies' other products.

In this section, I describe these search engines' common use in enterprises today.

Using SharePoint search

The Norwegian FAST company was the newest player in the enterprise search space before being acquired by Microsoft. FAST now is incorporated into Microsoft's SharePoint platform and is no longer available or supported as a separate search platform.

Integrating NoSQL and HP Autonomy

HP acquired the independent British firm Autonomy and has incorporated the software into many products. Autonomy is now a brand within HP. The HP Autonomy IDOL search platform incorporates the search engine products.

IDOL has more than 400 system connectors for search, supporting over 1,000 different binary file types of text and metadata extraction, as well as image, document, and video-processing capabilities.

Advanced functionality includes deduplication, and the creation of reports and dashboards. IDOL also works well with Hadoop HBase and Hive.

As the only enterprise search platform still available as a comprehensive suite of search products, HP Autonomy is the leading vendor in corporate search platforms.

Using IBM OmniFind

IBM OmniFind was at one point a very popular search engine with IBM customers. Many people may be familiar with the Yahoo! Desktop Search application, which was actually a limited version of IBM OmniFind provided free for desktop users.

I worked for IBM from 2006 to 2008, and at that time, we often used OmniFind on our laptops to manage a search index of our customer documents and emails. It was a great way to demonstrate the software to potential customers — as long as we were careful about we searched for, of course. Now OmniFind's functionality is included in the IBM Watson Content Analytics product. This product provides for significant data analytics and dashboard creation, although from an end user's perspective, the search functionality hasn't advanced in the intervening years.

Evaluating Google search appliance

Google provides a search engine called Google Search Appliance (or GSA, as it's often referred to). This appliance provides the familiar Google search experience for corporate data sources and internal websites.

Because it's easy to install and so many users are familiar with its features, GSA is very popular. It supports the usual Google features, including faceted navigation and also a limited set of corporate system search crawler connectors.

Its price is based on the number of documents you index for search, and there's a significant initial investment for GSA. However, if you have a large (but not overly large) number of intranet sites that employees search or an application that external users access, then Google Search Appliance may work well for you.

Storing and Searching JSON

Solr and MarkLogic support XML, JSON, text, CSV, and binary documents and provide searchable indexes over them. However, the leader in JSON storage and search is Elasticsearch. Elasticsearch provides a JSON-only document store with a universal JSON index. The complete package is provided by what is referred to as the *ELK stack,* which stands for Elasticsearch, Logstash, and Kibana. They are all Elasticsearch products.

The Logstash product processes log files and indexes them for search. As you can see in Figure 27-1, Kibana provides a very sexy dashboard set of widgets that allows you to design a search interface just by using a web browser.

In this section, I discuss the key features of Elasticsearch and why you may choose to deploy this for your search platform.

JSON universal indexing

Elasticsearch will index every property and value in any JSON document you store in its universal index. In addition to simply storing values as text, Elasticsearch will attempt to guess the data type of the property being stored.

This provides a quick start when storing and searching JSON documents. Elasticsearch, like Solr, is built on top of the Lucene indexer and search engine. Elasticsearch provides a distributed architecture for indexing large amounts of data using Lucene.

Elasticsearch makes a better attempt than Solr at providing a fully consistent master-slave replication of saved data. This means all replicas are consistent with any changes applied to the master as soon as a transaction completes. Transaction logs in Elasticsearch are also committed immediately to disk, minimizing the chances of data loss if a server fails immediately after a document is saved.

Scriptable querying

Elasticsearch doesn't provide a free Google-style query grammar. Instead, you create a structured query using an Elasticsearch-specific JSON format.

This format provides queries that return relevance-ranked results and filters that return exact matches to the filter terms. Many types of query and filter terms are supported. Filtering also allows the use of a query within a filter.

The script filter enables simple JavaScript Boolean terms to be submitted as text and executed in order to filter the documents. These can also be parameterized and cached, allowing for a facility similar to bound variables from the relational database world's stored procedures.

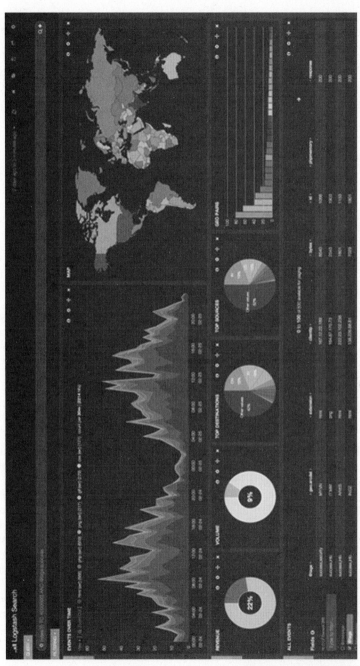

Figure 27-1:
Kibana
dashboard
application
from Elastic
search.com.

Evaluating Elasticsearch

Elasticsearch is a good place to start if you need to store data as JSON documents primarily for full-text searches or for range query searches. The ELK stack allows very rapid use of Elasticsearch for log file storing, search, and analytics in an attractive and high-performance front end.

Beyond log file use, though, you must plug Elasticsearch's HTTP-based REST API into your programming language and user interface layer of choice. Support is provided for a wide range of languages.

Elasticsearch doesn't handle binary documents or XML natively, so if these are among your needs, then you need to look at other solutions. No connectors are provided for Elasticsearch to pull in information from other corporate systems or applications.

Elasticsearch does handle JSON documents better than Solr. This is especially true with complex nested tree structures and parent/child relationships within documents.

Elasticsearch is also schema-less with a universal index, unlike Solr where you need to specifically instruct the search engine about the format and fields in the indexed documents. In Solr, schema changes also require a cluster restart — they cannot be done live. In Elasticsearch, you can alter them live as long as the changes don't break existing indexes.

If you have a variety of ever-changing JSON documents and need to search them, then Elasticsearch is a good choice.

Microsoft's entry into the JSON document NoSQL market with its DocumentDB service on Azure could prove a more attractive option to managing and search JSON documents as it matures over the next two years. At the moment, Microsoft DocumentDB has no free text search capability, preferring instead to use Structured Query Language (SQL) queries from the relational database world. If Microsoft were to take its FAST database technology and apply it to its DocumentDB product with its existing universal index, and then allow on-premise installations, then DocumentDB will become an attractive alternative in large enterprise deployments.

At the moment, though, Elasticsearch is the dominant JSON search engine, but it will have to adapt in order to pull ahead of Solr or MarkLogic, which both support a wider range of document formats.

Chapter 28

Elasticsearch

*E*lasticsearch is one of the more recent additions to the *enterprise search* world of products. Using Apache Lucene internally as the core indexing and search library, Elasticsearch provides a distributed search platform designed for NoSQL database-style storage and high availability.

In this chapter, I discuss this product specifically as Elasticsearch introduces a number of innovations over traditional search engines. Elasticsearch also uses several core architecture concepts common with NoSQL databases — having the ability itself to store and manage JSON documents.

Using the Elasticsearch Product

Elasticsearch is an open-source product that anyone can download and use. Elasticsearch, the company, provides support for this product as well as value-added products, including systems management software in its product, Marvel. This provides system administrators with information on the current health of the Elasticsearch cluster — and will therefore be of interest for large, complex *enterprise* installations of Elasticsearch.

In this section, I discuss the Elasticsearch product and complementary products ecosystem.

ELK stack

The Elasticsearch ELK stack suite comprises the separate but complementary open-source projects, Elasticsearch, Logstash, and Kibana, which do the following:

✔ Elasticsearch provides the search platform.

✔ Logstash provides the processing and extracts data from a variety of log file formats.

✔ Kibana provides an easy way to create a dashboard-based search and analytics application on top of Elasticsearch.

With this suite of products, you can quickly create an Elasticsearch application.

Using Elasticsearch

Elasticsearch is a rich search platform capable of indexing JSON data. Source records — whether they're database tables, CSV or text files, or extracted text from Microsoft Word documents — are stored as JSON documents and indexed in Elasticsearch.

Elasticsearch provides a highly available service with no single point of failure. Even if a server dies, the service is unaffected, thanks to Elasticsearch's support of consistent replicas and transaction logs. This ensures that no data added to Elasticsearch is lost, unlike eventually consistent systems such as SolrCloud, where it's possible under certain circumstances to lose data.

Elasticsearch provides document creation, update, patch, and deletion functions, along with a rich search and index API. Because these operations are based on common RESTful HTTP standards, you can access these APIs from a wide range of programming language client APIs.

Elasticsearch makes it very easy to add or remove servers to a cluster at runtime. Shards can be automatically redistributed as servers are added. Sharding in Elasticsearch also takes into account the physical location of servers — Elasticsearch is aware of machine and rack configurations and of the availability of zone/data center physical servers; and it adapts the shard locations automatically.

After an Elasticsearch cluster installed and running you'll need to manage its health over time. The Marvel application provided by Elasticsearch BV (the company), as a separate commercial add on product, enables you to monitor and manage an Elasticsearch cluster. Consequently, organizations can discover potential performance problems before their services go live.

Marvel also gives you the ability to look at historical data so that you can track spikes in usage and issues that occur intermittently over time. Marvel also includes a developer console that allows testing of REST requests processed by Elasticsearch.

Marvel is available to everyone who buys a development or production support plan from Elasticsearch BV, and not as an open source product.

Using Logstash

In Logstash, custom formats are handled through configuration files. These files specify how Logstash processes each log file line, and how to convert and store data within log files.

However, you can configure the Logstash application to process a broad range of common log file formats, including Linux syslog and Apache Combined log File (CLF) format. As a result, you can take many log files and store them consistently within Elasticsearch, ready for search and analytics to be applied.

Logstash, by default, creates a new index file in Elasticsearch each day. These logs are restarted (known also as rotated) at midnight, which gives you a convenient way to restrict the log entries you search to only those in a particular time period referenced by an index.

Using Kibana

After you store and index all your log information in a consistent manner, you need a way to slice and dice the information and then show it to end users. This is where Kibana comes in.

Kibana is a web application with a set of configurable widgets, or panels. You can create a search or dashboard page in Kibana without writing a single piece of code! You just place the widgets where you need them on a page.

As you can see in Figure 28-1, you can easily create some compelling dashboard pages in Kibana. You can even create and share dashboard pages and import dashboard configurations from other systems.

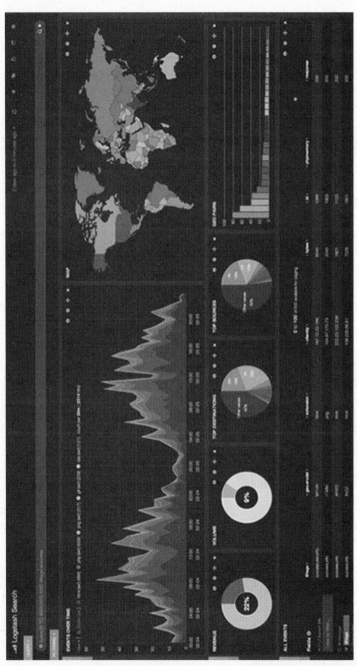

Figure 28-1:
A Kibana
Search
dashboard
page.

Finding Support for Elasticsearch

Elasticsearch is supported by the commercial entity, Elasticsearch BV. This company provides support, services, and add-on products as I discussed earlier in this chapter.

Various cloud service providers are also available for Elasticsearch, including Bonsai.io, Indexisto, Qbox.io, and IndexDepot.

Elasticsearch has a broad and dedicated community base that supports development and the creation of extensions. The community site — `www.elasticsearch.org` — contains a wealth of information about installing and using Elasticsearch.

Online communities such as `StackOverflow.com` contain thousands of messages about using Elasticsearch that are useful to people interested in Elasticsearch technology and in using it for their particular needs.

Evaluating Elasticsearch BV

Elasticsearch is a trademark of Elasticsearch BV, which is based in the Netherlands, with a major hub in the San Francisco Bay Area, and with branches throughout the world.

Many members of Elasticsearch BV also commit code to the Apache Lucene open-source project. So, these people are skilled in supporting customers with complex search indexing needs.

Elasticsearch BV provides both development and production support subscriptions. The developer subscription is aimed to help customers implement Elasticsearch in their own environments in order to make their applications more powerful. This support includes web and email support channels, support for Kibana and Logstash, and access to the Marvel management application.

Production support is available in Silver, Gold, and Platinum packages, each with its own Service Level Agreements (SLAs) for incident response times. For example, Platinum support includes 24/7 support with a guaranteed one-hour critical-issue response time. It also includes emergency patch access for urgent fixes.

Elasticsearch BV is the most comprehensive partner available for Elasticsearch deployments, and is where the experts on Elasticsearch mostly work. If you're considering Elasticsearch as a technology, then you need to evaluate the cost of the commercial version designed for large enterprise deployments, and the support provided by Elasticsearch BV. This support may vary at the different places the company is located — so be sure to check these issues before committing to Elasticsearch.

Part VII
Hybrid NoSQL Databases

In this part . . .

✔ Merging features from many categories.

✔ Creating multifaceted applications.

✔ Examining hybrid NoSQL products.

✔ Visit www.dummies.com/extras/nosql for great Dummies content online.

Chapter 29

Common Hybrid NoSQL Features

*N*oSQL databases are evolving. Much as relational databases added data types over time — like character (text) long objects (CLOB), binary long objects (BLOB), and XML data — NoSQL databases are adding support for new types of data.

If you've read other parts of this book, by now you probably understand that a given business problem can be solved different ways in each of the databases (key-value, Bigtable, graph / triple stores, and document databases) covered in this book. storing a document for a unique ID, for example, is a feature of both key-value stores and document databases.

Various databases can, therefore, technically be called hybrid in that they support multiple paradigms of data management. I restricted the list of hybrid databases in this chapter to those that provide significant functionality in more than one area — note that support for a new data type doesn't qualify as a hybrid database unless common management operations related to that type of data are also provided — column aggregate functions in Bigtable clones, for example. Also, document databases aren't automatically classified as key-value stores even though they can technically store values against a unique key. Likewise, not all databases that provide in-memory caching of property values are classified as column stores.

All that said, my purpose is be sure that neither I nor NoSQL vendors' marketing departments create confusion and leave you thinking that all NoSQL databases can provide all features for all kinds of problems. Instead, if you really need a hybrid approach, I want to help you correctly identify and select the right NoSQL solution.

The Death of Polyglot Persistence

In some cases, a single application has to communicate with a mainframe system, a relational database management system (RDBMS), and a NoSQL database management system (DBMS). However, as I mention in Chapter 2, the idea that a single app needs multiple NoSQL database management systems is temporary because NoSQL databases are rapidly evolving. For example, OrientDB has a database that blends a triple store and a document database. Why buy two products if one does the same job?

When relational database management systems first became mainstream, they tended to offer different advantages. For instance, some had support for triggers, whereas others had cascade delete capabilities. Over time, such features became standard in all relational database management systems. The same will be true for NoSQL databases as new features are added by vendors to encourage customers to choose their database from among the many.

One product, many features

Customers may find that they prefer a single-product approach because one rich product makes training developers and administering the IT landscape easier than using multiple databases would.

A single product also means that you don't have to become a coding plumber. You don't have to figure out how to join two different systems together. With a single product, vendors generally do these things themselves.

In OrientDB, which I discuss later in this chapter, adding an order document with a link to a product (say a product_id=29 document value) generates a triple that links the order to a product document in the system. Also, OrientDB blends this product data with the order document when the order document is requested by the application.

The makers of OrientDB provide this mechanism through the configuration of their server. I think you'll agree that not having to write code that communicates with two systems — one managing the relationships (triple store) and the other managing the data (document store) — will save you a lot of time.

Best-of-breed solution versus single product

The main risk with a single-product approach is that the product may provide weak functionality in every area rather than doing one thing well. Sometimes you do need advanced features, in which case, you want to use multiple products.

As an IT professional seen as your clients' "trusted adviser," it's your job to figure out where to draw the line between using multiple products and a single product.

It's very rare, though, that one application needs the ten most common features of each type of data store. (Although that certainly doesn't keep business analysts from writing requirements saying that the application needs all possible features!)

Advantages of a Hybrid Approach

Hyrbid databases can provide a number of additional benefits beyond minimizing the number of components in your application's IT infrastructure. In this section, I discuss these additional benefits.

Hybrid approaches provide important advantages, including the following:

- ✔ **Single strategic tech stack:** Implements a single data layer to power all your applications. As an IT professionals you've probably unknowingly been using relational database management systems to do this, but NoSQL means there's no up-front schema design, which gives you the flexibility to create an operational database and achieve fast application builds.

- ✔ **Common indexes / no duplication:** Storing a single index rather than having an index of the same data in multiple products is advantageous. Storing a document in an enterprise content management (ECM) platform means indexes are held in an RDBMS. Separate indexes will also exist in a search engine that indexes content held in that repository. A hybrid NoSQL system that supports search means a single set of indexes, which results in lower costs for storage and faster reindexing.

- ✔ **More real-time data through the stack (fewer moving parts):** Because indexes are updated as information is added to a hybrid NoSQL document database and search engine, fewer indexes as well as nearly real-time indexes are produced, or at least they're transactionally consistent. This real-time indexing powers alerting and messaging applications, such as the backbone of `HealthCare.gov`.

✔ **Easy administration (fewer moving parts):** Database admins need to be absolute experts on the systems they manage. The level of complexity in all products is great, and it increases over time. Therefore, having multiple products typically means the need for multiple administrators, each with different skillsets.

Single product means lower cost

A single product offers a number of advantages. If you add them up, the following cost-saving measures are huge. They can easily mean half the cost of implementing a new database layer:

✔ Less integration code between your application and its persistence layer

✔ Less ETL code to convert data formats between products

✔ Lower software license, maintenance, and consulting costs

✔ Lower training costs for developers and administrators (and a single API to access all your data)

✔ Lower salary costs because fewer experts for each system are needed

✔ Fewer moving parts with backups and maintenance, such as patches and security updates

You gain some of these benefits by adopting any kind of NoSQL technology. The ability to load data "as is" into a schema-less document store, for example, means lower ETL (Extract, Transform, and Load) costs. As soon as you introduce two NoSQL stores, though, moving data between them or merging data from each of them still entails more ETL costs than adopting a single NoSQL database.

ETL is very expensive. An entire industry has developed for ETL tools. There's also the related problem of data warehouses. Data warehousing exists because a single relational structure is hard to use both operationally and for business intelligence. A data warehouse stores the exact same information in a structure that enables faster aggregate reporting and statistics. Requiring two separate structures for the same data may not be the case of NoSQL databases in certain circumstances, though.

How search technology gives a better column store

Applying search technology to document stores for analytical operations is one example of how a hybrid approach provides additional benefits over just IT simplification.

A column store database performs rapid aggregate calculations, and it returns sets of atomic data (column families) of a whole row (record). Using column stores requires transforming data into a row and column structure, and supporting multiple instances of data within some column families (avoiding cross table joins like in an RDBMS).

You have to effectively do some ETL (Extract, Transform, and Load data) in order to store data in a way that makes it work better for the type of queries and analysis you do over it.

When Google approached the problem of indexing the web, what they *didn't* do was to let the administrators of every website know they had to adopt a single structure. Instead, Google stored what was there, and indexed it for retrieval via search.

By applying the same search technology to documents, hybrid NoSQL databases can provide an in-memory cached set of ordered column values that lend themselves not only to fast search, range queries and sorting, but also to high-speed analytical operations.

Because document NoSQL databases with search also update their indexes during the transaction that updates a document, these indexes are also updated in real-time, which is great for an analytics platform.

When looking at column stores for analytical operations, don't discount hybrid document and search NoSQL databases, especially if the source data is already in XML, JSON, or other document structures.

Document stores that also sport comprehensive search features tend to provide a set of analytical functions. Customers, being customers, always ask companies to do more with the same feature!

All common aggregation algorithms are present: mean, mode, median, standard deviation, and more — plus support for user-defined aggregate functions written in fast C++ that work next to the data, processing the data throughout the cluster.

How semantic technology assists content discovery

When most people think of accessing large sets of document data, they immediately think *search.* We're so used to using search that we even apply our own technical workarounds.

When you search for information about a health problem on Google, you type a phrase that you think will return the right result.

If I'm concerned a family member's diet may be placing them at risk of heart attack, I access the UK National Health Service website at www.nhs.uk. It has a range of excellent health FAQs.

In the search bar, I type "heart attack." When I get a page of results. I see that the first result is a page that describes heart attacks. Clicking through to that page reveals subpages, including one for risk factors.

Hang on, though. Why didn't I type "heart attack risk factors"? It's because I, like you, instinctively know that search engines aren't very good at getting the context.

For the same reason, people search for "NFL standings" rather than "Green Bay NFL record" — they know a simple search will get less noise and that we can as humans navigate from the general information picture (all NFL standings) and filter down to just what we need (Green Bay's standings).

Understanding context, therefore, is important in navigating directly to the most appropriate data. The way to describe these contexts is to use an *ontology,* which is a set of terms and definitions that applications use to describe a unique information domain.

This technology is associated with the semantic web and triple stores. It's not a graph store problem because you're not interested in analyzing the links or the minimum distance between subjects; you're just using the links.

Often, when publishing data, you know a lot about its context. Adding this information into a database helps later on when the data is queried. Understanding what people searched for previously and linking those queries to subjects as triples may also be advantageous.

So, back to my earlier scenario. If I want to search for "*heart attack,*" the most important keywords are "*risk factors*" and "*How can I prevent being at risk of a Heart Attack?*" By showing this semantic information in context with the content search results, I can shortcut the step of reading through results to manually filter content.

This is exactly what Google is doing now. Search for a common person or place or organization, and you'll see an Info Box next to the search results. These are semantically modeled facts culled by Google from information on the web.

The idea is to provide people with a set of answers rather than a set of search results. Imagine how rich and immediate semantic information will make the web for researchers or students in the future!

If you have a similar requirement for rapid discovery of content or for context-aware search, then investigate a hybrid document or triple store NoSQL database with search capabilities.

Chapter 30

Hybrid Databases in the Enterprise

• •

In This Chapter

▶ Selecting the right product

▶ Keeping your data intact and available

• •

*I*n the enterprise, hybrid databases have the advantage of fewer moving parts than using multiple databases in the same application. This is because they comprise a single system rather than separate entities that require manual integration.

There are still difficult problems to overcome, though. In this chapter, I identify the key issues to consider when looking at deploying a hybrid NoSQL database in the enterprise.

Selecting a Database by Functionality

Most people like to work with tick lists. For example, tick marks are great for comparison tables with multiple products listed next to their prices and functionality. You might use big green tick marks or red crosses to help identify the options with least functionality; then a purchaser could select the best compromise between price and functionality.

This type of "beauty pageant" can be distracting, though. It tempts you as purchasers to prioritize the number of functions available versus the value of those functions (or not) to your organization. What is needed is an assessment of the overall data management needs of your organization. This should include weightings for how important a feature is (critical, optional, nice to have). This analysis is more balanced, providing a better picture of both technical and business fit with your organization's needs.

This comparison mechanism is especially important when selecting a hybrid NoSQL database. This is because a single product likely covers a wider range of functionality, but perhaps at a lower depth of detail than in products covering just a single type of data management.

In this section, I describe the key challenges when selecting a hybrid NoSQL database, and how you can accurately analyze a product's fit with your organization now and in future software releases.

Ensuring functional depth and breadth

The number of functions it supports gives you an idea of a product's functional breadth, although this may not be a reliable method to determine how *useful* that functionality is. A good example is support for full-text search, which is a typical line item in a comparison of hybrid databases. It includes not only word searches but also multiple language support, word stemming, thesaurus support, complex Boolean logic, and a range of other topics.

The breadth-versus-depth argument is important when you're selecting a hybrid NoSQL database because, as the name suggests, these databases support a wider array of functionality than other NoSQL databases. So, it's important to ensure that the features provided truly have the functionality you require, and aren't just tick-box features designed to avoid a thorough analysis of the product's features.

I recommend dividing comparisons into sections, with the important functionality of each feature you want spelled out. This approach forces vendors to respond to the question you actually have, which ultimately is, will this database work for *me*?

Following a single product's roadmap

By product roadmap, I mean the long term view of upcoming features, or themes, for upcoming versions of database software. Typically products have rough outlines for 2 or 3 versions in to the future, over a 2 to 5 year period.

Tracking a single product's lifecycle is difficult, but tracking the several that you may use instead of a hybrid database is even more difficult. I've already mentioned that if you have multiple products that need to be integrated, the complexity means more expense. The situation is even worse when you consider that each product you integrate has its own roadmap of upcoming functionality, as well as dates when the current support of the version expires.

You must monitor each of the product's roadmaps for new functionality you want to take advantage of. You also need to consider how upgrading one component will affect the integration of another component. Often integration code updates lag behind the main product updates, so you don't necessarily want to upgrade as soon as a new version is released.

If you don't upgrade immediately, though, in a couple of years, your current version may no longer be supported, which makes it impossible to get support from vendors for the version you have. (Vendors always advise to upgrade to the latest version, or at least a supported version, in order to fix an issue.)

An advantage of hybrid NoSQL databases is that there's just a single product's roadmap to consider, which also means that each part of the product is tested thoroughly to be sure that it works with all the database's other features. In this way, you don't have to worry about whether the integration code between several distinct products will work after an upgrade cycle.

Building Mission-Critical Applications

Multiple issues are involved in putting a new solution into production. Businesses won't bet the bank on it, and executives won't bet their careers on implementing technology that may lose data. A down day is a death day when it comes to keeping services online in today's world.

In this section, I discuss how a hybrid NoSQL database can make overall system architectures more robust, by minimizing the number of parts of an end to end solution, and simplifying data management tasks.

Ensuring data safety

The first order of business is ensuring that data is kept safe. When databases indicate that data is saved, you need to be guaranteed that is the case. This guarantee requires ACID-compliant durability guarantees. Data needs to be written to disk, or at least to journals, in order to ensure that it is in fact safe.

The disks need some form of built-in failover, which you can do using a redundant array of independent disks (RAID) on a single machine.

There are various RAID levels, with the most common being

- ✔ RAID 0 is a single hard disk with no data duplicated, or an array of hard disks exposed as a single logical disk, but still without data duplication. This allows higher throughput than a single hard disk, but provides no additional durability guarantees.

- ✔ RAID 1 is where each disk has an exact duplicate.

- ✔ RAID 10 is where there is a RAID 1 array of two RAID 0 arrays. This provides higher throughput with one exact duplicate copy of each file.

- ✔ RAID 5 and 6 are technologies that allow multiple disks to be joined and data stored two or three times, but without reducing the storage space available by one-half or two-thirds. You achieve this level of space savings by using check bits rather than storing full copies of the data. This comes with the disadvantage of longer times to rebuild a new disk after failure.

- ✔ RAID 50 and 60 are several RAID 0 arrays configured as a single RAID 5 or 6 array. This provides higher throughput while ensuring greater data density.

These configurations trade off storage space, storage times, access times, and disk rebuild on failure times. For high performance environments, RAID 10 is typically used. RAID 50 is often used for high-density environments. RAID 60 takes longer to rebuild and requires more disks, so it's used less often than RAID 50.

When a failure of a single hard disk occurs, files held there are still accessible from the other disks in the array. If the system has a hot standby disk, the system can manage failover without requiring administrative help.

Ensuring data is accessible

There are occasions when entire systems fail or entire clusters disappear on a network. Workmen and excavating machines are the biggest culprits of these types of failures! They either dig up network cables or take out the power of the entire site.

To solve this problem, you can distribute data to other nodes (servers) in the same cluster and to other sites. By using multiple nodes within a cluster and storing multiple copies of data, you're ensuring that a cluster is highly available.

Many NoSQL systems don't immediately ensure that all their data is held on a second node in the cluster. Many, instead, distribute data after it's saved. This approach is called being eventually consistent, which could cause you to still lose data.

Every day more and more NoSQL databases support ensuring that their replicas are up to date within the bounds of a database update. This requires a *two-phase commit,* which is basically committing the change locally and then to a second node (or more) before confirming to the client that the update transaction is complete. MarkLogic Server is an example of a hybrid NoSQL database that supports two-phase commits within a cluster.

Between clusters that are geographically dispersed, though, the norm is to provide eventually consistent replicas. Eventual consistency between clusters is to even out the bursts or lag time for data flowing between clusters. If you don't even out this lag, replicating data to another cluster over the Internet will slow down local site database operations too. This is why the tradeoff of consistency versus lag time is often made in multi datacenter replication.

Using a separate cluster that is available for use only when the first cluster becomes unavailable is referred to as disaster recovery (DR). One or more DR sites can be replicated to, ensuring maximum service availability even if the replicas are a few seconds out of date.

Having local ACID compliant replicas within a cluster provides resilience in case of hardware failure. Having cross site DR database replication also means you don't have to worry about a single site being unavailable. Ensuring your chosen hybrid NoSQL database supports both of these mechanisms ensures maximum service availability.

Operating in high-security environments

When using separate pieces of technology and gluing them together, one of the more subtle (but infuriating!) problems you'll come upon is an *impedance mismatch,* which is when different systems have a different view of the same data or concept.

When it comes to security, this mismatch is most obvious between document databases and search engines. Many NoSQL databases support record-level (document) security. Some databases can also be used to enforce label-based access control (LBAC) within documents. This means parts of a document may require a higher level of security permissions, or roles, to access than others.

Separate search engines typically provide security at either the collection (set of documents) or document level. These two mechanisms therefore support access to the same information at different levels of granularity. Most of the time, search engines index updates lag behind the updates of the database they're linked to, which means that indexes are also out of date.

The best you can hope for in this case is a *false positive pointer* to a document. With a false positive pointer, a document ID or name is returned in the result set, showing you a document that you don't have clearance for, or a document to which security labels have not yet been applied (and thus visible to all).

The worst kind of scenario is one in which a document is marked as "Confidential" with a section within it marked as "Top Secret," and the top secret portion is leaked. Perhaps typing a word that happens to be in the top secret section shows a user with confidential-level access the full content of that paragraph in the search snippet. The top secret section shows up because the user has the appropriate level of access for the document, but the search engine doesn't "understand" that sections in documents may require higher security levels.

A hybrid NoSQL database that enforces the same security policies, roles, and permissions means this impedance mismatch is impossible. Whether you fetch a document by ID (an example of a database operation) or it happens to match a text phrase (an example of a search operation) is irrelevant. The hybrid NoSQL database will always enforce the same security policy against that document.

If you need to operate in a high-security environment, then using a hybrid NoSQL database will be easier than integrating multiple technologies. Some hybrid NoSQL databases, such as MarkLogic Server, are used in high-security environments in systems that are independently accredited for classified information. These databases probably have the right security controls for a range of commercial and government clients.

Chapter 31

Hybrid NoSQL Database Use Cases

•••

In This Chapter

▶ Directing readers to relevant articles

▶ Cataloging all available information

•••

Many use cases straddle the worlds of document NoSQL databases, triple stores, and search. As a result, combinations of these functions form the basis of the most common hybrid NoSQL databases.

In this chapter, I explain these use cases and how they combine the features of each world so that you can apply them to similar use cases in your own organization.

Digital Semantic Publishing

Publishing and managing a news website that changes on a daily basis is hard to do. Deciding exactly where each story should appear on the site is even harder. Stories on soccer may be relevant in one area, but what about stories about a soccer star's fashion label? These kinds of stories may belong in multiple areas on a website.

Traditionally, journalists and their senior editors decide where news stories are posted. However, in the fast-paced and ever-changing world of news, it's difficult for editors and journalists to categorize information in a timely way.

As a result, a more reactive way of publishing news stories is needed. Editors and journalists need to react to the various entities mentioned in news stories, allowing the relationships among these entities to drive where information is placed in a publication.

In this section, I discuss the challenges and solutions available for digital semantic publishing.

Journalists and web publishing

In web publishing, journalists have traditionally been asked to write a story and tag it with metadata, including

- ✔ What the story is relevant to
- ✔ Who is mentioned in it
- ✔ The names of relevant organizations or topics
- ✔ The most germane place on the website for the news story

Obviously, these tasks require a lot of time and effort. It's not as simple as typing names of people; you must find the exact name as it exists in some organizational taxonomy.

Digital semantic publishing on the web eliminates this problem. Digital semantic publishing is where entities (for example people, places, and organizations) and their relationships to each other drive the placement of an article that mentions one or more of those entities. This avoids forcing the individual journalists and editors from manually trying to learn and apply a complex and ever changing taxonomy (topic and sub topic hierarchy).

Therefore, digital semantic publishing provides a way for news publishers to store a set of interrelated facts separate from the stories themselves. In this way, facts drive navigation. These facts might include who plays for which teams, which organizations people belong to, which news stories they're mentioned in, and what fashion labels they're associated with.

As a result, users can simply use search terms that identify a story's main topics, and the story will show up in all relevant sections on the website. This capability means that, as they are preparing the story, journalists don't have to consider all the items that relate to it, freeing them to spend more time on journalism itself.

For example, the BBC Sport and BBC Olympics websites combine a document store and a triple store in a sophisticated web publishing application, making them great examples of digital semantic publishing. (Turn to Chapter 36 for more details on this NoSQL application.)

Changing legislation over time

Many documents change over time, and legislation covering an entire country is no different. Laws are revised by the legislature and clarified by the courts. Some elements of laws are activated by the secretary of state (they're called a Statutory Instrument in the UK, similar to Executive Orders in the United States) for a particular department. Activation happens at a time decided by the government of the day.

Determining which laws and particular clauses are applicable at any given time is a very complex task. Many pieces of legislation affect other existing clauses throughout the body of law. This is particularly difficult when your legal system dates back a thousand years, like it does in the United Kingdom.

The `www.legislation.gov.uk` website uses a document NoSQL database and a triple store to hold the legislation, as well as relationships between clauses and future and past modifications from Acts of Parliament and Statutory Instruments. The website even lets you know about legislation going through Parliament and upcoming clauses to be activated at a future date.

These complex interrelations can occur between any Act for any reason, which means that the possible combinations of relationships aren't known at design time. A schema-less approach to the content of acts and the relationships between them is, therefore, advantageous.

Metadata Catalogs

In many systems, it isn't possible or desirable to replace multiple systems with a single new system. When a single view of all available information is required, you need to pull in the relevant data pointers from each source system and join them together.

This is particularly important in the media and intelligence worlds. Video and audio files are maintained in their own specialist systems. Users, though, generally want to search across all programming from a particular company in order to see what is relevant for them.

In this section, I describe how a metadata catalog approach is different to consolidating (copying) data from source systems in to a single master database to rule them all, and why you would consider applying the metadata catalog use case in your organization.

Creating a single view

Perhaps there's a film about Harry Potter, a TV interview with J.K. Rowling, and a syndicated program interviewing the cast of the Harry Potter movies. A search for Harry Potter should show all programs, no matter what the source repository.

This single view approach is designed to provide a user-friendly interface. Consumers don't need to know what source systems or separation exist between content systems. This makes searching for content a seamless and consistent process and increases the likelihood for content to be discovered and played, which is vital for increasing the use of public and commercial broadcasting services.

Intelligence agencies also closely guard their information, yet they must provide a catalog of their intelligence reports to other agencies for searching. So the high-level metadata on each piece of intelligence must be combined to help other agencies discover what intelligence is available on a particular subject. Once the reports are discovered, analysts can request access to the source material they need in order to perform their tasks.

Replacing legacy systems

After a single view of existing data is created, you may find opportunities to look at older legacy systems and switch them off in favor of a new catalog. In fact, it isn't unusual for metadata catalogs to expand and include entire records of legacy systems before the source systems are switched off. This is particularly true of costly mainframe systems that were used to manage documents in a way that makes it difficult to migrate from these systems to a relational database management system (RDBMS). These migrations are best done over time and in a way that's transparent to users of the services. A common pattern is to have several RDBMS schemas configured for the same data, each organized slightly differently, depending on the application accessing them. Typically, doing so involves representing the data at different levels of granularity.

Replacing these multiple RDBMS systems with a single hybrid NoSQL database may be desirable. Doing so could provide one or more of the following benefits:

- Lower cost by storing the data once
- Simpler data management, altering the view through automatic denormalization or at query time (called *schema on read*)

✔ More comprehensible mental model for data organization

✔ Less complexity when one schema needs changing

✔ Fewer different integration points for downstream systems and user interfaces

A recent media company's metadata catalog implementation I was involved with replaced three MySQL databases (and their sizeable hardware environments), along with a large set of APIs built on top of those three databases, with a single NoSQL hybrid database cluster and one API. The new system provided the following advantages:

✔ Wholly accurate search over all metadata records

✔ Denormalizations of metadata records at the program availability level, in line with user expectations

✔ Shorter time to achieve availability for new program information online

✔ Less outlay of hardware

✔ Easier to maintain API codebase

When the use case is correct, a hybrid NoSQL database approach, as compared to traditional approaches, can save a great deal of money in terms of maintaining code and hardware.

Exploring data

In many of the use cases throughout this book, I assume that the format of the data is known prior to the application being designed to access that information. In most cases, this is a fair assumption; however, there are some situations where the structure may not be known prior to the design of the application, for example:

✔ A dump of digital data from a hard disk in computers obtained when police execute a search warrant on a house

✔ Data and contact information from an arrested suspect's mobile phone (in countries where this is legal!)

✔ Messages on social media where the underlying data format changes, depending on the application that creates it

✔ Data feeds from external organizations where the format is out of your control and changes rapidly (such as CSV format files on http:// data.gov.uk that change monthly without warning)

✔ Largely free text information, such as that found in emails and mailed correspondence

✔ Binary documents that allow unstructured information (PDF, Word, and XHTML documents are typical examples)

The preceding content types are wide-ranging, but they must have these two features in order to be accessed:

✔ Text and metadata structures must be understood, or converted to a format (JSON, XML, or plain text, for example) that can be natively understood and indexed.

✔ A search engine that, at a minimum, understands free-text content, but that can also understand metadata extracted or the inherent structure within the document (such as the JSON of a tweet or XML nodes in an XHTML web page).

Being able to perform both of the preceding processes enables users to immediately access value in all stored data, even if the inherent structures aren't yet known, and so cannot be built in to a system's design. This is an example of using an *exploration application*.

After the data formats are better understood, specific indexes and user-interface components can be added to the application to take advantage of emerging structures, including metadata fields such as the date created, the author, or GPS coordinates at which an image was taken.

From day one, an exploration application enables end users to take advantage of data captured. This data can be searched immediately, and analysed later to determine fields that are present. These fields could be configured in an application later to make it easier to categorize or search data. This avoids a complex testing and rollout process, ensuring a system can handle all data before it is first released.

Hybrid NoSQL databases, such as MarkLogic Server, that support document storage and search along with binary file extraction features provide a good foundation on which to build exploration applications.

Chapter 32

Hybrid NoSQL Database Products

*H*ybrid NoSQL databases fall into two categories:

- ✔ Those that use a non-relational data type and triples to store relationships and metadata about those records
- ✔ Those that integrate search with document structures (whether they are key-value stores or document databases)

Using a triple store approach to provide schema agnosticism in the relationships mirrors the way that NoSQL databases provide schema agnosticism in their own records' data models. A triple store approach to relationships between records goes some way towards providing cross record information links, avoiding some of the need for producing denormalizations.

OrientDB, ArangoDB, and MarkLogic Server all take the document-oriented approach, using triples to store relationship information either within, or independently of, the document records they describe.

There is a level of depth required in multiple NoSQL areas (such as document, triples, and search) that is required to be a true hybrid NoSQL database.

In this chapter, I describe the most common data management use cases that hybrid NoSQL databases are used for.

Managing Triples and Aggregates

Rarely do I gush about NoSQL databases, but I really like OrientDB's simplicity in terms of synergies between a document database and a triple store. Many NoSQL databases are criticized for being unnecessarily complicated or esoteric, so it's refreshing to find one that solves complex problems in compact and easy-to-use ways.

For example, document NoSQL databases are often used to achieve denormalization, which means that, rather than follow the relational model and split data into constituent parts, you put all the data in a single document.

Product orders are typical examples. An order may include a product id, a name, a price, the quantity ordered, customer and delivery details, and payment information. It makes sense to model information in a single container (document) so that all the information can be accessed at the same time.

In some circumstances, though, it still makes sense to treat the information as discrete documents. What do you do then? Do you manage many denormalizations ("probably" is the honest answer!), or do you keep atomic structures, such as relational tables, and piece them together at query time?

Merging data at query time isn't fun, as anyone who has written a complex system in relational databases can tell you! Complex inner and outer joins are hard to get right at query time, and it's even harder to make them run fast.

Generating triples from documents

OrientDB has a nice solution to the problem of managing these compound document use cases. As well as being a full-featured document NoSQL database, OrientDB gives you the ability to configure it so that it generates the triples (relationships) between documents as they're added, and to materialize views automatically at query time based on those relationships. All without nasty complex SQL-like queries or complex triggers to maintain multiple denormalized documents.

OrientDB actually achieves this through *lazy loading* of the child documents, transparent from the calling code. This means that the OrientDB client API will receive the definition of a compound document and only fetch the parts needed from the server when the host application accesses them.

Lazy loading avoids materializing every relationship before returning the full document to the client. For many applications where a user drives accessing parts of a document this approach is likely a better performing one overall.

In the preceding example, you can configure OrientDB so that any JSON document being added that has a product_id field also generates a triple (relationship), thereby linking the document and the relevant product document it refers to.

Enforcing schema on read

Schema on read means that, as an app developer, you can design an app so that when the details on a customer's latest order are shown, the application asks for the order document and indicates that the product details should be embedded within the order document. This procedure puts data merging activities into the database where they belong and relieves application developers of having to deal with all the complex code and modeling of client-side manual data aggregation.

If you have numerous JSON documents that need to be maintained individually but combined at retrieval time, or if you want triples generated automatically, then consider using OrientDB.

Evaluating OrientDB

OrientDB is available both as an open-source product and as a commercially supported product. The company that makes it is based in the UK and is relatively small, although it succeeded in being included in the 2013 Gartner Magic Quadrant for Operational Database Management Systems.

I have only one criticism about OrientDB: It provides only its proprietary API for accessing triples. I'd liked to see a more open-standards approach, such as support in the core platform for the Resource Description Format (RDF) and SPARQL semantic query standards.

I definitely recommend that you take a look at OrientDB if you need a database that goes beyond JSON document storage and that requires complex relationship modeling.

Combining Documents and Triples with Enterprise Capabilities

MarkLogic Server is one of the oldest NoSQL databases included in this book. In fact, MarkLogic has been around even longer the term NoSQL.

MarkLogic was originally an ACID-compliant XML database with a built-in search engine. It was developed for the U.S. government's clients that wanted the enterprise features in XML documents that they used in their relational DBMS systems.

MarkLogic adopts a lot of the approaches to indexing and search that you see in standalone search engines.

Full Disclosure: I work as a principal sales engineer for MarkLogic, so obviously I have a bias; however, as author of this book, I cover both MarkLogic's strengths and its weaknesses. (The Publisher wouldn't let me do otherwise!) Some of these strengths and weaknesses are mentioned in Chapter 17, such as MarkLogic's historic dependency on the XQuery language, not familiar to many developers. (JavaScript is supported in the version 8 release of MarkLogic Server.)

Combined database, search, and application services

MarkLogic's abundant uniqueness is why I included it in this book. First, it's commercial-only software, which is rare in the NoSQL world, in which most NoSQL databases are perceived as being open-source, meaning they have free developer licenses.

MarkLogic Server is a single product that combines a document-orientated NoSQL database, a sophisticated search engine, and a set of application services that expose the functionality of the server.

MarkLogic currently supports XML, binary, and text documents. At the time of this writing, the MarkLogic 8 Early Access version also includes support for native JSON storage — although an automatic translation between JSON and XML had been available for two years.

The primary reason I include MarkLogic in the hybrid section is because it has a built-in triple store with support for both the W3C graph store and SPARQL protocols and for ingestion and production of RDF data in a variety of formats. This means MarkLogic Server is both a document-orientated NoSQL database and a triple store, as well as a search engine — all in a single product. You're free to use only document operations or only semantic operations. You can use both at the same time, and combine this data format support with free text, range query operations (less than and greater than), and geospatial search.

These are two layers in MarkLogic Server:

✔ The database layer provides ACID compliance, compressed storage, and indexing during a transaction.

✔ The evaluation layer is a query layer that supports several query languages.

✔ There is a high-level, Google-style grammar search API (the Search API) and a lower-level structured query (CTS API — CTS is an abbreviation for MarkLogic's former name, Celoquent Text Search). This layer also provides support for the W3C SPARQL 1.0 and 1.1 API and the W3C graph store protocol for semantic queries.

In terms of the programming language used in the evaluation layer, the server is written in C++ and uses the XQuery native language (and thus XPath) and XSLT. MarkLogic Server 8 adds server-side JavaScript support to this mix. Anything you can currently do in XQuery, you'll be able to do in JavaScript.

Schema free versus schema agnostic

Most document NoSQL databases are schema agnostic — that is, they don't enforce schema. MarkLogic is a schema-free database. You don't normally enforce XML schema, but you can do so if you wish.

MarkLogic hailed from the XML standards world, so as you might expect, there's a lot of XML standards support. If you need to enter data into the database and still validate (compare) a document to a schema and generate a compliance report, you can do so with a schematron approach. Although this isn't one of MarkLogic's standard features, it's been implemented for several customers in the evaluation layer as a pluggable extension module.

Providing Bigtable features

The fastest way to perform aggregate functions, sorting, and search is to use an in-memory data representation. Column stores do this by storing ordered columns or column families in RAM. Search engines do this by storing one or more term lists (including forward, reverse, and text indexes) in RAM.

In-memory databases, in contrast, store all data in RAM, so you can quickly churn through it. The problem with in-memory databases is that if your data runs beyond the amount of RAM you have in a cluster, issues with the system's stability or with data consistency arise.

MarkLogic's indexes are used both for normal database queries — like `Give me document with ID 'MyDocument'` or `'where owner=afowler'` — and search engine operations — like "Give me all suspicious activity report documents that talk about places in this geospatial polygon, that mention 'pedestrians' and that are related to vehicles with ABC* on the license plate."

The same indexes are also used for range queries, sorting, and aggregate functions. Storing these in memory makes accessing them fast, and ACID compliance ensures that they're also kept on disk keeping them safe should a system failure occur.

Consider a common column store operation like counting the number of kernel panics in a log file from a particular system over a specified day. You perform an exact-value-match query to match the system name, and a range query to set the upper and lower limits of the time of the log entry. You then perform an aggregate function over the result — in this case, a simple count (summation) operation.

Aggregate functions can be much more complex — such as calculating a standard deviation over a set of matching range index values, or even a user defined function written in C++ and installed in a cluster.

Once you have range indexes, and thus in memory columns, defined and associated with a document, you can do another interesting thing. Take the document id as a record ID, and a set of range indexes as columns. Using this approach, you can model a relational view of the co-occurrence of these fields within a particular set of documents.

MarkLogic Server uses this approach to provide Open Database Connectivity (ODBC) driver access. This allows business intelligence tools to query MarkLogic Server's documents as though they were relational database rows.

MarkLogic Server handles in-memory data aggregation at high speed, much like a column store. Therefore, you can use MarkLogic Server both as an Operational Database Management System (OpDBMS, a term used by Gartner to refer to both relational databases and NoSQL databases used for live operational workloads) and as an analytics/data warehousing database.

Securing access to information

Many of the first MarkLogic customers were in the defense sector. This sector realized early on that they needed the same business capabilities across unstructured and semi-structured documents as they had in their relational database systems.

A key requirement in defense is security of the data. I cover this functionality in detail in Chapter 17, but I include a summary here for convenience.

MarkLogic provides granular access to information by supporting the following functionality at the document level:

- ✔ **Authentication:** Checks users to be sure they're who they say they are. This is done either in a database or through an external mechanism like LDAP or Kerberos.

- ✔ **Permissions:** A list of roles with whether they have read or update access to documents, URIs (directories), and code modules.

- ✔ **Authorization through role based access control:** Users are assigned roles, and these roles are associated with permissions at the document level. User roles can be set in MarkLogic Server or read from an external directory server through LDAP.

- ✔ **Compartment security:** Enforces AND logic on roles rather than OR logic. Basically, a user must have all roles attached to a named security compartment in order to have that permission on a document, rather than just one role with that permission. This role logic mode is useful for combining citizenship, job function, organization, and mission involvement criteria required for any user to access information.

These permissions are indexed against the document like any other term list in the internal workings of the MarkLogic Server search engine. This makes permission checking just as fast as any other search lookup, and just as scalable.

MarkLogic Server is also used in security accredited systems at a very high level in defense. It's also the only NoSQL database to achieve independent accreditation through the NIAP Common Criteria at EAL 2. This is an industry standard, recognized throughout NATO countries, that states that a product and its development process has been checked so that it complies to industry best practice for producing systems used in secure environments.

Evaluating MarkLogic

A key advantage of MarkLogic is that you can use the same database cluster for both types of operations. In the relational world, you have two separate databases, with different structures (schema) — each requiring timed pushes to an alternatives database warehouse structure, typically only updated every 24 hours.

MarkLogic Server provides a wide range of functionality spanning document ingestion, conversion, alerting, search, exploration, denormalization, aggregation, and analytics functions. It does so in a commercial product with strong support for open W3C standards across the document, search, and semantic areas of functionality.

As a hybrid NoSQL database MarkLogic Server spans several NoSQL areas — document management, search, and storing triples. MarkLogic Server also supports fast in memory data aggregate operations, and access to its data from legacy relational, SQL query based, Business Intelligence (BI) tools.

If you need a wide variety of functionality spanning a single or combined areas within document, search and triple store capabilities then you should consider MarkLogic Server.

Chapter 33

MarkLogic

• •

• •

MarkLogic Server functionality ranges from simple document storage, to search, to semantic triple store capabilities. Document lifecycle is supported through creation, conversion, entity extraction, alerting, search, content processing, storage tiering, and disposition.

Often the difficulty in fully understanding MarkLogic Server relates to which areas of functionality are relevant for which business solutions. It's easy to become overwhelmed by the science and list of functionality. So, you need to focus on the areas that are likely to provide you with the most value, both in the short-term and in the long-term as your NoSQL installation (inevitably) expands.

In this chapter, I discuss the key areas of technology within MarkLogic Server, and how it provides a comprehensive hybrid NoSQL database.

Understanding MarkLogic Server

MarkLogic Server is a single product that serves three main areas:

✔ **Document NoSQL database:** Persisting data and providing consistent views of data, this database stores and provides access to your JSON, XML, text, or binary documents.

✔ **Search:** Provides content and/or semantic search, including full text, range (greater than, less than) and geospatial.

✔ **Application services:** Provides access to functionality through the REST API and programming language wrappers, and provides high-level APIs (for example, a Google-like text string search grammar) for end users.

MarkLogic Server is the only product mentioned in each of the Gartner Magic Quadrants for enterprise search, operational database management systems, and data warehouse systems. MarkLogic Server is also mentioned as a leader for NoSQL databases in the Forrester Wave for NoSQL.

Universal Indexing

MarkLogic Server includes a universal index of all content. All text, XML, and JSON document content are indexed for their structure, the elements and attributes present, and their values. The universal index also includes full text indexing with many options for including indexes for specific cases, such as 2 (Ad*) and 3 (Ada*) character wildcards.

This universal index is MarkLogic's secret sauce. It's what allows you to load your content into the database without needing to tell MarkLogic how that data is structured before loading it.

You load the data "as-is," and the structure, value, and text queries can immediately be used to search and explore your data. Later on, you can add specific range indexes for your application needs.

MarkLogic Server can store binary documents efficiently, but the universal index doesn't automatically process them for text searching. To do that, you need to enable one or more of the Content Processing Framework's (CPF) content filtering pipelines.

CPF moves documents through predefined states. It's basically a finite-state automata. Various pipelines are available, including for converting Word documents to Docbook XML and for extracting text from PDF files.

Over 200 binary file formats are supported for extracting text, ranging from office formats to photos (extracting metadata about the camera, for example), and to email and other formats.

The universal index allows very fast resolution of text query terms. Each word is stored in a reverse index. Instead of saying, "Look through all documents and list their words — now, which ones include 'Fred'?" you say, "Store all words in every document, and keep a list of document IDs for each word."

This term list makes search engine lookups very fast. Say that you have a complex "and" query of 200 terms. And queries are where all terms must match a document in order for it to be included in the results.

Rather than churn through the documents (boring!), you fetch the list of terms and perform a simple (fast!) intersection of the lists. The resulting shorter result set includes all documents that match your whole query! Simple.

MarkLogic uses its indexes for document retrieval, search, and sorting operations. Rather than have a document database with its own indexes and a separate search engine with its indexes — some of which will be duplicated — you have a single set of indexes.

Range indexing and aggregate queries

Often you don't need to index the exact values of elements and attributes, or words and phrases. Instead, you need to perform a range operation like these:

- ✔ Find me all documents updated in the last week.
- ✔ List all articles published in August 2009.
- ✔ List all employees who are between 5 feet and 6 feet tall.
- ✔ List all types of cheese with a Wendy Rating greater than three stars.

My wife, Wendy, loves cheese!

These are all queries that fall before or after a single value, or that lie between two values — a value range.

MarkLogic stores range indexes similarly to those in the universal index, except that the values are stored in order, which makes finding lists of matching documents even faster.

Rather than scanning the entire index for all values and checking that they are between the two limits of your range query, MarkLogic finds the lower limit value, then the upper limit value, then aggregates the document IDs of every list of terms in between, which results in much faster search resolution.

These indexes are also cached in memory. They can be combined with structure, value, and term queries in a single index resolution — that is, one hit on the indexes.

Each range index obviously has its own type. All the basic XML types are supported — integers, positive integers, W3C dates and date-times, floating point numbers, and so on.

There are also two types of special range indexes. The first is a geospatial index. Rather than index a set of single values, this indexes two — one for longitude another for latitude. You are, in effect, indexing a 2D plane, which also makes geospatial searches fast.

MarkLogic Server supports the World Geodetic System 1984 (WGS84) standard for longitude and latitude, and considers the uneven curvature of the Earth. Various operations are supported, including basic point and radius and bounding box, and complex polygon searches. MarkLogic also has an optional license for polygon-polygon intersection and other advanced geospatial operations, although most customers outside of the defense industry rarely use it.

Range indexes aren't just used for searching, though. They are key to performing fast aggregation functions. MarkLogic Server supports several of these:

- Count (document or fragment frequency)
- Sum
- Maximum and minimum values
- Correlation
- Mean and median averages
- Standard deviation, variance and co-variance (including population functions)
- Custom aggregate functions through creating your own user-defined functions (UDFs) in C++

Combining content and semantic technologies

A key example of combined content and semantic search is around document provenance. Say that you're a publisher and you find a mistake in a published article. This mistake is in regard to incorrect experimental results around a specific scientific term, making the proof of a scientific theory questionable.

This scientific theory claims that if your author's belly becomes any larger, it will start to have its own micro climate, called the *Adamosphere*. As you can guess, the results of the article are suspect. (I'm slim, honest!)

You could do a content search to pull back all documents with the term Adamosphere, but you'd spend ages checking to see if the mistake is referenced in the article. Likewise, you could find all documents that refer to the article, but then you'd have to manually find just those that mention the specific term.

The World Wide Web Consortium's (W3C) Provenance Ontology could help you here. Say that, with every newly published document, you create a set of triples to indicate that a new document is a derivative work or refers to a list of other documents.

You could save a lot of time by using the SPARQL query language to search all references; then you could use the resulting list of documents and do a content search to find the exact documents that need to be corrected.

It's also possible to do this combined search in a single call to MarkLogic via its XQuery API, thereby executing a search that includes a SPARQL term. This assumes the triples are embedded within the document, though, because such a query uses search index resolution at the document level.

Adding Hadoop support

MarkLogic supports various technologies for storage, including local disk (SSD and spinning), shared disk (NAS, SAN) and cloud (HDFS, Amazon EBS, and Amazon S3).

MarkLogic also supports tiering data automatically on the fly without any downtime or transactional inconsistency. You can use any range index in a rule to define when data is moved between tiers.

Doing so enables you to use, for example, a fast local disk for the last 90 days of trades, a shared and slower disk (say a NAS) for trades up to one year, and HDFS as an inexpensive albeit slower storage layer for older information.

Using MarkLogic with HDFS has some advantages over using the HBase NoSQL database with HDFS. First, the indexes stored on HDFS are also cached in RAM, so you may avoid a remote HDFS fetch penalty when querying data held on HDFS.

MarkLogic Server also has a map/reduce connector. This enables map reduce jobs to call data held in MarkLogic Server (whatever the storage mechanism). This option exposes current inflight data to your map reduce analyses.

These map/reduce jobs are fast, too, because you can use MarkLogic Search to reduce the amount of data operated on in your map/reduce job, rather than churning through all the stored data just in case it's relevant.

MarkLogic HDFS forests (a storage directory, akin to a shard — many forests form a database) can also be used as an archive format. You can take these forests offline and move them to a tape tier, or they can be kept in HDFS but not updated by MarkLogic. This reduces the number of forests the MarkLogic tier is managing.

MarkLogic provides a JAR file for its proprietary storage format so that map/reduce jobs — outside of MarkLogic — can access the data held in these offline forests. No need to reattach to MarkLogic before accessing the data in them, or indeed the index values!

Replication on intermittent networks

Not all systems can rely on a constant connection to their networks. This is particularly true in the defense industry's working environment — for example, forward operating bases with limited satellite communications, naval vessels, or even Special Forces soldiers with laptops in the middle of nowhere. Before these operators are detached, they want to search for and replicate useful information to their laptops or base portable servers.

Replication configurations of this kind aren't entire replicas of a whole data center like traditional replication is. Instead, it's a subset of data specified by a query, a collection, or a directory of information. You can prioritize these datasets for replication. Doing so is particularly useful if you've added information over time.

However, returning to the military scenario, an operator may have only a brief window of time to connect to a higher echelon of command. During this time, the operator needs to replicate high-priority items first, followed by lower-priority items.

This is where query-based, flexible replication comes in, because it allows users to specify and prioritize multiple replication datasets.

Ensuring data integrity

MarkLogic Server is built as an ACID-compliant, fully consistent database with data durability guarantees. Making a change in MarkLogic Server updates all available replicas within the transactional boundary, including all search indexes, which provides entirely accurate search results.

MarkLogic Server takes this ACID compliance one step further and guarantees *fully serializable* transactions. I discuss fully serializable transactions in Chapter 1. *Fully serializable* means that a long-running transaction sees the database's state at the point in time when the query started. Even if a short transaction updates information or deletes it, this long-running transaction still sees the database state at the point in time when the transaction started. This approach allows for repeatable reads within the same transaction.

MarkLogic Server supports *multiversion concurrency control* (MVCC). I discuss MVCC in Chapter 2. MVCC is an internal database versioning mechanism that provides for very high write and update rates, while maintaining access to existing information for reads (that is, without blocking the information until the writes are finished).

MarkLogic Server also uses an in-memory stand. A stand is a storage area within a forest, which is a MarkLogic term for a shard. There are many stands within a forest, which is the unit of partitioning in MarkLogic Server. This means all writes happen in memory with only the transaction log being written to disk in case of system failure. This provides ACID consistency guarantees while ensuring fast data ingest and query speeds.

Compartmentalizing information

MarkLogic Server's universal index has a hidden index for document security permissions. This indexed list of permissions is always consulted by MarkLogic Server for all database read and search operations, ensuring that data doesn't leak to those without permission to access it.

MarkLogic Server provides both classic *role based access control* (RBAC) and compartmentalization — that is restricting access to a group of people with a very specific set of roles.

A typical document using standard RBAC lists the roles that have permission to read a document. A user with any one of those roles will have access to a document.

However, if one or more document permission roles belong to a named compartment, the user must have all those roles in order to read the document — this role check uses AND logic. For example, this approach is particularly useful if you want to give access to information only to users with all the following roles: the UK role in the Citizenship compartment, the Senior Analyst role in the Job Title compartment, and the Chastise role in the Operation compartment.

MarkLogic's document transformation functionality (using XSLT, XQuery, or JavaScript transform modules) also provides a way to proactively redact parts of a document upon request or search. This approach is useful in situations where you want to provide access to a summary but not to the raw information. You can also use this functionality during flexible replication to transform data before sending to or receiving from another MarkLogic cluster. Using transforms on flexible replication is therefore a good way to move some information from a high security system to a lower security system (such an information movement system is called a *Guard* in the defense industry).

For more on the inner workings of MarkLogic, go to `developer.marklogic.com` and check out Jason Hunter's paper entitled, "Inside MarkLogic Server," which you can download at no cost.

MarkLogic Corporation

MarkLogic Corporation is the commercial company behind MarkLogic Server — and my employer! Headquartered in San Carlos south of San Francisco, California, MarkLogic has worldwide field offices, support, sales, consulting, and engineering staff.

MarkLogic Corporation is, by revenue, the largest NoSQL company, according to the latest Wikibon analysis of the Hadoop and NoSQL database markets.

Finding trained developers

A historic irony in MarkLogic is that, although it's arguably the most open-standards-compliant NoSQL database — having been built on published open standards, including XML, XPath, XQuery, and XSLT — a problem has been finding trained developers for these languages, especially XQuery experts.

However, MarkLogic Server version 8 will embed a JavaScript engine in MarkLogic Server. JavaScript support will provide all existing functionality of the core server to server-side JavaScript developers. So, JavaScript developers will be able to create database triggers, content processing scripts, search alert handlers, and reusable libraries in the database.

JavaScript is the most commonly used scripting language available today. Although it has limitations for processing XML, it's very adept at providing an easy-to-understand language for general scripting and JSON document management functions.

Support for server-side JavaScript should go a long way in alleviating the shortage of expert MarkLogic Server developers, and in reducing barriers to adoption throughout the market.

Finding 24/7 support

MarkLogic Corporation provides 24/7 global support at customer sites. An interesting thing about all MarkLogic support engineers is that they are full-blown product engineers with access to the support code — they just happen to work on the support team. This means they can often find and suggest workarounds and fixes for system issues without having to wait for product developers to wake up halfway around the world.

MarkLogic also provides free online training for its products. Custom courses can be designed by its own developers. All presales personnel can deliver one-day MarkLogic Foundation courses to instruct staff on how to install and use MarkLogic Server. MarkLogic has also introduced a developer certification program, with training pathways and certification tests.

MarkLogic's Consulting Services team provides customers with expert services, project management, and business analysts. During the early stages of a new deployment, many customers particularly value this expertise, especially in terms of "sanity-checking" on decisions about sizing and system design.

Using MarkLogic in the cloud

MarkLogic Server is available in traditional core-based license packs for development (non-production) and perpetual licenses for cluster production systems.

MarkLogic Server version 7 also introduced yearly term-based licensing and a 99-cent per hour, per vCPU (Virtual CPU, which is like half a CPU processor core) subscription option on Amazon Web Services.

You can also use MarkLogic perpetual and term licenses on public and private cloud installations, which is useful because the 99-cent Amazon option doesn't include support or advanced options.

MarkLogic's term and perpetual licenses are available in two models:

- ✓ **Essential Enterprise:** This model is typically designed for applications. It requires up to nine servers of 8 CPU cores each and has optional license models for semantics and language packs.

- ✓ **Global Enterprise:** This model supports any number of servers in a cluster; options include semantics, language packs, tiered storage, and advanced geospatial alerting (including polygon-polygon intersection, which is primarily used in defense solutions).

Even though they include a yearly maintenance charge, over time, the perpetual licenses work out to be less expensive than the annual term licenses, because the maintenance charge is less expensive than the annual term license.

To compare the licensing options available, go to www.marklogic.com/pricing.

Part VIII
The Part of Tens

the part of tens

In this part . . .

- ✔ Surpass RDBMS.
- ✔ Correct misunderstandings.
- ✔ Connect with the world.
- ✔ Visit `www.dummies.com` for great Dummies content online.

Chapter 34

Ten Advantages of NoSQL over RDBMS

In This Chapter

▶ Saving development time

▶ Increasing flexibility

▶ Reducing cost

I've said throughout this book that NoSQL databases are not a direct replacement for an relational database management system (RDBMS). For many data problems, though, NoSQL is a better match than an RDBMS. I point out the most useful advantages in this chapter.

Less Need for ETL

NoSQL databases support storing data "as is." Key-value stores give you the ability to store simple data structures, whereas document NoSQL databases provide you with the ability to handle a range of flat or nested structures.

Most of the data flying between systems does so as a message. Typically, the data takes one of these formats:

✔ A binary object to be passed through a set of layers

✔ An XML document

✔ A JSON document

Being able to handle these formats natively in a range of NoSQL databases lessens the amount of code you have to convert from the source data format to the format that needs storing. This is called *extract, transform, and load* (ETL).

Using this approach, you greatly reduce the amount of code required to start using a NoSQL database. Moreover, because you don't have to pay for updates to this "plumbing" code, ongoing maintenance costs are significantly decreased.

Support for Unstructured Text

The vast majority of data in enterprise systems is unstructured. Many NoSQL databases can handle indexing of unstructured text either as a native feature (MarkLogic Server) or an integrated set of services including Solr or Elasticsearch.

Being able to manage unstructured text greatly increases information and can help organizations make better decisions. For example, advanced uses include support for multiple languages with facetted search, snippet functionality, and word-stemming support. Advanced features also include support for dictionaries and thesauri.

Furthermore, using search alert actions on data ingest, you can extract named entities from directories such as those listing people, places, and organizations, which allows text data to be better categorized, tagged, and searched.

Entity enrichment services such as SmartLogic, OpenCalais, NetOwl, and TEMIS Luxid that combine extracted information with other information provide a rich interleaved information web and enhance efficient analysis and use.

Ability to Handle Change over Time

Because of the schema agnostic nature of NoSQL databases, they're very capable of managing change — you don't have to rewrite ETL routines if the XML message structure between systems changes.

Some NoSQL databases take this a step further and provide a universal index for the structure, values, and text found in information. Microsoft DocumentDB and MarkLogic Server both provide this capability.

If a document structure changes, these indexes allow organizations to use the information immediately, rather than having to wait for several months before you can test and rewrite systems.

No Reliance on SQL Magic

Structured Query Language (SQL) is the predominant language used to query relational database management systems. Being able to structure queries so that they perform well has over the years become a thorny art. Complex multi-table joins are not easy to write from memory.

Although several NoSQL databases support SQL access, they do so for compatibility with existing applications such as business intelligence (BI) tools. NoSQL databases support their own access languages that can interpret the data being stored, rather than require a relational model within the underlying database.

This more developer-centric mentality to the design of databases and their access application programming interfaces (API) are the reason NoSQL databases have become very popular among application developers.

Application developers don't need to know the inner workings and vagaries of databases before using them. NoSQL databases empower developers to work on what is required in the applications instead of trying to force relational databases to do what is required.

Ability to Scale Horizontally on Commodity Hardware

NoSQL databases handle partitioning (*sharding*) of a database across several servers. So, if your data storage requirements grow too much, you can continue to add inexpensive servers and connect them to your database cluster (*horizontal scaling*) making them work as a single data service.

Contrast this to the relational database world where you need to buy new, more powerful and thus more expensive hardware to scale up (*vertical scaling*). If you were to double the amount of data you store, you would easily quadruple the cost of the hardware you need.

Providing durability and high availability of a NoSQL database by using inexpensive hardware and storage is one of NoSQL's major assets. Being able to do so while providing generous scalability for many uses also doesn't hurt!

Breadth of Functionality

Most relational databases support the same features but in a slightly different way, so they are all similar.

NoSQL databases, in contrast, come in four core types: key-value, columnar, document, and triple stores. Within these types, you can find a database to suit your particular (and peculiar!) needs. With so much choice, you're bound to find a NoSQL database that will solve your application woes.

Support for Multiple Data Structures

Many applications need simple object storage, whereas others require highly complex and interrelated structure storage. NoSQL databases provide support for a range of data structures.

- Simple binary values, lists, maps, and strings can be handled at high speed in key-value stores.
- Related information values can be grouped in column families within Bigtable clones.
- Highly complex parent-child hierarchal structures can be managed within document databases.
- A web of interrelated information can be described flexibly and related in triple and graph stores.

Vendor Choice

The NoSQL industry is awash with databases, though many have been around for less than ten years. For example, IBM, Microsoft, and Oracle only recently dipped their toes into this market. Consequently, many vendors are targeting particular audiences with their own brew of innovation.

Open-source variants are available for most NoSQL databases, which enables companies to explore and start using NoSQL databases at minimal risk. These companies can then take their new methods to a production platform by using enterprise offerings.

No Legacy Code

Because they are so new, NoSQL databases don't have legacy code, which means they don't need to provide support for old hardware platforms or keep strange and infrequently used functionality updated.

NoSQL databases enjoy a quick pace in terms of development and maturation. New features are released all the time, and new and existing features are updated frequently (so NoSQL vendors don't need to maintain a very large code base). In fact, new major releases occur annually rather than every three to five years.

Executing Code Next to the Data

NoSQL databases were created in the era of Hadoop. Hadoop's highly distributed file-system (HDFS) and batch-processing environment (Map/Reduce) signaled changes in the way data is stored, queried, and processed.

Queries and processing work now pass to several servers, which provides high levels of parallelization for both ingest and query workloads. Being able to calculate aggregations next to the data has also become the norm.

You no longer need a separate data warehouse system that is updated overnight. With fast aggregations and query handling, analysis is passed to the database for execution next to the data, which means you don't have to ship a lot of data around a network to achieve locally combined analysis.

Chapter 35

Ten NoSQL Misconceptions

In This Chapter

▶ Blowing away misinformation

▶ Bringing clear facts

As I mention in earlier chapters, NoSQL is a rapidly evolving market with products undergoing constant change. Having so many NoSQL databases available is a double-edged sword. With so many differences out there, common misconceptions form and become lore. I highlight the most common misconceptions in this chapter.

NoSQL Is a Single Type of Database

NoSQL is a catch-all term for a variety of database types that exhibit common architectural approaches. These databases aren't intended for related table, rows, and columns data. They are highly distributed, which means data is spread across several servers, and they're tolerant of data structure changes (that is, they're schema agnostic).

You can find several types of databases under the NoSQL banner:

- ✔ Key-value stores provide easy and fast storage of simple data through use of a key.
- ✔ Column stores provide support for very wide tables but not for relationships between tables.
- ✔ Document stores support JSON and/or XML hierarchical structures.
- ✔ Triple (and graph) stores provide the same flexibility to relationships that document NoSQL databases provide to record structures.

NoSQL Databases Aren't ACID-Compliant

ACID compliance is the gold standard of data safety. By ensuring that operations are atomic, views of data are consistent, operations don't interfere with each other, and data is durably saved to disk, you protect your data. People often think NoSQL databases do not provide ACID compliance.

Many NoSQL databases provide full ACID support across clusters. MarkLogic Server, OrientDB, Aerospike, and Hypertable are all fully ACID-compliant, providing either *fully serializable* or *read-commit* ACID compliance.

Many other NoSQL databases can provide ACID-like consistency by using sensible settings in client code. This typically involves a *Quorum* or *All* setting for both read and write operations. These databases include Riak, MongoDB, and Microsoft DocumentDB.

NoSQL Databases Lose Data

This misconception occurs when NoSQL databases are used incorrectly or when less mature products are used. Some NoSQL products are less mature, having only been around for fewer than five years, so they haven't developed data loss prevention features yet.

The guarantee of durability in ACID compliance is vital for enterprise systems, and ACID-compliant NoSQL databases provide this guarantee. Therefore, you're assured that no data is lost once the database confirms the data is saved.

Furthermore, eventually consistent databases can also provide data durability by careful use of a write ahead logging (WAL). Many NoSQL databases provide this capability.

NoSQL Databases Aren't Ready for Mission-Critical Enterprise Applications

On the contrary, many organizations are using NoSQL databases for mission-critical workloads, including the following:

- ✔ Defense and intelligence agencies storing and sharing information
- ✔ Media companies storing all their digital assets for publication and purchasing in NoSQL databases
- ✔ Media companies providing searchable metadata catalogs for their video and audio media
- ✔ Banks using NoSQL databases as primary trade stores or back office anti-fraud and risk-assessment systems
- ✔ Government agencies using NoSQL databases as the primary back ends for their health care systems

These are not small systems or simple caches for relational systems. They are cases for which NoSQL is well suited. Of course, some NoSQL databases are more ready for enterprise systems than others, which is why I wrote this book!

NoSQL Databases Aren't Secure

Not so! Many NoSQL databases now provide record-level and even data-item-level (cell) security. Microsoft DocumentDB, MarkLogic Server, OrientDB, AllegroGraph, and Accumulo all provide fine-grained role-based access control (RBAC) to access records stored within these NoSQL databases.

Many NoSQL databases provide integration to existing Lightweight Directory Access Protocol (LDAP), Kerberos, and certificate-based security systems. Support for encryption over the wire in all client-to-server communications, and internode communications within a cluster, is also provided by these databases.

Some NoSQL databases are even accredited and used by defense organizations. Accumulo came from a National Security Agency (NSA) project. MarkLogic Server is independently accredited under the U.S. Department of Defense's (DoD) Common Criteria certification.

Not all NoSQL databases provide this functionality, though I expect that the majority of them will in the future. For now, you have choices that enable you to secure information.

All NoSQL Databases Are Open-Source

There are numerous open-source databases in the NoSQL world. Many commercial companies have attempted to replicate Red Hat's success by offering a subset of their products' capabilities to be used for free under an open-source license.

Many of these companies' platforms don't support open standards, though. Also, most of the code is contributed by those companies. Limited features are provided in the base version by these "open-source" companies.

There are many fully commercial companies in the NoSQL space. Microsoft, MarkLogic, Franz (Allegrograph), Hypertable, and Aerospike are all great commercial companies offering NoSQL databases, and they're being very successful doing so.

NoSQL Databases Are Only for Web 2.0 Applications

Their use in new web and mobile application stacks have made NoSQL databases popular. They're easy to use from the start, and many operate under a for-free license agreement, making them attractive to startups.

Social media applications commonly use NoSQL databases. Social media applications bring in web published data and aggregate it together in order to discover valuable information.

The vast majority of use cases, though, aren't Web 2.0-type applications. They're the same applications that have been around a long time, but where relational databases no longer provide an adequate solution. This includes scenarios where the data being stored is very sparse, with many blank (null) values, or where there is frequent change over time of the structure of the information being stored.

NoSQL Is Just Hype

Microsoft, Oracle, and IBM each have their own NoSQL database on the market right now. Although susceptible to bluster, these companies invest in technology only when they see a profit.

Established players like MarkLogic with years on the market have also proved that NoSQL technology isn't just hype and is valuable to a range of real-world customers across industries in mission-critical systems.

NoSQL Developers Don't Understand How to Use an RDBMS

There is a common misconception (by evil relational database application developers; you know who you are!) that NoSQL is used because developers don't have a grasp on the fundamentals needed to configure relational databases so that they perform well.

This is completely incorrect. NoSQL comprises a range of approaches brought together to answer fundamentally different data problems than a relational database management system (RDBMS) solves.

If you're comparing an RDBMS to a NoSQL database, then you're comparing apples to motorbikes! NoSQL databases will not replace RDBMS. They are intended for data that's structured fundamentally different, as well as for different data problems.

Updated RDBMS Technology Will Remove the Need for NoSQL

Many of the highly distributed approaches of NoSQL are being blended with RDBMS technology, which has resulted in the emergence of many NewSQL databases.

Although NewSQL is helping to deal with NoSQL developers' criticisms of RDBMS technology, NewSQL is organized around the same data structures as an RDBMS is.

NoSQL databases are for different data problems, with different data structures and use cases.

Chapter 36

Ten Reasons Developers Love NoSQL

In This Chapter

▶ Saving time

▶ Saving money

▶ Saving headaches

*T*he popularity of NoSQL databases arises from the sheer number of developers who are excited about using them. Developers see NoSQL as an enabling and liberating technology. Unlike the traditional relational approach, NoSQL gives you a way to work with data that is closer to the application than the relational data model.

Developers adopt NoSQL technologies for many reasons, some of which are highlighted in this chapter.

No Need to Write SQL

Writing Structured Query Language (SQL) — and doing it well — is the bane of many enterprise developers' existence. This pain is because writing very complex queries with multiple joins across related tables isn't easy to do. Moreover, in light of regular database changes over time, maintaining complex query code is a job in and of itself.

Enterprise developers have invented a number of ways to avoid writing SQL. One of the most popular ways is through the use of the Object-Relational Mapping (ORM) library, Hibernate. Hibernate takes a configuration file and one or more objects and abstracts away the nasty SQL so that developers don't have to use it. This comes at a cost in terms of performance, of course, and doesn't solve all query use cases. Sometimes you have to fall back to SQL.

NoSQL databases provide their own query languages, which are tuned to the way the data is managed by the database and to the operations that developers most often perform. This approach provides a simpler query mechanism than nested SQL statements do.

Some NoSQL databases also provide an SQL interface to query NoSQL databases, in case developers can't break the SQL habit!

Don't Have to Spend Months Designing Schema

Schema agnosticism in NoSQL databases allows you to load data quickly without having to create a relational schema over a period of months. You don't have to analyze up front every single data item you need to store in NoSQL, as you do with an RDBMS.

Less Data Transform Code (ETL)

A common problem with relational databases that comes from having an up-front schema design is that you have to force nonrelational data into rows and columns. This shredding mechanism, along with other code methods that preprocess information for storage and post-process it for retrieval is referred to as *extract, transform, and load (ETL)*.

This code forces developers to take their nice shiny object and document models and write code to store every last element. Doing so is nasty and also leads to highly skilled developers writing poor performing and uninteresting plumbing code.

NoSQL databases allow you to keep the stored data structures much closer to their original form. Data flowing in between systems is typically in an XML format, whereas when it comes to web applications, data is formatted in a JSON document. Being able to natively store, manage, and search JSON is a huge benefit to application developers.

Easier to Maintain Code

All the code that you write must be maintained. By keeping database structures close to the application code's data formats, you minimize the amount of code, which in turn minimizes the maintenance of code and regression testing that you need to do over time.

When data structures change on an RDBMS, you have to review all SQL code that may use the changed tables. In NoSQL, you simply add support for the new elements, or just ignore them! Much easier to maintain, thanks to the schema-agnostic nature of NoSQL databases.

Execute Code Close to the Data for the Best Performance

An RDBMS provides stored procedures for executing code on a database server. This code is executed in one place. This useful approach is the basis of many analytical and complex data-management applications.

Many NoSQL databases allow this type of code to be distributed across all servers that store relevant data, which allows for greater parallelization of the workload. This approach is especially important for large ingestions of data that need processing and for complex aggregation analytics at query time.

User-defined functions (UDFs) and server-side scripting in a variety of NoSQL databases provide this distributed capability. UDFs are similar to Hadoop's MapReduce capability, except UDFs can happen in real time rather than in batch mode and doesn't require the same outlay in infrastructure that Hadoop plus a database would require.

Lots of Open-Source Options

In many enterprise software areas, the choice of a solid open-source solution is lacking. Only one or two widespread options may exist. Availability of skills and local in-country support are even bigger problems.

However, there are a myriad of open-source NoSQL databases. Many of these have full-fledged commercial companies that offer support and have offices globally. So, if you do need support or more features, you can move to those versions eventually.

This reduces the cost of adopting NoSQL technology and allows you to "try before you buy." This availability of open-source alternatives has caused commercial companies in the NoSQL space to offer free but well-featured versions of their software or to offer special startup licenses to small organizations.

Easy to Scale

You don't need to get a costly DBA to spend days refactoring SQL and creating materialized views in order to eek every inch of performance out of NoSQL systems.

Key-value stores can handle hundreds of thousands of operations per server. All types of NoSQL can scale horizontally across relatively cheap commodity servers. So, it's much easier to scale your database cluster with NoSQL than with traditional relational databases.

In addition, because of their ability to scale, NoSQL databases also fit well into public and private clouds. NoSQL databases are designed to be flexible and expand and contract as the uses for your application change. This capability is often called *elasticity*.

Eventual Consistency Data Model

Although I believe that mission-critical cases require ACID compliance, not every application needs to do so. Being able to relax consistency across very large clusters can be useful for some applications.

NoSQL databases allow you to relax these constraints or to mix and match strong consistency and weak consistency in the same database, for different record types.

Esoteric Language Support

Pretty much all databases support the main programming languages such as Java and C# .NET. Many databases support the likes of PHP, Python, and Ruby on Rails.

NoSQL has a flourishing set of language drivers for an even wider range of programming languages. I've counted more than 34 different programming languages and platforms that are supported by NoSQL databases. If your organization has a domain-specific language, you may well find support for it in a NoSQL database.

JavaScript End-to-End

JavaScript use has exploded in recent years. It's a convenient scripting language both on the web and, thanks to Node.js, on the server-side.

Many NoSQL databases now support full end-to-end JavaScript development. This means your organization can now use the same pool of programming language skills to craft web applications and middle tier data APIs and business logic, as well as handle back-end database triggers and MapReduce-based analytical processing next to the data.

As a result, in comparison to other database technologies, the total cost of ownership (TCO) of NoSQL is lower.

Index

● *U* ●

● *V* ●

About the Authors

Adam Fowler is a principal sales engineer at MarkLogic Corporation, an Enterprise NoSQL database company, located in the UK. He previously worked for small UK e-forms companies like edge IPK (now part of Temenos group) and for larger vendors in the enterprise content management (ECM) and business process management (BPM) spheres such as IBM FileNet.

While working for IBM FileNet, he coauthored an IBM Redbook on IBM FileNet P8 Platform and Architecture and wrote much of the platform, content, use cases, and security information in the book.

He is an enterprise Java software engineer by training and worked on content management and student management systems for several companies and universities in the UK.

He is passionate about enterprise class software solutions that solve really difficult problems for customers. He works primarily in the public sector in both civilian and defense areas, but has previous experience in diverse areas, including media, retail banking, retail insurance, and reinsurance.

In his spare time, he's a cadet forces instructor with Trent Wing Air Training Corps (ATC), where he instructs teenagers on drill, dress, discipline, and adventure training activities in the UK and abroad.

Adam lives in Chesterfield, which is a borough of Derbyshire, United Kingdom, and he works throughout the UK. He tries to spend as much time as possible with his wife, Wendy, and Leo, their young labradinger, which is a cross between a Labrador retriever and an English springer spaniel.

Dedication

To all lovers of using new technology to solve really hard problems.

Authors' Acknowledgments

First, I want to thank my wife, Wendy, for putting up with me over the past year as I retreated into the study to write (and, yes, agonize over) this book. Wendy, I would not have finished this book without your support.

Also, my thanks to the many great people at MarkLogic who supported me in writing this book and to the other passionate people working for NoSQL companies who communicated with me via Twitter and email to provide timely input for the book.

Publisher's Acknowledgments

Project Editor: Pat O'Brien

Copy Editor: Melba Hopper

Technical Editor: Allen G. Taylor

Editorial Assistant: Claire Brock

Sr. Editorial Assistant: Cherie Case

Project Coordinator: Patrick Redmond

Cover Image: ©iStock.com/cosmin4000